Other books by Duane Acker

Can State Universities be Managed? A Primer for Presidents and Management Teams. 2006, American Council on Education Series on Higher Education.

Animal Science and Industry, first edition, 1963; seventh edition with co-authors, 2005, Prentice Hall.

TWO AT A TIME

Reflections and Revelations of a Kansas State University Presidency and the Years that Followed.

Duane C. Acker

iUniverse, Inc.
New York Bloomington

Two at a Time

The sketches of Anderson Hall and The President's Home on the front cover were by former K-State Dean of Architecture and Design Emil Fischer and courtesy of the K-State Foundation. Background scenes for the back cover are the Washington Monument from the window of my USDA office and our first field of soybeans from the breakfast table of our farm home. The latter is from a charcoal by Doug Russell, assistant professor of art at the University of Wyoming.

iUniverse books may be ordered through booksellers or by contacting:

iUniverse
1663 Liberty Drive
Bloomington, IN 47403
www.iuniverse.com
1-800-Authors (1-800-288-4677)

ISBN: 978-1-4502-1966-2 (sc)
ISBN: 978-1-4502-1964-8 (dj)
ISBN: 978-1-4502-1965-5 (ebook)

Printed in the United States of America

iUniverse rev. date: 08/03/2010

Shirley and Duane Acker at a January 31, 1986, dance in the Kansas State University Union Ballroom. The dance was sponsored by the K-State orchestra for University faculty and Manhattan townspeople, and in recognition of Shirley's January 29 birthday.

Table of Contents

Acknowledgements xi

Introduction xiii

Chapter I. The Summer of Discovery 1

- Just a Loan 1
- Why and How Here? 3
- What is a Financial Statement? 6
- On Whom Do I Depend? 9
- Who Were the Deans? 12
- Dean Weber's Reminder 14
- The Bank did What? 15
- Regents, The First Nine of Thirty 17
- Michener's Book 19

Chapter II. Year 1, Expectations and More Questions 24

- Expectations 24
- Was the Board Stacked? 27
- What About the Castle? 30
- Can the Women Practice? 32
- An RV for Football? 33
- Mold on the Library Wall? 34
- Don't Embarrass the Governor, But 35
- Who Changed K-State's Building Priorities? 36
- Aren't You Playing God? 40
- Tea, Donut, and a Dozen Eggs 41
- Cookies and Bars for a Thousand 42
- The New Athletic Director that Didn't Show 44
- One Department of Athletics 45
- Why is the Athletic Dorm Losing Money? 46
- What do the Demographics Show? 48
- Where are the National Merit Semifinalists? 48
- Is Duane There? 51
- Where Did My Time Go? 51

Chapter III. The Web 53

- The Statesmen 54
- The Watchers 55
- The Protesters 56

Chapter IV. Intercollegiate Athletics 59
Coach Hartman Comes Back to Town 59
The Would-be Successor 63
Freedom of the Press 64
Goodby, Coach Rainsberger 65
Confirming Information 67
The New Coaching Staff in Trouble? 69
Dedication of Edwards Hall 70
The First Bowl Game in 85 Years 71
How About Title IX? 72
The Sit-In 75
How About No Athletics? 78

Chapter V. Political Theatre 79
Where to Send the Bill 79
Margarine for the Dairy Dedication 81
The Castle: Raze or Stabilize? 83
The Chamber and Projected Enrollment 87
They Towed Whose Car? 89
Reserved Seats for Governor Landon 91
The Right Gift for President Reagan 92
The 4-H Style Show and the Governor's new Wife 95
Who Gets the Sales Commission? 97
Charlie, Go to H___! 98
Consultants and the Doctor of Education 99
Cutting the Trees at Cedar Crest 101
A Spare Axe Handle 102
Two More Buildings 104
The Lone Vote Against Bramlage Coliseum 106
One Ulcer or Two 110
Regents in Heaven? 111
Did K-State Beat the Projections? 112
Nichols Hall, from The Castle 114
Follow-up Thoughts 116

Chapter VI. Leadership and Management 119
Incentives and Budget Policy 119
The Master of Fine Arts 121
Seamless: Teaching, Research, and Extension 122
Offense and Defense in Administration 124
An Internal Auditor and Why 125
One Leader for Agriculture 127

A Parallel at Oregon State....129
A Provost and Why....132
Games Universities Play....135
Data Dilemma....137
A Parallel in the Business College?....140
Delayed Consequences?....142
From Two Vice Presidents to One....143
A Mistake?....145
A Kansas-Nebraska Veterinary College....147

Chapter VII. The Campus Beyond....151
A Buffer for the Herds and Flocks....153
K-State in the Philippines....155
Who Can Take Off Chains?....156
The Konza Prairie....158
K-State in Nigeria....161
My Stool Won't Flush....162
China: Mopeds and Doilies....163
From Phillipsburg I'd Prefer to Walk....166
Plow Twice....168

Chapter VIII. Building A Tradition....173
Two Helpers from KU....174
The Wish List....176
The Donors' Direct Descendants?....177
A Maori Blessing for the Roast Pigs....179

Chapter IX. University Guests....181
Red Skelton....181
Shirley Temple Black....184
American Security and Energy Policy....186
The Non-Landon Lecture....187
Jeers and Howls!....190
No Impossible Dreams....192
Tip O'Neill and the Chrysler Bailout....194
The Decision to Bomb Libya....196

Chapter X. Faculty and Staff....198
Specific to New Faculty....199
A Party for Town and Gown....200
A Eulogy in a Proper Setting....201
Deserved Recognition....203
My Special Guest....204
Academic Freedom and Tenure....205

Where Tenure Doesn't Belong 208
Distant Temptations 209
Local Temptations 210
The Faculty's Golden Years? 211
Are Notes Worth $100,000? 213
Inflation in the Grade Book 214

Chapter XI. Students and Surprises 218
Early Morning Calls 220
Teaching in Their Second Language 220
Back to the Classroom 222
Charge to the Class of 1979 223
What the Mailman Brings 229
At the Water Cooler 229
Academic Advising: Nine Steps 230
The Football Team is Stealing our Rock 233
No Homeland 233
Murphy's Laws 235
Kansas State, Harvard, and Yale 236
Classes Cancelled? 238
Out of Film 240
Residue from the Canoe Race 241
Freedom to Choose 242
Teams and Trophies in Academics 244
No 7:30 Class! 247

Chapter XII. Apprehensions and Satisfactions 249
What Experiences Next? 249
I Wish I Could do That! 252
The Halls of Ivy 255
Satisfactions, Pride, and Credit 258
Cookies from Big Mama 269
A Rancher's View 270

Chapter XIII. After the Presidency 272
On the Potomac 272
Corn, Beans, and Alfalfa 275
Community and Rural Development 276
Professor Again 277
Taking up the Pen—and the Laptop 278

Citations 280

Index 287

ACKNOWLEDGEMENTS

Though the gist of this book is of my recollections and perceptions, it could not have been accomplished without generous help from many former Kansas State University colleagues and others.

Before citing those persons, however, I express appreciation for all of the K-State campus and statewide faculty and staff, students, and statewide clientele; Kansas legislators, Governors Robert Bennett and John Carlin, their executive branch staff, U.S. Senators Bob Dole and Nancy Landon Kassebaum, and Congressman (now U.S. Senator) Pat Roberts; Kansas Board of Regents members and staff; Manhattan and Junction City area citizens; and others who helped make Shirley's and my experiences in the K-State presidential and spouse roles rewarding and memorable.

On an early assembly of materials I had drafted for this book, Richard Seaton, Elizabeth "Beth" Unger, Robert DeBruyn, William "Bill" Johnson, and Carroll Hess each gave me valuable feedback on appropriateness and fairness of content as well as on structure. They also gave me encouragement to proceed.

Unger, Rita Bath, Robert "Bob" Snell, John Graham, Kathy Treadway Holen, Mary Molt, and John Pence each provided valuable information related to intercollegiate athletics. Especially on women's athletics, Unger provided details on events in which I had not been personally involved.

Ronald Downey came through with enrollment data for the years I lacked, plus confirming and supplementing information on enrollment tabulations. For the chapters related to students and to faculty and staff, Miles McKee, Charlie Griffin, Craig Brown, David Littrell, Raydon Robel, Pat Bosco, Joan Shull, Gregory Dennis, Stanley Dennis, Lori Daniel, Candace Becker, and Gayle Spencer each gave me important information and suggestions.

Hess and David Norman, who had served respectively as chief of party for K-State's Philippine and Botswana efforts, shared final reports and other documents. Lynne Lundberg, Larry Weigel, Tim Lindemuth, Jennifer Fabrizius, Kyle Butler, Don Rathbone, Ruth Dyer, Roger Mitchell, Barry Flinchbaugh, Mike Johnson, Doyle Rahjes, Melvin and Randi Dale, Debbie Soper, Charles Hostetler, Rex Armstrong, and June Palacio provided names and/or information that let me complete and insure accuracy in several sections.

I especially appreciate and thank University Archivist Anthony Crawford, Reference Specialist Pat Patton, and Cindy Von Elling for their untiring efforts in locating and copying documents and photos for this work. Though I do not know who shot the photos used, I am certain that some were by two whose work I admired, University Photographer David Von Riesen and a K-State student, Pete Souza.

As important as specific information was the general encouragement on this effort that I received from the early reviewers mentioned above; from Ralph and Mary Ellen Titus, Cindy Harris, Charles Reagan, and William Richter; from Paula Moore of the American Council on Education; and from my wife, Shirley, and daughters, Diane Nygaard and LuAnn Deter.

To each one, and to others who may not be named but who contributed in one way or another, I am grateful.

INTRODUCTION

What goes on behind those vine-covered, limestone walls of Anderson Hall, the administration building at Kansas' land grant university? Most are familiar with K-State's football stadium and basketball arena, and have a good picture of what happens in the campus classrooms and laboratories. But what goes on behind the scenes?

Besides appealing to the legislature for increases in faculty salaries, officiating at commencement ceremonies, and announcing increases in student tuition, what do a president and all those vice presidents deal with? Both the public and perhaps a majority of faculty may wonder.

There may be other questions. Who sets priorities or makes decisions regarding new buildings or programs? How are those millions of dollars that taxpayers provide allocated? Who monitors the spending? How do a president and staff cultivate potential donors for scholarships, art centers, or sports arenas? How does a university attract more high-ability students?

What does a university do with tenured faculty or deans who can not get along with each other? How do long-time vice presidents and deans behave when a new president shows up? Who does the president call on when the governor's wife calls with a problem?

What about the Board of Regents; do members fight for their own alma mater or for the total Regents' System? Do regents, legislators, or governors meddle in the University? How do local merchants and the chamber of commerce see "their" university?

How does a university keep its coaches and well-intentioned boosters from violating NCAA and conference rules? How does a president keep the egos of successful coaches or tenured professors in check? Is faculty tenure really needed? Who really runs the place?

What about the President's Home? Is it simply a cozy place where the president and spouse can spend quiet nights reading? Or, does it have a university-wide purpose?

For eleven years, with my wife, Shirley, as an unpaid partner, hostess, good-natured friend, encourager, and keen observer, I had the privilege of serving as president of nationally respected Kansas State University, referred to by most of the University family only as K-State. And, I choose to tell you a bit about our experiences.

The reader is reminded that the initial setting for this series of stories is the year 1975. That year the dollar was worth four to five times its value today and state appropriations provided most of K-State's budget. Tuition levels allowed a student of modest means to earn a degree in four years with only a part-time job plus a small scholarship or loan. Football coach's salaries were more in line with those of deans and presidents, and the academic year salary of a full professor was about $20,000.

This was before cell phones and the internet. The university's "main-frame computer" occupied a whole room with extra air conditioning and, at least at K-State, no department could purchase a more modern computer without the personal approval of the financial vice president. A student or faculty member would look you in the eye and say "Good morning" when met on campus, not have wires in both ears and their head down texting on their I-pod.

There were also similarities with today. There were excellent instructors (and perhaps one or two not so good), dedicated advisers, and faculty who brought students into their research labs, animal pens, and field plots. For faculty there was also a university bureaucracy and too few parking spaces. Especially, it was, as today, a great university.

This book may complement, but certainly not be a substitute for, official histories of K-State. Much of the content is documented from pocket notebooks and materials in my files or otherwise gathered. However, to limit such a work to that which can be documented unduly limits what I believe needs to be shared—perspectives from one who was there at important times in the life of the University.

Some of the recorded anecdotes are humorous; a few are tragic and expose the human frailties that appear in a population of more than twenty thousand people. The latter remind one that a university population, though perhaps more academically able than the average of society, is part of that society. Every organization has overly aggressive people who push the envelope too far. They also remind that, for universities to retain the credibility that society expects, faculty and university leaders at all levels must try to function as models for their colleagues and students.

Several sections describe problems that I faced early in the presidency, especially in athletics. The reader should infer from those descriptions no criticism on my part for the actions or decisions of my predecessor, Dr. James McCain. Such would be improper and unfair. McCain had a highly successful presidency; his leadership skills served the University extraordinarily well.

I think of a university's leadership as a continuum; successive leaders advancing their university toward its purpose and goals in accord with the circumstances of the time. I am thankful for the positive steps taken before my time at K-State and I would applaud the steps that would be taken after my time.

The first three chapters focus on our first year in the presidency, the setting and the questions and answers that would, in general, outline what was ahead. From there, material is arranged in sectors—athletics, political theatre, etc.—and generally in sequence within sector. For certain episodes some background or foreshadowing is included in order to make the story complete. There is also some cross-referencing, so the reader may find more information related to the item at hand. For most of the dates mentioned, I am confident of accuracy. However, for some, I could be off a year or two. Though the memory of the event and outcome are vivid, I may lack calendar notes or documents to confirm.

The College of Home Economics was re-named Human Ecology during my presidency and the reader will find reference to both names. The K-State Endowment Association was also renamed, to the K-State Foundation. Except for the section describing the change, I have used the name, K-State Foundation.

The presidency of a major state university brings with it some responsibilities beyond the university, itself, to speak out or to be present in support of state priorities or issues that may face higher education or the president's subject matter discipline. A few of these experiences are included. The last two chapters share some thoughts and satisfactions as we completed our self-imposed ten-year limit (it became eleven) and describe some of what happened to the Ackers after leaving the presidency.

Chapter I

The Summer of Discovery

Just a Loan

4 p.m., June 30, 1975

Grace Lindquist, secretary to retiring President James McCain, called mid-afternoon as the movers were yet unloading boxes and furniture in the garage at what would be, after necessary rewiring and some remodeling was completed, our new home on the Kansas State University campus, "The president is going down to a four o'clock meeting with the Foundation executive committee on some athletic department issues and wondered if you would like to go along."

I had learned a sport or two was being dropped because of financial problems. This was an opportunity to learn more. "I would be pleased to," I said.

En route to the First National Bank upstairs meeting room, McCain told me there was a financial shortfall in athletics and that he needed some help from the Foundation "to tide them over." He wanted to get it wrapped up so I would not have to deal with it.

In my years as K-State's associate dean of agriculture a decade earlier I had met a few of those in the meeting room, including Foundation executive director Ken Heywood, Director of Athletics Ernie Barrett, Foundation Chair Al Hostetler, and local abstractor, Robert Wilson. I find no record of others in attendance, but I believe the small group included Dr. Bob Snell, chair of the athletic council, local attorney Richard Rogers and businessman Jack Goldstein. I shook hands with all, and sat down to listen.

McCain told the group he needed some help from the Foundation for athletics and asked Barrett to outline his situation. Barrett's presentation was short; athletics needed enough money to pay the previous fall's yet unpaid charter flights for football, bus trips for other sports, and visiting team guarantees. At this writing I find no record of the dollar amount, but it covered a mass of unpaid bills, back for most of a year!

There followed a moment or two of stunned silence, then banker Al Hostetler spoke up, "But the Foundation already has three loans to the Department, Ernie, that aren't current!"

That opened a flood of questions, "How will you pay off this loan?" "When can you bring current payments on the other loans?" "What caused the problem?"

Barrett offered no answers. He was only optimistic about the coming fall; with a new football coach there would be increased ticket sales, more income. "Let's think positive" was a repeated theme. He just needed some help. Next year will be a good year!

It was a difficult meeting. A long-time and successful president, on the eve of his retirement, was asking for help. He deserved to retire with a feeling he had solved a serious problem. Foundation trustees were dedicated to helping the University. Yet, they had fiduciary responsibility to protect and wisely use the Foundation's private funds.

In the discussion I learned that the executive committee had earlier approved three loans, none current in re-payment, to an operation that now had nearly a year of unpaid bills. And in this meeting they were being given no useful data, no plan, and no schedule for loan repayment. Should they approve the loan?

After much consternation, the loan was approved, but with several conditions, including 1) that the Athletic Council chair co-sign the note and 2) that the Department bring the other three loans current.

I could not imagine any thinking council chair being willing to co-sign a note in such a circumstance. As to bringing the other three loans current, it was obvious from information presented that was impossible. Having those conditions on record, however, would let the assembled trustees feel a bit better about their action. And, McCain could retire feeling content.

I was not impressed. Nor did I believe any problem had been solved. It was apparent that intercollegiate athletics would be occupying much of my time in the immediate days ahead—for a new president, far more than it should.

Why and How Here?

Five months earlier, yet in my first year as vice chancellor for agriculture and natural resources at the University of Nebraska, I was invited to submit my resume for consideration for the presidency of Kansas State University. Should I submit my resume?

To go back to K-State as president would be a thrill and a great opportunity, but it would also carry some risks. I had had a totally positive experience as associate dean of agriculture and director of resident instruction from 1962 to 1966. We had had increases in new students and in student retention, good relationships across campus, and many friends from my travel across the state.

However, I had some concerns. The first was that I had seen too many campus jealousies related to K-State's large agriculture budget and faculty, relative to student enrollment, and agriculture's political clout in obtaining state funds. I wondered, "Would one with an agricultural background be readily accepted campus-wide?"

Of course, most who had exhibited those jealousies likely did not know or had given little thought to the fact that much of the agricultural funding was federal formula allocations or state line items to the Cooperative Extension Service (CES) and the Agricultural Experiment Station (AES). The College's instruction budget was, by comparison with other colleges of the University, modest.

Though the Agricultural Engineering curriculum was in the College of Engineering, that department's research and extension programs were parts of the AES and the CES, both of which reported to the dean of agriculture (title changed in 1966 to vice president for agriculture). The same was true for extension and research in Home Economics and Veterinary Medicine. And, in contrast to agricultural experiment stations in many other states, the Kansas AES then was providing most of the research funds for the college of Arts and Sciences, largely in the physical and biological sciences, and for Veterinary Medicine.

Though President McCain had worked hard to increase political and financial support for engineering and other colleges, the budget and faculty size disparity between those units and the total agricultural programs remained very large, larger than at many other land grant universities. The Engineering Experiment Station and Engineering Extension budgets at that time were yet modest.

The College of Business had been elevated from department status in 1962, the Colleges of Education and of Architecture and Design a few years later, during my time as an associate dean. I did not know how much budget progress McCain had made with each.

Would my identification with agriculture bring undue concern to those faculty or administrators with such jealousies? Would I be perceived as fair in my judgments and dealings with all colleges and units? Or, would I be perceived as too loyal to the several agricultural units?

My second major concern was McCain's long tenure, twenty-five years in the presidency. I recalled a comment by one of my early mentors, Iowa State's Associate Dean Roy Kottman, when he resigned from Iowa State to succeed a twenty-five-year dean at the University of West Virginia, "A long tenure is usually followed by a very short tenure!" After two years as West Virginia dean, Kottman had moved on.

In my nine years away from K-State, though fully occupied as dean and director of agricultural programs at South Dakota State University (SDSU) and vice chancellor for those and related programs at the University of Nebraska, I had been cognizant of developments at K- State. The most obvious and public was in athletics. McCain had made a major thrust for football, with a new coach, a new stadium, and aggressive player recruitment. K-State had had some winning seasons, beating traditional Big 8 powerhouses Nebraska, Colorado, or Missouri. Such dramatic success had attracted both national media attention and, in time, an investigation that had resulted in a recent conference and NCAA (National Collegiate Athletic Association) probation for major rule violations.

As chair of the SDSU athletic council, I had attended a special NCAA conference on the steady rise in intercollegiate athletics rule violations. The violation patterns described, plus K-State's announced probation, had bothered me. I still had pride in and concern for K-State.

During those nine years, K-State had made tremendous progress in other areas, including new buildings, enrollment increases, and, with an enrollment-driven formula for state funding, new faculty positions. The CES and AES, though, had not had parallel increases in state funding or faculty positions.

Nation-wide, Extension was under intense scrutiny. Both Congress and many state legislators worried that Extension had not adapted its programs to technology advances, farm consolidation, and Rural America's demographic changes. In many states, Extension funding had been held level or had decreased.

In the research arena, Congress was providing major funding increases to the National Science Foundation and National Institutes of Health. Money to USDA was moving from the traditional formula (based on farm numbers and rural population) for experiment station allocations to competitive grants and contracts.

How about K-State's central administrative personnel? Most in central administration had been with McCain most of his twenty-five years in the presidency. Max Milbourn had been McCain's assistant and legislative contact from the beginning and Vice President for Finance Dan Beatty and Information Director Ken Thomas most of that time. Could they adapt to a new leader?

Chet Peters had advanced from director of placement to dean of students and vice president for student affairs during that time. Paul Young, who was departing for the University of Arkansas when I arrived in 1962, had returned as vice president for facilities.

John Chalmers, who had come as dean of Arts and Sciences in 1963, had replaced John Lott Brown as vice president for academic affairs in the late 1960s. I had been contacted for interest in that job but had declined. I was then in the middle of a rich experience at SDSU and did not feel I would be content in the academic affairs role. I was not willing to give up state-wide work with industry leaders, legislators, and other university supporters.

The other significant change had been the retirement of Glenn Beck, the person who, as dean of agriculture, had brought me to K-State in 1962. He had taken several years leave in the early 1970s to lead programs in West Africa for the Rockefeller Foundation, then returned to his vice presidency a year or so before retiring. He would be replaced by Roger Mitchell, a former Iowa State University colleague, Mitchell coming on board just weeks before I was hired.

It was no secret there was considerable stress between Chalmers and some of the campus leaders in agriculture, largely on budget allocations and program direction, but not limited to those issues.

Though I recognized the risks, my concerns were dampened by the good experiences I had had in moving to new jobs, to K-State as associate dean and since. At SDSU, each of my three administrative associates had been in their jobs nearly eight years. Though I had known only two of the three, and them only through professional meetings, we had meshed quickly and smoothly.

At Nebraska, I had become the first vice chancellor for a new structure, an Institute of Agriculture and Natural Resources. The five central Institute administrators who would report to me, plus a special assistant, had each been in their offices for several years. I had had good professional acquaintance with two and modest acquaintance with a third. The other two, before restructuring, had reported elsewhere in the University. Not only did they not know me, they were concerned about how the new structure would work. From the first day, though, we were on track with the first three and within a few months there was mutual confidence with all.

My work with industry leaders, legislative committees, and state agencies had been comfortable and productive in both states. In Nebraska I had had close contact with and virtually unlimited support from members of the University's board of regents.

My previous time at K-State, my eight years as dean and director at SDSU, and my brief time at Nebraska had been highly productive and had yielded appreciated support and positive feedback from faculty, administrators at all levels, and statewide leaders.

As important in considering a university presidency, during all of our university years Shirley had received many compliments and seemed to relish her role, hosting and being well acquainted with students, faculty, and university supporters. We both enjoyed the Midwest and the University environment. Our daughters were both in college and would soon be on their own. These reinforced our feeling that a presidency was the next step and that it would be a good step. I submitted my resume.

After a series of March and early April interviews with a twelve-member committee that had chosen six finalists, and an evening for Shirley and me with the full Board of Regents, I would have a final interview with the Board at the Kansas City Airport Marriott.

A chance meeting between my fourth floor hotel room and the downstairs meeting room, where members of the Kansas Board of Regents would invite me to become K-State's eleventh president and I would accept, was surely an omen to what would demand my attention the first weeks and years of the presidency. As I entered the elevator, its lone occupant exclaimed, "Duane, what are you doing here?" It was a person with whom I had worked closely at SDSU just a few years earlier, SDSU's Director of Athletics, Stan Marshall!

It had been an honor and thrill to accept the invitation to become K-State's president.

* * * * *

As we drove back to the campus that evening, McCain told me he had athletics' finance officer reporting directly to Dan Beatty, Vice President for Finance, rather than to Director of Athletics Barrett. It was the only way he could feel comfortable about Department finances. I did not question McCain; he was leaving the presidency and it would now be my problem. But, how could a director of athletics not be responsible for the Department's finances?

What is a Financial Statement?

8 a.m., July 1, 1975

First thing this morning, I stepped in to ask Beatty to brief me on athletics' finances. I hit a nerve. "Don't ask me about athletics' finances! I've got nothing to do with it! The president wouldn't do what I told him had to be done so I'm not involved!" He was adamant.

I had known Beatty from my first tour at K-State, but not well. I knew him to be honest, conservative, and cautious in handling university funds, and that he could be trusted. I also knew that a vice president is likely to be on edge the day a replacement for his long-time boss arrives. Will he still have a job? Can he work with the new president?

For my own benefit, I should have been able to say, "Dan, as of now you are totally responsible for getting to the bottom of the athletic department's finances." However, this moment was not the time. He alluded to that, "If I would have to be responsible for athletics, then I'm not the person for this job."

Beatty, remaining adamant, followed up, "You need to get hold of Brad Rothermel, the assistant director of athletics. He's their finance man."

I placed a call to Barrett; he, not Rothermel, reported to me. However, Barrett had left town on a fund-raising trip (a surprise and disappointment, considering my presence and the issue at the previous day's meeting), so I asked Rothermel to come over to brief me on the Department's finances. I was to learn that Rothermel had a doctorate in Physical Education; his knowledge of finance I would also soon learn.

Most income to an athletics department is from ticket sales, payments from host universities for "away" games, a share of bowl and tournament receipts through the conference, and donations. Modest state funds are often provided. In the case of K-State, the Department also operated an athletic dormitory, so records should show room and board income. Department expenditures would range from team equipment to travel to food and staff salaries, presumably categorized by sport and, in this case, the dormitory. It was a sizeable operation.

I expected Rothermel to bring me a statement of cash flow (money in and out by months), a statement of profit or loss, by fiscal year, and a statement of financial condition, certainly one at the close of the previous fiscal year and perhaps the current year as of May 31.

Rothermel brought little paper, nothing organized for a briefing. But he was a pleasant fellow and asked, "What would you like to know?"

I mentioned the Foundation trustee's meeting the evening before and that it had prompted some concerns, "What is the Department's current financial condition?" I asked.

"What do you mean?"

I clarified, "How much money does the Department have now? How much money is due the Department? What are the Department's debts?"

Rothermel's only response was that the Department had several accounts, some in the University and some in the Foundation. But he gave me no data!

Why haven't last year's game guarantees to visiting teams been paid?" I asked, "Is there any money in the Department to pay those? Is there any money to pay those charter airline or bus trips I heard about last evening?"

It was obvious Barrett had not briefed Rothermel on the meeting or the Foundation's conditional loan. I asked more questions and got few answers, none that were precise. He neither had nor mentioned documents of income, expenditures, or balances.

Rothermel soon seemed as frustrated as I. "I don't understand what you really need to know," he said. I had to agree.

"What I want, Brad, is a complete financial statement for the Department of Intercollegiate Athletics!"

Rothermel's response to that told me the whole story, about both his financial acumen and the Department's financial management, "What's a financial statement?"

I went back to Beatty, shared with him my frustration and told him I had to have his help. Beatty was still adamant that he was not involved and I understood why. But, he did call for University Controller Ralph Perry to come down to join Rothermel and me. I had also known and respected Perry.

"Ralph, I want you to take Brad and show him what a complete financial statement is. Then work with him to get one put together for athletics. When you get it finished—soon, I hope—you and Brad bring it back to me."

Perry proved to be, during my time at K-State, the salt of the earth, honest, direct, able, and loyal to the University in all respects. In time, though he gave me some data, he emphasized there simply were not enough records for him to be satisfied that he had a picture that was even close to complete.

Now we had two problems, not enough money and not enough records! In a public entity, when financial records are inadequate, there are two possible reasons, "don't want to know" or "don't want others to know." Was it one or both?

What next? I had an important and highly public athletics department that had dropped sports for lack of money, had a stack of unpaid bills, had three loans not current, the director had left town the morning after his new president had been apprised of serious financial problems, the Department's finance officer could provide no useful information, and my finance vice president would have nothing to do with it!

* * * * *

There would surely be other issues with which to deal, opportunities and needs far beyond athletics. How about the other K-State administrative people on board, whose help I would also need?

On Whom Do I Depend?

On whom in Anderson Hall, besides Beatty and Perry, would I depend? Who, besides Beatty, would report directly to me and, by no other action on my part, be accepted as my management team? The team included:

Chet Peters, Vice President for Student Affairs, a K-State graduate in agricultural economics and a natural for the job. When I arrived in 1962 as associate dean, Peters had just been promoted from director of the University placement center to dean of students, responsible for the residence hall system, student organizations, placement center, and the student health facility. We quickly meshed; our student-oriented philosophies paralleled. His focus, as mine, was student development, to challenge the most able and provide the environment for every student to reach their potential. His title had been appropriately elevated to vice president in the intervening years. Chet would prove to be a gem in all respects. He kept a positive and constructive attitude in himself and in those people and units for which he was responsible.

Groundbreaking for the Chet Peters Recreation Complex, February, 1979. Behind me (the one with the shovel) are Student Body President Sam Brownback, Student Affairs Vice President Peters, Cindy Bingham, student chair of the Recreation Services Council, Raydon Robel, director of Recreational Services, and Facilities Vice President Paul Young. Fortunately, most of our ground breakings and building dedications were in warmer weather.

Dan Beatty was a graduate of Michigan's Hope College and had moved from the state budget office in Topeka to be K-State's business manager in the early half of McCain's administration. I had not worked closely with Dan, but knew him to be respected and cautious. He understandably focused more on dollars than on programs and had spent little time being involved in "what happened where," on campus or at outstate research or extension facilities. Dan had his systems and traditions, most not open to change. It quickly became apparent he did not trust presidents to be prudent with dollars or to have interest in fund status. I had to remind him that I had had plenty of experience making budget allocations, keeping commitments within dollars available, and that I did want to know major fund status on a regular basis.

Paul Young, Vice President for Facilities, was a former mathematics professor and associate dean of Arts and Sciences. He had left K-State for a vice presidency at the University of Arkansas about the time I had arrived as associate dean. I had become more acquainted with Paul in the intervening years at land grant meetings and in his later role with the Mid-America State Universities office in Kansas City. McCain had brought Paul back in the late 1960s or early '70s to replace C. Clyde Jones in the facilities job. Paul and his wife, Edna, had invited Shirley and me out to dinner during a May visit we had made to Manhattan and he had shown us the plans for the President's Home renovation, which the legislature had funded before my selection. That visit and his arranging an apartment for us while the renovation was underway provided the only close association I would have with any Anderson Hall staff prior to my arrival as president. I would find Paul to be totally loyal, with exceptionally good judgment and analytical skills. He had the difficult and generally unappreciated responsibility for construction and maintenance of physical facilities, with a budget far too small.

John Chalmers, Vice President for Academic Affairs. Chalmers had come to K-State as dean of Arts and Sciences in 1963 from the academic affairs job at the University of Wyoming. Other than his year or two at Wyoming, I was not aware of other land grant university experience. In my earlier K-State role, the working relationship with Chalmers, often regarding some course in his college in which our freshman and sophomore agriculture majors were enrolled, had not been the most satisfying. He was a former Rhodes Scholar and seemed to have little patience with those who were less than top students, or with the state's community colleges. Chalmers worked well with Beatty on budget issues, but his disdain for student affairs and facilities was ever present. I was determined, though, to do all I could to find common ground in a working relationship, believing that my background could complement his, bring about a balanced focus on student development and even enhance our community college relationships. Time would prove me wrong.

One other person carried the vice president title, **Roger Mitchell**, who had arrived to lead the College of Agriculture, Agricultural Experiment

Station, and Cooperative Extension Service shortly before I was selected. In contrast to the other vice presidents, his role was not university-wide. This vice presidency had replaced a dean title in early 1966, and the very fact that it was not accompanied by an office in Anderson Hall had allowed, over time, an erosion of its "direct reporting to the president." The vice president for academic affairs had assumed or been given increasing budget allocation and program guidance prerogative that would prove difficult to undo. More regarding this position is discussed in a later section.

Assistant to the President **Max Milbourn**, in that role during essentially all of McCain's twenty-five years. Milbourn told me he had been assistant to University of Wichita President William Jardine (a former K-State president), and had moved to K-State to teach journalism and help McCain. Milbourn would be considered the quintessential presidential assistant, accommodating, loyal, neat in appearance and manner, sensitive to people and circumstances, and easily liked. He had been the major link to the Kansas legislature. I would soon realize that K-State needed a more aggressive presence in dealing with the legislature, especially with appropriations committees and emerging legislative leadership. Though I would bring in another person for that role, Milbourn remained totally loyal and supportive. He was a gentleman in all respects.

Director of Information **Ken Thomas**. Thomas had been in this role at least from my time as associate dean, paid in part by Extension, and so was the University-wide coordinator of all information services, including Extension media, KSAC, and the University News Bureau. Thomas was able and had long-standing relationships with local media, but would have difficulty responding to new priorities.

How about the college deans; did they not report to the president? No. Except for the dean of the College of Agriculture, who reported jointly to Chalmers and Mitchell, they reported to Chalmers, the academic vice president. With the University's 1960s growth and McCain's establishment of the vice presidency for academic affairs, deans' reporting route had been shifted from McCain. By my making no change in structure or personnel at my arrival, I believe I handicapped the deans. Both the structure and other demands on my time, such as athletics, the legislature, regents, alumni, and interest groups, gave little opportunity for direct interaction with each dean. Consequently, they were without an adequate link to me and my perspectives, or the feedback I received from both students and those statewide interactions. It was my error in not budgeting my time to insure that opportunity.

The director of athletics, **Ernie Barrett**, also reported directly to the president. Barrett was a former All-American K-State basketball star, gregarious, and Mr. K-State to athletics supporters and many alumni. He had been an assistant basketball coach and major fund raiser for the Department, and promoted to director of athletics several years earlier.

Grace Lindquist, the president's secretary. Totally efficient and well known both among key alumni and campus leadership, she was another gem, especially during my first months in the office. Her transfer of loyalty was evident and complete on Day One. She was reticent to move outside her formal role, to offer advice. However, in a variety of ways she clued me in to some problems of which I should be aware. She was also generous in her evident approval and support of some of the early decisions I made. When she chose to retire, after a few years, I would feel her loss.

A few years after I had left the presidency one of my Manhattan friends commented, "You made your job more difficult by not building your own team right after you took the job." He was right.

By no means do I suggest that I should have built a totally new Anderson Hall leadership team. A newly-named president at one of the New Mexico state universities had tried that in the early 1970s, asked all central officers for their resignations. There resulted such an uproar that he resigned from his new post before arriving on campus.

Nor do I suggest that any of the vice presidents and directors lacked valuable and appreciated skills. As with all of us, some may have had a few blind spots, but each was capable and had obviously been chosen for their strengths.

Who Were the Deans?

2 p.m., July 1, 1975

That few of the stories which follow do not involve deans is, in itself, a message. The deans did well what deans do, lead and manage their colleges and faculty. This is a credit to my predecessor in naming able people to dean posts, some fortunate selections during my tenure, and effective leadership by the college deans and their close administrative colleagues. In those instances where deans' functions demanded my time or involvement, I was there. However, other demands on a major university president's time and presence require that most matters pertaining to deans' daily functions, such as budget, facilities, or personnel, have to be delegated to a provost or vice presidents. This was especially the case my first year.

I consider the Department heads and deans the most important managers in a university. They are the people who recruit and hire the faculty, orient those new people to their jobs, and encourage, support, and initiate reward for their good work. I was therefore glad that presidential secretary Grace Lindquist had arranged a meeting with the deans my first day on the job. The vice presidents on hand (Chalmers had chosen to be on vacation my first week) were also in the meeting, but I had already spent a bit of time with each who was there and my focus was on the deans. A few words about each:

Bernd Foerster, Dean of Architecture and Design. A new face to me, he had replaced Emil Fischer four or five years earlier. He was quiet and cautious in this setting. I would find him an innovator and an encourager of faculty ideas, but also a worrier about the status of his college within the University.

Carroll Hess, Dean of the College of Agriculture. I had known Carroll slightly during his graduate school days at Iowa State and he had come from Minnesota to replace me when I had left K-State for SDSU. (The job title had changed at that time. The dean of agriculture position had been re-named vice president and my position, associate dean and director of resident instruction, re-named dean of the college.) With Hess' good reputation of working with students, I had been pleased to see him chosen for the job.

Doretta Hoffman, Dean of Home Economics. Doretta had been a joy to work with during my time as an associate dean, but her health was rapidly deteriorating at my arrival as president. She was represented in this meeting by Associate and Acting Dean Ruth Hoeflin, another who had been a joy to work with in my earlier time. Hoffman would be with us but a few weeks; Shirley and I would be with her family and close friends when her remains were buried in a small country cemetery west of Alta Vista.

Sam Keys, Dean of Education, was another new face to me. He was steady, forward looking, dedicated to advancing his college, and also quiet and cautious in this setting. Keys would resign from the deanship at the end of the year, but retain his professorship in the college.

Robert Lynn, Dean of Business Administration, was also new to me, having replaced C. Clyde Jones when the latter had become a vice president. Lynn was focused on his job, cooperative, and always positive. He had a difficult job, handling growing enrollment in a rather new college and with limited space in rather outmoded Calvin Hall. He would do it well.

Don Rathbone, Dean of Engineering. Rathbone had been on board only a year or two, but I had heard a number of good things about him and had sought him out during a brief visit to the campus in May. It had not taken long for me to agree that K-State was fortunate to have his leadership on board.

Bill Stamey, Dean of Arts and Sciences. A key thread in the basic fabric of the University, an outstanding math faculty member, a fellow associate dean during my earlier time at K-State, and well regarded by faculty in other colleges. He had replaced Chalmers on the latter's promotion to the academic affairs vice presidency about six years earlier.

Don Trotter, Dean of Veterinary Medicine. I had worked closely with Trotter, then a department head, and other veterinary department heads in my earlier K-State years. I had later tried to hire him to head my veterinary science department at SDSU. He and his wife, Marilyn, had spent a full day with us; we had a good job lined up for her on our SDSU child development faculty. I had been confident they would join us at SDSU but, in the end, they just could not leave K-State. I was glad to see him in the dean role.

Robert Kruh, Dean of the Graduate School, was also a new face to me. I would quickly learn that Kruh was highly respected, dependable, and fully cooperative with faculty and deans of the colleges. Kruh's and his office's role would expand, emerge as increasingly important in seeking and coordinating the use of federal funds for research and in the operation of a related K-State Research Foundation.

This meeting allowed me to get acquainted with those deans I had not known, and them with me. However, from an information exchange standpoint it was perhaps the least useful of many meetings I would have. All were cautious about this new guy in the chair. I wanted to hear about their issues, perhaps the opportunities or problems they saw ahead. However, most, even those with whom I felt acquainted, were not about to expose their issues and their thoughts, especially among their colleagues, this early in the time of a new president.

As I look back on the circumstance, especially having read myself referred to as "clean sweep Acker," in one of the *Manhattan Mercury* pieces at the time of my appointment, I should have delayed such a group meeting until there had been time for me to interact with each one on some of their individual issues. In regard to that *Mercury* reference, I never learned if that "clean sweep Acker" was in reference to some personnel changes the writer, Bill Colvin, had learned I had made at SDSU or Nebraska. Or, was it a clue to some action Colvin thought I should make at K-State?

* * * * *

A couple long-retired deans, M.A. "Cotton" Durland of Engineering and A.D. "Dad" Weber of Agriculture, came to visit. Though both had left their dean's positions even before I had come to K-State in 1962, their perceptions regarding such issues as athletics and university needs were "right on," and their evident interests in my tasks were highly appreciated.

Dean Weber's Reminder

July, 1975

"Sometimes all that is needed is your presence." That thoughtful reminder was gently offered by a gentle person, retired dean and vice president A.D. "Dad" Weber, in a brief courtesy call my first or second week in the presidency.

Dr. Weber had returned to the campus in 1962 from a two-year assignment in India, to serve as vice president for international programs. I had known him only by reputation and by watching him judge cattle competition at Chicago's International Livestock show during my college years. By coincidence, it had been Weber's departure for India in 1960 that had triggered a series of personnel moves in agricultural leadership and, in time, my filling the associate dean position.

Weber's advice this day was both timely and apt. He had no doubt watched me work as associate dean and had noted my tendency to jump into issues "with both feet." He was reminding me that the number of issues in which a president might become engaged is endless and that others should and do carry responsibility for leading or handling most. I should let them do their job. I should limit my involvement in those situations to a show of interest or support, perhaps by my presence at a key meeting or event.

Though I had not had the privilege of working closely with Weber during my earlier years at K-State, I shared the high regard for him that was evident among those who had. I appreciated his courtesy call and his willingness to share this admonition.

At this writing, thirty-plus years later, I confess that it was often difficult to identify the "sometimes" to which Weber referred. In several cases, an issue would have been better served, and I would have been better served, had I charged others to lead. At the same time, I do recall countless cases where I did follow Weber's reminder and felt satisfaction and pride in the resolution that others achieved.

* * * * *

After reading about the next event, would the reader feel that I should have followed Weber's advice on the problem and charged someone else to make the phone call?

The Bank did What?

Late July, 1975

The word got around the campus that Acker seemed to be determined to get to the bottom of athletics' finances. I had been asking plenty of questions. Both Snell and, in his absence, Donna Thompson, vice chair of the athletic council, had been asked to co-sign that Foundation note and had understandably refused. And, it was public knowledge that student holders of modest swimming scholarships had been left high and dry in more ways than one when budget problems had prompted dropping the sport.

Because the Foundation received and held some money for the athletics department and its loans to the Department were delinquent, long-time Foundation Executive Vice President Ken Heywood was also concerned. Both Foundation and University financial staff had been cautioned by McCain to be especially vigilant regarding expenditures from athletics' accounts.

Once people in a system believe the top officer is serious about addressing an obvious problem, information begins to seep out. Among several pieces of information that reached me was a document that showed expenditures for a spring 1975 track or cross country team trip McCain had instructed be cancelled. McCain had declared that any existing funds or donations that might come in had to be used to pay existing bills!

However, the team trip had been taken! According to the documents, Barrett had taken a Foundation check, showing the Department of Athletics as payee, to the local Union National Bank, endorsed the check, and walked out of the bank with the cash. That cash had apparently helped finance the team trip, in contradiction to my predecessor's instruction.

I had served on two bank boards, but did not need that experience to tell me that in exchanging cash for a check made out a university unit, the bank was out of bounds. As it was explained to me, and from my personal review of the substantive documentation, the evidence was clear. I could hardly believe a bank would take such risk. Most important, I could not allow a repeat of such.

Fortunately, I had become acquainted with the bank president, Bill Stolzer (later chair of our President's Club) and called him. I described what I had been told and seen, and said I had difficulty believing it. "There was no problem," Stolzer responded, "Ernie needed the money for a team trip."

Though it was obvious Stolzer simply wanted to be helpful to Barrett and the team, I still had difficulty accepting that a bank would convert what was clearly University funds to ready cash. The bank was not my problem, though; the University's operation was. I had to pursue the topic, "If Don Good, highly respected head of Animal Science, walked in with a check made out to his department, would you cash it and let him walk out with the cash?"

"Oh, that's different," Stolzer responded; "we all know athletics is different. We just needed to accommodate."

I was stunned, but followed up, with some firmness "Bill, the athletics department is part of the University. Should your bank ever be confronted with a similar situation, I urge, in the strongest terms, that you not cash a check made out to any unit of the University."

As I hung up the phone, I felt that Stolzer still did not believe what the bank had done should be considered serious. And, how did that new president find out?

I had a bigger problem than I thought; the loose handling of athletics' finances extended into the community. How far? Regrettably, it extended far beyond this one bank event. And, also regrettably, I would learn about most far too late. I had not asked enough questions of enough people.

* * * * *

I should describe the nine members of the Kansas Board of Regents who had decided that I was the one they wanted to take over the leadership of Kansas State University. Who they were, their priorities, and how they saw Kansas State University, relative to other universities in the Regent's System, would be significant factors in my effectiveness.

Regents, The First Nine of Thirty

I had not known any of the nine during my earlier time at Kansas State, and I did mot meet them until a search and screening committee had narrowed the nominees and candidates down to six people, five others and me. Most had strong personalities; together, they comprised an interesting lot. Here is how I would characterize each.

Henry Bubb, not the Board president, but who assumed the position of senior statesman. A University of Kansas graduate, head of a large Topeka-based savings and loan (S&L) association, and a long-time power in Republican politics, he seemed to have two purposes for his remaining time on the Board. The first was to see that KU be held supreme in all real and symbolic features, relative to K-State or other system universities. The second would be to remind me periodically that a certain professor of personal finance in K-State's College of Home Economics, Richard L.D. Morse, had no business telling students, let alone the public, how banks or S&Ls calculate interest rates on savings accounts or loans.

Glee Smith, a Larned attorney, KU graduate, former president of the Kansas Senate, and a master politician with unlimited energy and the ability to be at the right event and say the right thing. He had been appointed early in the year by new Governor Robert Bennett, but worked and acted without reservation. Smith was the kind that would, when he was due at a Washington, D.C. meeting the next day, remain in Larned to introduce and listen to me at a Kansas State alumni dinner, then go by private plane to Wichita or Kansas City so he could catch an early morning flight to D.C.

Dr. Jim Basham, Ft. Scott M.D., an early graduate of the KU medical school and a long-time board member. He was depended on by board colleagues for virtually all judgments regarding the medical school. Basham was a quiet but strong supporter of K-State, especially its Cooperative Extension Service.

His awareness of Extension was helped by the fact that his wife's sister was a K-State Extension specialist.

Paul Wunsch, another KU law school graduate and former Senate president, with a law office in Kingman. His age would show, in both his attendance and his attentiveness to the issues, but he was loyal to his university and the Republican Party.

Elmer Jackson, a Kansas City, Kansas attorney, KU graduate, and chair of the Board during my interviews. Jackson was serious, conscientious, and deliberate, but clearly not well acquainted beyond the bounds of the Kansas City metropolitan area. He was not easy to characterize because of his quiet nature.

Jess Stewart, Wamego undertaker, KU graduate, and brother-in-law of Manhattan attorney and former state senator Richard Rogers. Stewart seemed to defer on most issues to those with more public role experience. Stewart's term was to end in December and, being interested in reappointment, he would be careful to visit our campus in the early fall and express interest in K-State. However, he would not receive reappointment.

John D. Montgomery, a Democrat and publisher of the *Junction City Daily Union* and clearly an equal to Glee Smith in his political skills and connections. Though he was a KU graduate, the economic and social impact of K-State on the Junction City community kept him a strong supporter. He would give me much personal support as I handled some difficult issues my first year.

Walter Hiersteiner, from Fairway, a Kansas City western suburb, and vice-president of a Kansas City, Missouri, envelope manufacturing company. Several of his patented envelope designs were prominent on his office wall. He was the other new member on the Board and a break from the KU line-up, a graduate of the University of Iowa and Harvard Law School. Hiersteiner exhibited a strict and positive business orientation. Though he had little familiarity beyond the Kansas City metropolitan area, he worked at getting acquainted with visits to the campuses and devoted a Sunday to K-State' summer term commencement.

Prudence Hutton, Newton, was the lone K-Stater on the Board and, by rotation, became board president July 1, 1975. She was also the first woman to serve on the Board in recent years and it was clear that her senior colleagues were not used to the idea. In the 1975 political environment it would be fair to suggest that her appointment was to provide "the token woman" on the Board. Though only one-ninth of the Board, she had at least twenty-five per cent of the collective insight to universities, both academics and athletics.

This single board guided Kansas' six state universities. Regent members were appointed by the governor and confirmed by the state senate. Membership is generally one of the more sought political appointments, but no more than a majority of one can be of a single political party. Their major job was to hire, monitor, and set compensation for institution presidents and approve university policies, major programs, and State appropriation requests.

Universities are large and amorphous; it takes a new regent considerable time to get acquainted with one university, let alone six. For a president, that is both good and bad. The good is that members have little time or desire to micro-manage; they usually have to limit their activities to system-wide issues or major policy issues of individual universities. The bad is that when a president really needs some regents to "go to bat" on an issue to advance his or her institution, they may have neither sufficient acquaintance nor willingness to play the role. I would experience much of the good—very few incidents of insertion to management—and, from time to time, some of the bad.

During my eleven years in the presidency, regents would come and go. I count thirty who were members during those years and I may have missed one or two. This meant that considerable of my time was devoted to my getting acquainted with each and to getting each of them acquainted with and interested in K-State's missions and programs.

Though a few of the thirty were disappointments, I felt satisfaction in knowing, working with, and helping most of them help K-State. Beyond that, I continue to appreciate their willingness to devote two days per month, plus a lot of travel and reading time, to Kansas' higher education system.

* * * * *

Soon after I had briefed those board members on the financial and other problems in K-State athletics, at least what I had learned so far, Regent Hutton loaned me James A. Michener's book, *Sports in America*. Most people have read other of Michener's books, such as *Iberia, Centennial*, or *Return to Paradise*, but are surprised when I mention his book on college sports.

Michener's Book

August, 1975

This book is a good read, interesting, revealing, and analytical. Michener expresses well the physical grace, art, and style of athletic performance, such as the synchronized smoothness of a baseball double or triple play, the broken-field running of the skilled football carrier, or the coordination of the discus thrower.

Equally well done is his description of emotional fan loyalty, including the progressive graduation of some fans' loyalty from the home high school team to their university team and, for some, to a professional team. For the latter, he illustrates with University of Wyoming football and the Denver Broncos.

Though I had been chair of SDSU's Athletic Council and representative to the North Central Conference and otherwise involved with athletics (helping coaches recruit players and, as Iowa State's faculty council chair, helping Athletics sell more tickets to faculty), Michener's book added to my perspective.

I had read former University of Oklahoma President George Cross' book, *Presidents Can't Punt*. (Cross had hired Bud Wilkinson.). Over the years, I had watched media reports of conference and NCAA rule violations and probations. During my time as chair of the North Central Conference, I had participated in a special NCAA conference on the escalating violations among member universities.

These experiences and observations, plus the immediacy and depth of K-State athletics' financial situation (a negative net worth eventually established at about $500,000, equivalent to $2,000,000 in 2009), the Department having dropped some sports, on probation for football violations, and the University having hired before my arrival a football coach with some history of violation investigations, made it clear I needed to crystallize and articulate a set of guiding principles for athletics.

Of course I wanted all sports to be competitive and for basketball and some other teams to be competing for the top end of the conference. Athletics must also get on firm footing in finances and rule abidance in all sports. In short, K-State athletics must balance the checkbook and follow the rules! On the latter issue, football was my major concern.

For these things to occur, I would have to function differently from some university presidents. History suggests university presidents can be placed into three categories: 1) Win, but make sure I don't know the details. If serious violations bring sanctions, defend the coach, keep contributors happy, and blast the NCAA. 2) Keep athletics subordinate so there is little incentive to violate rules. Accept being in the bottom half of the conference. Keep alumni focused on other university programs. 3) Set realistic goals for winning or conference rank, expect abidance with the rules (NCAA, conference, and university), and demand financial accountability. I chose the latter.

Though a university's academic excellence is rarely judged by its athletics program, a university's integrity may be. Michener's book and what I had observed prompted me to crystallize and articulate my goals and my posture as president. In presentations on and off campus, as well as in direct conversations with Barrett and his department, I took every opportunity to articulate my goals and my posture:

- Top half of the conference in all sports, a contender for conference championship in two. Goals are long-term; they may not be achievable in the first or second year. K-State was there in men's basketball and had been in football, but the latter on a thin foundation and probation had resulted. Track was in good shape.
- Responsible financial management. Balance the checkbook. Be cautious on expenditures; the director able and willing to say "No."
- Adhere to the NCAA and Big 8 rules, as well as university policy. After all, K-State had chosen to be a member of the Big 8 and the NCAA. Through its successive faculty representatives and athletic directors, it had helped set the rules and had agreed to abide by them. Though some rules may appear complex and open to interpretation, those features get blown out of proportion by universities trying to defend patterns of rule violation.

With the history and culture I faced, I would need more than articulated goals and posture; I would need to establish consequences:

- If there is a pattern of violations in a sport, that coach must be terminated.
- If there is a pattern of violations that does not get caught and stopped in early stages by the athletic director, the director must be terminated.

These consequences, too, were clearly articulated. However, they were, no doubt, not always heard.

The word, pattern, is key. Individual violations can happen, by carelessness, inattention, or misinterpretation of a rule by a coach or by some outside party. However, if there are repeated violations, evidence of a pre-determined method of violation that is routinely used or a gradual escalation of such, the pattern becomes evident. There is obviously some subjectivity to this, but every conference or NCAA sanction I had observed had resulted from either an egregious, one-time violation or an obvious pattern of violations.

For integrity in athletics, no coach's job can be immune from a pattern of errant fan or supporter behavior. No coach should say or imply "Help me recruit but don't tell me how you do it." The coach must be motivated to say, "Help me legally; don't jeopardize my job. (And, don't jeopardize my university's integrity.)"

The director is responsible for setting the tone and the ethic, for leading the program, and for coordinating department operations. NCAA, Conference, and university rule abidance is a key part of the task. As with coaches, the A.D.'s job cannot be immune from errant behavior by fans and supporters. Fans and supporters need to know that!

This may indicate far too much attention to rule violations and, to some, my posture may seem too harsh. However, rule violations seem endemic in university athletics, and K-State's football probation was Exhibit One.

This does not suggest rule abidance is the only task of a coach or A.D. Recruiting and coaching skills are the core for the coach. For the A.D., marketing, financial management, and fund raising are major leadership tasks.

Simply stating my posture would not make people believe it or insure they would be guided by it. What president would not say that rules need to be followed? What president would not say there would be serious repercussions from repeated violations by coaches? What president would not say they wanted to win within the rules?

What would it take to make the director, coaches, and supporters believe and follow my posture?

* * * * *

I had read two other books related to my new job. The first was *The President is Calling,* by Milton Eisenhower, a K-State graduate who had been K-State's president from 1943 to 1950. In the book he related that when he was offered the K-State presidency, he and his wife listed all the factors for and against accepting. He said that what tipped the balance to accept "was my belief that at last I would have the opportunity to do some serious studying and write several articles each year. I was to learn that serving as a university president was, in fact, far more difficult, time-consuming, and worrisome than anything I had experienced."[1]

The second was *Where Has All the Ivy Gone*, by Muriel Beadle, wife of a new president at the University of Chicago. The title of her book had been prompted by what she and her husband had encountered when they arrived at Chicago. All the ivy had disappeared from the academic buildings and when she had asked why, she had been told the ivy was damaging the mortar.[2] I would find the same at K-State and would be told the same!

* * * * *

After my college sophomore year, twenty-five years earlier, I had had a modestly parallel summer of discovery. It was my first university employment and I was the Audubon County, Iowa, extension youth assistant for the summer months. I discovered some of my talents and limitations. I learned the strengths of my one professional colleague and supervisor, the county extension director, and where I should focus my efforts. I discovered how to make good use of the office secretary. I discovered that most 4-H leaders accepted my ideas for demonstration projects, but one or two would say my ideas would not work.

I also learned that summer about the importance of financial records. My office, in the basement of the Audubon post office, happened to be next to a temporary IRS interview room. My concentration would sometimes be interrupted by heated exchanges next door, apparently involving misleading or missing financial records, the conversation transmitted through a less than sound-proof connecting door.

This summer of 1975 I had discovered strengths of my Anderson Hall colleagues and areas where I should focus my efforts. I also discovered who among them would accept my ideas for their sector and the one or two that would invariably respond, "That won't work here at K-State."

I had discovered enthusiastic and able faculty and student leaders. One early example: Shirley and I had joined our former neighbors, music professor Paul and Joan Shull, in the old stadium one evening our first week to watch the student performance of *Jesus Christ, Superstar.* Student body President Bernard Franklin played the lead.

Chapter II

Year 1, Expectations and More Questions

In a state university the year usually refers to the academic year. In late August when nine-month faculty and students return and new enrollees arrive, things begin to roll. Some classrooms and offices have been re-painted over the summer, deans and vice presidents have had their usually brief summer vacations and lines of cars appear in front of the residence halls to deposits bags and boxes along with sons and daughters.

In addition to my on-campus discoveries during July and August, Shirley and I had been to countless alumni events across the state, I had had a number of visits with regents and legislators, and long-time presidential assistant Max Milbourn had arranged get-acquainted luncheons with Topeka and Kansas City business leaders. All of these things had given me some base from which to crystallize what I felt we could and should expect, at least in the first years of our presidency.

A formal installation ceremony is common for a new president and, so it could involve students and faculty, it had been arranged for late September in Ahearn Field House. That would be an opportunity to share some of my expectations.

Expectations

September 26, 1975

My formal installation ceremony included a series of charges by representatives of the faculty, students, and alumni and by Prudence Hutton, chair of the Board of Regents, followed by my response. The charges were, in essence, their expectations of me as the new president. It seemed appropriate that I respond with my expectations, of the students, the faculty, alumni and, at the close, members of the Board.

Following are my comments (with some minor editorial corrections from a copy I find on file). The comments were, of necessity, brief. No one wanted a fifty-minute professorial lecture in the hot and packed Ahearn Field House.

"That students, alumni and faculty have stated expectations in this public setting is appropriate and for Chairperson Hutton to state on behalf of the Board of Regents their charge to the new president in this public setting is essential. Their statements are not surprises to you or me. They summarize and formalize thoughts, opinions, feelings, concerns, and desires of most of you in this field house, and the rest of the K-State family.

Kansas State University has a heritage worthy of pride. Its contributions touch every Kansas home and homes around the globe. Each of us, as professor, secretary, off-campus worker, student, alumnus, or friend, is proud to deepen and strengthen that heritage. We want to merit continued support by the citizens of Kansas and the U.S.

I do acknowledge and accept these statements. They are reasonable, clear, substantive, and achievable. But, if my acceptance is to imply that the expectations will be fulfilled, that the charges are to be followed, then my acceptance must be accompanied by your acceptance.

You have asked me to lead this university, and I accept with eagerness. But, leadership is shared by many, especially in a university. And, if you are to share it with me, as you must, then I must also suggest some expectations.

Students. I expect students to:

Know and respect faculty as people — humans with strengths and weaknesses, biases, and frailties, and with untapped talents that you might help tap; and with feelings — that show and that respond to praise and acknowledgement of their work.

Accept membership in the academic community, to sip from the cup of knowledge, to taste each sip, to discriminate among the cups from which you may drink. But, to be ever thirsty! To seek out learned and scholastically excited people — faculty, students, and other professionals, in person and through the scholarly journal in your field. By the time you are a senior, perhaps a junior, to subscribe to your professional journal.

To mature, by experiencing, encountering, interacting, by voicing on university issues, but to mature in the cadence of time, not by rushing or shortcutting or grasping.

And, to realize that we — teachers, scientists, leaders and our American society — also are maturing.

Faculty. I expect faculty:

To read. To know their discipline and the place of that discipline or sub discipline within the academic community and within society, to have familiarity with related and complementary disciplines or societal needs, to glean from this year's literature material for lectures, lab experiences, or extension assignments, and to harness basic research, wherever done, in applied research for Kansas.

To know each student as a person and to respect each one, regardless of age, as an adult client. To take your students where they can go in your discipline, you must know where they are now — the courses they have completed, the concepts they hold, their academic skills, their fears, and their aspirations, and, by this means, insure that each student is given an opportunity to succeed.

To do these things is an application of ethics. We present ourselves as scientists, as learned men and women, as able to do and use basic research, and as effective teachers. To be less is less than ethical.

Loyalties in higher education have shifted. Through the 1940s faculty loyalties were primarily to their institution. The 1950s brought a noticeable shift, with more loyalty to the discipline. And, in the 1960s, with high demand for faculty, loyalty to ourselves. In the 1970s, the pendulum is swinging back to the discipline and the institution.

Alumni. Communication is rarely adequate. So we often speak more, write more. But half of communication is receiving—listening, reading, observing, and interpreting. We want your ear and your reading time, so you can play the role you want to play in understanding K-State and its needs.

To be effective leaders in guiding the University's role, we need your help. Alumni, yes, and also commodity, industry, and professional groups. Repeatedly, the directions such groups suggest to us are directions we have known we should take and perhaps we have already begun the shift. Recommendations from off-campus and from students often prod us to proceed, reinforce our confidence to proceed.

Summary. Each of you has a special interest. You may be a graduate student in sociology, you may be an associate professor of accounting, an undergraduate in home economics education, a department head in engineering, a herdsman at one of our livestock units, or a county extension agent. You wonder how your interest, your unit, and your future will fare with a new president.

You may be a wheat producer, an architect, a county official, an editor or an enrollee in extension classes. You wonder if your needs, for new varieties, new technology, information, or night classes, will continue to be met.

Does the new president bring with him the experiences, interests, and convictions that will help or hinder your interest or need? The new president does bring experiences, interests and convictions. They have been laid out in full view.

I have worked in several vineyards. These vineyards have varied in size, complexity, and geographic location. Whatever vineyard has been assigned me, I have worked it.

To be productive and vigorous, the plants of a vineyard must be fed and watered, given trellises on which to climb, be pruned and shaped, and the vineyard replenished with new stock.

The vineyard now assigned me is Kansas State University, extending to all corners of Kansas. I will work it, using all the talents given me and with your help.

My expectations of the Board of Regents are especially high. Each member has impressed me with their dedication to higher education, including research and extension and, specifically, to be forceful in helping K-State reach its full potential as a land grant university.

I expect that the individual members of the Board will:

<u>Listen</u>. They will question, challenge, and demand evidence. But evidence provided to support recommendations will be seen and heard, absorbed and considered.

<u>Set and monitor missions</u> for each university and college for which they are responsible. Only the regents, with advice and counsel from all quarters, can exercise this responsibility.

<u>Reward effective leadership and management</u> as well as the effectiveness an institution may demonstrate in adhering to and fulfilling its missions.

<u>Insure that each regent's responsibility to all of higher education will transcend</u> their individual station in life or their respective loyalty <u>to individual institutions</u> or disciplines."

* * * * *

By this date, three months after assuming the presidency, I had seen enough institutional loyalty among certain of the Board members to place this item last for emphasis. Though my expectations of students, faculty, and alumni would be reached and exceeded, my expectations in this last area would be met, from time to time, with some disappointment.

Was the Board Stacked?

K-State alumni, Manhattan townspeople, and several administrative and faculty colleagues thought it was. Among the more vocal was Manhattan's State Senator Donn Everett. Though most of the appointments of present board members had been made by his predecessor, George Docking, Jr., also a KU graduate, new Governor Robert Bennett was getting the blame; he had appointed two more KU graduates his first month in office.

I could not afford to develop a case of paranoia; such would not help my effectiveness. During my earlier time at K-State I had been bothered by some evident KU paranoia on campus and felt it a waste of emotional energy. The University of Kansas was a highly respected university; so was K-State. I chose to believe both Docking and Bennett simply chose people they knew and trusted and that had supported their election.

In my work with state agencies and legislators in South Dakota and Nebraska, I had been repeatedly told that the land grant university (or land grant focus of the University of Nebraska) was the most useful to them and their responsibilities. The land grant university enjoyed enormous respect in the legislatures and across each state.

Among those appointments which a governor makes, an appointment to the Board of regents is generally considered the most prestigious. And, governors tend to appoint their larger donors to the more prestigious posts, if that is the donor's preference. Though both Docking and Bennett were wise politicians, they simple were not sensitive to or chose to not consider the reality of university loyalties.

In dealing with regents, I was in for a real change from the Nebraska experience. The Nebraska board had contained several real characters, some whose antics and comments about university matters brought them both media attention and, from time to time, faculty ridicule—and, not surprisingly, public support for re-election. However, their support for my Institute of Agriculture and Natural Resources and me was unanimous, complete, and aggressive. In terms of the areas for which I was responsible, Extension, Experiment Station, Water Resources, and Geological Survey, as well as the College of Agriculture, mine was "the only game in Nebraska!" They wanted it to be a winner!

As K-State president, I was one of six state university heads, each responsible for advancing his or her university. And, unfortunately, one or two of my fellow presidents believed and acted, in many dealings with the regents and the legislature, that it was a zero sum game, "Anything you get, I don't get." Or, "Anything you don't get, I might get!"

Another contrast: My Nebraska regents were generally long timers, elected for six-year terms and often re-elected for second and third terms. Most Kansas regents, as appointees of the governor, served a shorter time. A new governor rarely reappointed those chosen by his predecessor. Also, there were several mid-term resignations during my presidency. This meant there were more shifts in board focus and posture.

For both the regents and a university president, the Board's executive director is a key person. Max Bickford, the first of three with whom I would work, was a K-State graduate and former school superintendent and had been in that job a number of years. He was outwardly blunt and direct, but with a heart of gold, sincere and fair in all his dealings. I soon learned, though, that he was distressed at the direction and some of the decisions of the Board. It became clear he had been told to stay out of any policy discussions, to not even offer an opinion. He would soon leave the position, to be replaced by a former state senator and assistant to the KU chancellor, John Conard.

In all respects, being part of a six-university system, unsettlement in the Board office, more turnover in board membership, and the potential for university loyalties to manifest themselves in board actions, it was clear I was facing a different circumstance from my Nebraska experience.

My first Board of Regents meeting, September 26, 1975. To my left at the table is Finance Vice President Dan Beatty. Behind me and to my right, in order, are Regents' Academic Officer Joe McFarland and Facilities Officer Warren Corman and Wichita State Vice President (and K-State graduate) Roger Lowe. To my far right, in the back row, is K-State Student Body President Bernard Franklin. Chairing the Board and with back to the camera is Prudence Hutton of Newton. This was my first board meeting as president and Corman was giving the board some background on a capital improvement project.

In contrast, I had no worries about how K-State would or could be treated by the Kansas legislature. The Nebraska legislature was a unicameral and that influenced how we related and functioned with members, but the South Dakota legislature was structured as Kansas'. Though it had become clear in my first months that we would need to be more aggressive in working with the Kansas legislators, it would be familiar and generally supportive territory.

Though the Board of Regents may be stacked and university competitiveness would characterize many board dealings, I had no worries about future dealings with the Kansas legislature. That feeling would prove to be absolutely accurate.

* * * * *

It is common, and understandable, that when a new department head, dean, or president arrives, those faculty or students who may have felt their issue or sector had not had the attention it deserved would decide "Now is the time to press." That had happened on several issues, and the burned out shell of Nichols Gym was one.

What About the Castle?[1]

September 29, 1975

I had wondered why the burned-out shell of what had been Nichols Gym, along the south edge of K-State's campus, had not been demolished and the site cleared soon after its December, 1968, fire. Vines encased the shell, exposed structural steel was rusting, the overheated stone above burned-out windows and doors was chalking away, and a heavy wire fence surrounded the hollow structure. It was, to say the least, unsightly, on an otherwise attractive campus.

For years before the fire, Nichols Gym had been referred to with disdain. After the fire, the disdain had apparently turned to affection for the burned out shell; students wanted Nichols rebuilt, its architecture and physical history retained. Successive student generations, especially students in the College of Architecture and Design, had picked up the call to "Rebuild the Castle!" Student rallies and Nichols champions apparently had made it difficult for the K-State administration to seriously consider demolition.

Within a couple weeks after fall semester began, Kent Foerster, an undergraduate in political science and son of Dean Bernd Foerster, asked that I attend a rally in front of Nichols so he and others could, by the presence of a large group, underline to me their belief that it should be reconstructed. I pledged to the assembled group, mostly students but also a few faculty and townspeople, that I would not guarantee when a resolution would be achieved, but there would be a resolution![2]

I would learn that a yet-useable swimming pool in Nichols' basement, protected from the weather by a concrete floor above, was the reason the site had not been cleared right after the fire. The natatorium attached to Ahearn Field House had not yet been built. Then I wondered, "Why wasn't Nichols demolished when the natatorium was completed?"

I had found on file several committee reports on options for the Nichols shell, including reconstruction. But the burned out shell had remained.

Nichols had apparently been ignored on the official campus planning agenda. Reconstruction was not on the five- or ten-year Capital Plan, nor was there a new building planned for the Nichols site.

During the next year students and some alumni would tell me they wanted Nichols rebuilt. However, from some townspeople, faculty, and other alumni I would hear, "For heaven's sake, get rid of that eyesore. Do something!" The K-State Alumni Association devoted a column to Nichols in the *K-Stater*, asked interested alumni to send me a letter if they were enthusiastic about restoration. I received six letters or cards, but no checks or pledges.

I asked University Attorney Dick Seaton for advice. Seaton had long and strong roots in the University, had sound judgment, and was one who would tell me what he thought. Such candor is not always easy to find. Seaton's advice was given with a broad smile, "Just name another committee; that has worked before." Seaton knew I would not be willing to continue to look at an unsolved problem. But to rebuild, I needed a specific use and I needed cash.

Foerster would be willing to move his College of Architecture and Design to Nichols, but the University's long-range plan was for that college to occupy more of Seaton Hall as new engineering buildings were constructed. The only realistic suggestion was to use Nichols for an art center.

Though our planning staff was convinced reconstruction would be more costly per square foot than new construction and, further, that the structure was unsound, I sought the opinion of Martin Eby, Sr., a K-State alum and successful Wichita contractor. His company had done similar reconstruction. His staff estimated reconstruction cost about equal to new construction, but emphasized the obvious configuration constraints.

The University was facing other high-priority needs, such as new chemistry and biochemistry laboratories, which could not be accommodated in a rebuilt Nichols because of both location and those dimensional constraints. Higher priority and special use buildings, such as Engineering I (Durland) and a three-structure veterinary medicine complex, had taken priority, and Plant Science, a classroom-office building and Engineering II were already in line. Would Nichols have to wait another decade? Or should it, at long last, be razed and the site cleared?

Whatever the eventual solution, I would likely need state money for it, and the legislature and the governor would be involved.

* * * * *

Back to athletics. Not only was it necessary to get to the bottom of athletics' finances (by late July known to be at least $365,000 and later determined to be about $500.000), the organization structure meant that even such a problem as competition for court use by the men's and women's basketball teams would get to my office.

Can the Women Practice?

October, 1975

Ranked second in the country and drawing 3,000 to 4,000 more fans than men's basketball in the early 2000s, K-State women's basketball coaches, players, and fans deserve a lot of credit. Also deserving credit are the late K-State Vice President for Student Affairs Chet Peters, Judy Akers, the women's coach when I returned to K-State as president, and other key persons whose involvements are described later.

There had been no intercollegiate women's program at SDSU and only the beginnings at Nebraska, so I was not surprised that K-State was yet at an early stage. However, I was surprised at the structure. Women's intercollegiate athletics was under Peters; the Department of Athletics was exclusively for the men's sports.

I was also surprised by the disdain and even some animosity toward women's sports within the men's athletic community, including some staff and donors.

At my seventy-student Wiota, Iowa, high school and in our school's conference, every basketball night was a double-header, the women's game preceding the men's. All were proud of our women's team; twice they brought home the state championship trophy. Our men's team made it to the state tournament but once.

The absence of women's intercollegiate sports had not bothered me in earlier years. Though I had been chair of the athletic council at SDSU in the late 1960s and early '70s, athletics had not been my major focus. But, as K-State president in the latter 1970s, the status and the treatment of women's sports was very much my responsibility. And, K-State's existing structure made it even more my responsibility, sometimes almost daily.

I had learned that a few years earlier, though the women's games were on the Ahearn court, the team had to limit their practice to the adjacent gymnasium. Recent negotiations, however, had allowed the women to practice on the Ahearn court at noon or early afternoon, "when the men didn't need it."

From early in the semester, I got complaints that the women were on the Ahearn court when the men wanted to practice. Some complaints came from the Department, but most from supporters of the men's program, obviously prompted by coaches or players. Women were holding the court too long, the men needed the court more before travel days, or other complaint.

The next complaint was about a student assistant charged with sprinkling the dirt running track that circled the Ahearn court. He was reported flipping the hose nozzle toward the women practicing on the court. Childish!

With both Barrett and Peters reporting to me, I would hear from both. There needed to be one department of intercollegiate athletics and one director, responsible for developing and leading the total program, gaining satisfaction from and feeling pride in both men's and women's sports. But, there would be some pain to get there.

* * * * *

We would learn of more operational problems, usually problems that further hurt, not helped, athletics' finances. Following is an example.

An RV for Football?

Late October, 1975

Bob Snell came in to report another problem in athletics, an issue about which he felt I should be aware. Snell, as chair of the Athletic Council and faculty representative to the Big 8 Conference, was keeping a close watch on department operations, especially anything involving financial commitments.

A group of five southwestern Kansas boosters were giving Athletics a used recreation vehicle (RV). Snell had questioned Barrett and Coach Rainsberger about why they needed it and they had their justification, to pick up football recruits at the Kansas City airport. Recruits would be impressed; their 100-mile drive to the campus would be in comfort.

They had a second reason. Coaches' wives, who followed the team to away games, could travel together and have a comfortable place to wait for their husbands after the game.

For recruits coming from the Kansas City airport, both Snell and I guessed there would be a few women along to help with the conversation, but they sure would not be coaches' wives!

Donors want to be helpful and they also want to be friends of the coach; Rainsberger had apparently expressed the need and these supporters had responded. And, there are tax benefits from donating an item to the University.

We had no idea the age or condition of that RV. Suppose one has a used RV of some value, perhaps $20,000. Four others put in $4,000 to buy a share. The group gives the RV to the University and each person takes a $4,000 tax deduction.

I am not suggesting a donation value of $20,000 was used; I do not recall learning the figure. The RV's market value was the donors' and IRS' problem, not ours. Our problem was the Department's finances and the need to rein in expenditures. Compare the operating cost of an RV at 8 mpg. vs. 22 for a sedan, to and from the airport. What about maintenance cost and insurance? And, though we had empathy for the coach's wives' comfort, did we really have the obligation to provide an RV?

Snell had the list of donors and I recognized most of the names. One, Earl Brookover, of Garden City, had served on the presidential screening committee and I had known him since my earlier time at K-State. I placed a call to Brookover, outlined what Snell and I were facing. I had assumed Brookover had not been the RV owner, and that was confirmed in our visit. I also knew, and Brookover's K-State friends knew, that he could always be counted on to kick in a few dollars for a K-State need, athletics or otherwise.

His response was what I had counted on, "I understand your problem. In fact, I wondered about this when I was asked; it seemed a bit strange." He followed up, "You do what you need to do. If you turn it down, that won't bother me."

Unfortunately, it was too late; the transfer had already occurred. The Foundation's acknowledgements of the gift were already in the mail.

This had added to my concern about the ability of the Department to manage its finances. The issues that Snell and I would discuss, en route with our wives to the K-State-KU football game at Lawrence on November 1, was getting longer.

* * * * *

To K-State students, as they walk along Lover's Lane or through the tall oak and hackberry trees to the west of the President's Home, that impressive limestone structure in a well-landscaped setting may be an item of wonder, "I wonder what it is like inside." A couple coeds decided one evening to try to find out.

Mold on the Library Wall?[3]

Late October, 1975

Shirley and I returned from a sorority dinner to find two girls sitting on the bottom stair step in our foyer. They had rung the bell and explained to Marilyn Funk, our student helper, that they had discovered some mold on one of the walls in Farrell Library. They thought the president should be made aware. Marilyn had invited them in to await our return.

We moved into the living room and they told me about the mold, in an upper corner of the main reading room. Apparently a minor leak had continued for some time and accumulated moisture on the plaster had resulted in some mold. We talked about the library and their residence hall life, their classes, and other items for perhaps fifteen minutes. We had a good visit.

Unfortunately, I was scheduled at one of the fraternities that evening for a conversation with its pledge class. (My calendar for that first year shows thirty-five dinners or discussions at fraternities, sororities, and residence halls, plus sixteen student club banquets or events that we would generally both attend.) I tried to avoid evening commitments unless both Shirley and I could attend, but this upcoming visit with fraternity pledge class was an exception. I had to interrupt the conversation, but drove the two young women by their residence hall en route and thanked them for their concern about the mold in Farrell.

Two years later one of the two girls approached me in the K-State Union. "I have a confession to make," she said, "Do you remember the evening when two of us came by your house to tell you about the mold on the library wall?"

I assured her that I did, and recognized her as one of the two. The confession: "We had left the library and were walking by your house when we had this uncontrollable urge to see the inside. We decided the mold we had noticed on the library wall would be a good excuse."

* * * * *

Regent Executive Director Max Bickford had seen to it that I meet Governor Bennett in Topeka that April day my appointment was announced. During the summer and early fall I had met and worked with several of his budget and administrative staff, but had had few occasions to spend time with the governor. Fortunately, by the time of the late season Nebraska football game at K-State, the improvements in the President's Home were sufficiently complete that Shirley and I could host a brunch prior to the game and the governor and his wife would be among our guests.

Don't Embarrass the Governor, But ...

November 8, 1975

Having endured years of cigarette smoke in my office and from group entertainment in our home, we had decided when we moved from South Dakota State to the University of Nebraska in 1974 that henceforth there would be no smoking in our home, our car, or my office. I had included in my introductory remarks to Nebraska faculty that what might appear as an ash tray in my office would be, instead, a candy dish. The word had passed on to K-State.

Today was the Nebraska-K-State football game and we had invited the Kansas regents, a few legislators, Governor Bennett and their spouses, and several of their Nebraska counterparts to a pre-game brunch at our home.

It would be a full day, starting with a 9:30 meeting for key legislators that the Kansas Farm Bureau had organized to push some university needs. It would end with a 6 p.m. dinner for members of Crew, an enthusiastic group that hoped to rise from a club sport to conference competition.

Bennett and his wife, Olivia, arrived at our home about 11:30, the governor holding his trademark cigarette in a holder. We greeted them, invited them to join other guests gathered beyond the foyer and on the porch.

What should we do about the cigarette? Shirley and I agreed, "Now or never!" I pulled the governor's driver aside, "We don't want to embarrass the governor, but we don't allow any smoking in the house. There are several smokers on the porch."

"No problem" he responded, "that's what I'm here for." He moved on to lead the governor and his wife to the porch. We wondered, of course, what the governor's reaction would be.

The brunch had gone off without a hitch and nothing more had been said about smoking. The Bennetts and several regents then joined us in what was then the president's box for the game. It wasn't really a "box"; it was the back two rows of chair seats in the west stadium's center section, protected only from the west wind by a block wall and from rain or snow by the press box overhang.

At half time, the governor leaned over, "You know," he said, "you are one of Olivia's favorite people!" That caught me by surprise, "Why is that?

"You don't allow any smoking in your home!"

* * * * *

Though Bennett caught some criticism for stacking the Board of Regents and he did not endorse everything we sought for K-State, he became a strong supporter of K-State and many of my efforts. I considered him an excellent governor. I do not know that being "one of the governor's wife's favorite people" helped the outcome of the next issue, but our "no smoking" policy for the President's Home had not hurt.

Who Changed K-State's Building Priorities?

November 13, 1975

A list of future building priorities for the University existed when I arrived as president. Heading that list were 1) a classroom-office building, later to be named Bluemont Hall, and 2) the first section of a plant science building, to be named Throckmorton Hall.

The campus sorely needed more classrooms and more office space for the College of Education and the Department of Psychology, the sequence seemed logical, and I was not about to make a change. Further, I knew a bit about where political power resides in a Great Plains state; much is in agriculture. If I could hold this priority sequence, there might be enough political support for the plant science building that we could get legislative financing for both in an early legislative session.

This day I would be surprised, and both the chance to get both buildings financed and my credibility with faculty would be put at risk.

I arrived at the capitol building early for a 1 p.m. capital improvement request hearing with the governor's budget director, Jim Bibb. I expected Regent Executive Director Max Bickford and Facilities Director Warren Corman to also be there. However, as I approached the Capitol about 12:30, I met Corman coming out the door.

"It's already done." he said, "We finished some other items early, so we proceeded with the K-State request." Then he added, "By the way, we switched your top two buildings, put Plant Science first."

I was stunned, "Warren, you've just killed me with my faculty!"

He was surprised at my reaction, "We just thought that with your background in agriculture, you would like to push for that plant science building."

I started to explain to Corman. Psychology and the College of Education were to move into that classroom-office building and we sorely needed the classroom space. Beyond that, some faculty members were suspicious of me being from agriculture. They would say, "Ah, ha!"

I soon realized that, though Corman was sincere and honest, he just did not understand the campus sensitivities regarding building priorities. I did not even try to explain political strategy. Though moving Plant Science to first priority would increase odds for getting it financed, the classroom-office building could be delayed for years.

I headed to the Board office, Corman following, and protested to Bickford. I had cooled down—some, the hearing was over, and it was apparent Bickford and Corman thought they had been doing me a favor. I just needed to find a way, soon, to get our priorities back in place.

A week later, Governor Bennett was in Manhattan to speak to the Rotary club. As I rode with him from Rotary to the campus for his scheduled interview on University radio station KSAC, he asked, "Why did you change the building priorities for K-State?" His knowledge and recall were amazing; though he had not been at the hearing, he knew the details.

"I didn't."

"Who did?"

"The regents' office."

"The regents, themselves, or the staff?"

"I presume the staff." (I had no reason to believe this had been at a board member's instruction.)

"What is your priority?"

"Classroom-office building Number One, Plant Science Number Two."

Bennett was cautious, "It probably won't make much difference," he said, "We likely won't have enough money to fund many capital improvements in the next couple years."

Our request was for architectural planning money; construction funds would come later.

Bennett continued, "Besides, even if you got planning money, universities have a tendency to change their minds on design or location when they get the construction money."

Though I had reservations about the chosen site for the classroom-office building, I was not about to re-open that issue. Hence, my quick response, "Governor, all I can say is that if planning money is provided for one or both, they will be designed for the sites already identified. And, when we get construction money, they will be built as planned, on those sites!"

Bennett's early January budget message to the Kansas legislature included planning money for both buildings! Planning funds for both were appropriated by that 1976 legislature and construction funds followed on schedule.

Breaking ground for Throckmorton Hall, May 20, 1978. To my right are Regents Frank Lowman of Hays and Jack Reeves of Garden City. To my left, in the light jacket, is Governor Robert Bennett. On my far left is Jolana Wright Montgomery of Junction City, a granddaughter of former Dean Throckmorton, and her son, John Gray Montgomery, Jr.

* * * * *

By mid December I had spent far more time on athletics than on any other issue. I find in my pocket date book at least twenty-five appointments or meetings regarding athletics issues from July 1, and that date book is likely incomplete. I depended on Grace Lindquist to maintain the complete calendar. Snell's name was the most common in that date book, but there were multiple entries regarding athletics, including Barrett, local auditor Joe Mills, Vice President Peters, Foundation staff, and even sports reporter Fred White.

Problems had continued on a steady stream during the fall, more than the few described on these pages. They ranged from Foundation funds used to remodel a private home kitchen to reserving hotel rooms for a batch of coaches, failing to cancel the reservations when plans changed, and having to pay for the rooms. Some details may be provided elsewhere, but they all pointed to dollar and operations problems.

In the end, I decided I would have to make a top management change in the Department of Athletics. It was a responsibility I could not duck or delay. Management was clearly not Barrett's strength, but he was well known, well liked, and seemed to be most effective in making friends and soliciting donations.

My hope was that he could help kick-start a new and major fund-raising drive as an assistant to the President. I felt Barrett could be more valuable to the University in this new role than as a line officer in department management.

At 9:30 on Tuesday morning, December 16, I had Assistant Max Milbourn join me for a meeting with Barrett. I told Barrett that his talents in representing the University and in fund raising were his strengths and that I would reassign him to a new position as assistant to the president for that University-wide fund-raising role.

At 10:15 I met with Track and Cross Country Coach DeLoss Dodds, told him of my reassignment of Barrett and asked him to serve as acting A.D. About 10:30 I met with the total athletics staff to inform them of the change.

Though Barrett initially agreed to the reassignment, there was a storm of protest from those who felt the cloak of Director of Athletics simply belonged on this former basketball All-American. That, and pride, would not let him stay. He resigned within a few days. (Barrett would later return. His recognized strengths, making friends and soliciting donations, would serve K-State well.)

Aren't You Playing God?

January, 1976

The question, "Aren't you trying to play God when you remove a person from their post?" surprised me. It came from a loyal friend of Barrett.

I could well understand the empathy the questioner had for Barrett. No matter how the public announcement is phrased, if it is not voluntary, it is not a happy time. I had anticipated some static from the move, but had never considered what the question suggested, this business of playing God.

Staff reassignments are not rare in business, nor unknown in universities. As a dean or a vice chancellor, I had reassigned people. If all considerations make clear one can make better use of a person's talents, or should relieve a person from a job they are not equipped to handle, such is a manager's responsibility.

In many cases, however, there has been an initial error, appointing a person inadequately equipped for the job. Management, saying yes and no, making personnel decisions, and monitoring operations, is not everyone's forte. I had been the guilty appointing party more than once.

During my time as a dean I promoted a senior professor to head a branch research station. His professorial skills were not the skills needed for personnel management or for dealing with farmer clientele. He was soon crosswise with both his staff and area producers. For two years I spent days and miles of travel putting out fires. I had caused the problem; I had to solve it. I reassigned him back to the campus. He was a good person, honest, sincere, and hard working. Though he had been eager for the branch station position, I had made an error in the appointment.

How did I answer that question, "Aren't you trying to play God?"

"No, I'm just doing what the regents hired me to do, trying to help every part of the University function as well as it can." I also added, "If one is playing God when they remove a person *from* a position, then one is playing God when they appoint a person *to* a position." In neither case are we trying to play God. In administration, we just try to do our job.

I have also advised deans and others facing difficult but necessary personnel decisions of two points 1) The person in the job probably knows things are not working, but does not want to admit it. When you make the move, you remove the pressure they are under. In a different role they will likely live a happier and more satisfying life. 2) You may not look forward to the conversation, but twenty minutes of awkward conversation is better than another year of frustration, for both parties.

* * * * *

Next is a reminder, that support from students and "the country" is important for a university president, the latter especially so for a state and land grant university president. I was fortunate that in my years as associate dean I had been in more than 100 Kansas communities recruiting students and speaking. I had a lot of friends and acquaintances across the state.

Tea, Donut, and a Dozen Eggs

January, 1976

My secretary, Grace Lindquist, stepped in to say two students wanted to see me. She moved aside for two young men bringing me a cup of tea and a donut.

I motioned them to chairs, thanked them for their thoughtfulness, and asked what had prompted the visit. I had been roasted that morning by a *Collegian* editorial regarding some of the actions I had taken with athletics. These two students had agreed with my action, believed the editorial unfair, and just wanted to let me know that.

I did not ask if the visit was their idea or if it might have been prompted by a discussion of the issue with a faculty member. As a whole, faculty had been concerned about apparent free-wheeling in athletics and any action I had taken to bring about rule abidance and financial accountability had earned general faculty applause. Some thoughtful faculty may well have responded to these students, "If you feel that way, why don't you take the president a cup of tea and a donut and let him know?" (My weakness for donuts was well known.)

There were other gestures of appreciation and support for our several moves in athletics. One of the sports writers had quizzed me about all the changes in athletics I had made and I had responded, "That's what I'm being paid for." Matfield Green rancher and K-State graduate Wayne Rogler mailed me the clipping with my quote underlined and a note in the margin, "That's right!" And, the next time Rogler was on campus he dropped by our home with a dozen eggs.

There was also a post card from one of our county Extension staff with the simple supportive message, "President Acker: When the going gets tough, the tough keep going!" And, when I arrived at an Emporia hotel to speak at a local service club meeting, K-State alum and Flint Hills rancher Lloyd Lewis, whose daughter was an outstanding K-State student, handed me a frozen package of steaks to take home.

* * * * *

In the President's Home that first year and most years that followed, it was Shirley and the young women or couples that lived in our home who provided the refreshments. The refreshments were more than one cup of tea and a donut; K-State had well over a thousand campus faculty, plus a good many across the state, whose presence and work we wanted to acknowledge.

Cookies and Bars for a Thousand

February, 1976

One of the first couples to arrive at a series of faculty open houses Shirley and I hosted a month or so after we were settled in the President's Home was Economics Professor Wilfred Pine and his wife, Beatrice. I had met Pine years earlier, during a visit he had made to the Iowa State University campus, and the Pines had been most gracious to us during our first tour at K-State.

Pine was a native Kansan, a K-State graduate, and one of the more highly regarded senior faculty. His comment as we greeted them, therefore, set us back a bit. With no little emotion, he said, "I've never before been in the President's Home."

Shirley and her student helper, Marilyn Funk, had been preparing for these and other open houses from the time we had moved into the house, even baking bars and cookies in a basement kitchen before the first floor kitchen was complete.

Shirley and I had decided early that we would invite a student to live with us in the Presidents' Home, to help in household and hosting duties in return for their room. A bright, windowed bedroom plus a bath on the second floor, a side entrance, and a back stairway to the basement kitchen allowed privacy for both the student and us.

One could say it another way: There was no university budget for help to clean and ready the 5,500 square foot home for the hundreds of faculty, students, and university friends we would want to host. There was, though, attractive and available space that would attract a willing student.

During our eleven years in the K-State presidency two young women and two couples were with us long enough to be, in many respects, part of the family. With our two daughters away in college, they gave Shirley some sorely needed help and both of us the satisfaction of watching and working with young people at their best. That we can a quarter century later name them without reference, Marilyn Funk, Heather Spence, June and Moki Palacio, and Sharon and Paul Geist, tells of our regard for each.

Our first guests in the refurbished home, at Shirley's insistence, had been the people who had done the work, the physical plant carpenters, painters, plumbers, and electricians, and their spouses. Eager to see the redecoration job finished, Shirley had donned jeans and gloves and worked alongside them, scraping and sanding.

That had been a most enjoyable and rewarding evening, both for our guests and for us. Each worker not only saw the finished product, each could let their spouse see and admire what they had done.

Our second group had been deans, vice presidents, and directors, the people with whom we worked closely in our daily duties, and their spouses. Secretaries are not to be overlooked; a late afternoon just before Christmas, those deans', vice presidents', and directors' secretaries were our guests for coffee and cookies. Few of them had been in the President's Home and, of course, they were even more interested in Shirley's decoration schemes and furniture arrangement than most deans and vice presidents would be.

But faculty are the core of a university. The rest of us are there to see that faculty, well over a thousand among our eight colleges, have the resources and support to do their jobs. We had set aside six Saturdays or Sundays in February, and planned for two groups of 100, faculty and their spouse or friend, each afternoon or evening. Invitations for specific times had gone in the mail a couple weeks earlier and I had sent word through deans and department heads that, should any one have a conflict, we hoped they would come at one of the other scheduled times.

Though the house seemed large, the living room, sun room, back porch, and even the dining room serving area were filled with people and conversation. Great Plains people love to visit, even those not native to the Great Plains.

By the time the last of the first group was out the door, we usually had but a few minutes to pick up the napkins, rearrange a few chairs, refill the coffee pots, and replenish the trays. The doorbell would ring and Shirley and I would be at the door to greet the second group.

Though there was work, especially for Shirley and her helper, Marilyn, we thoroughly enjoyed it. Many of our guests were people we had known well ten years earlier; they brought us up to date on themselves and their families. We enjoyed as much the new acquaintances, many who would, in one way or another, become good friends.

In any business or public entity, a normal staff concern is whether they count, whether they are appreciated and recognized. In a university, to be greeted by name in the hall by the dean, the department head, or even by a senior colleague, is part of that recognition. To be invited to their home has an even more positive impact. We believe that is a major reason a campus home is provided for a university president. And, that was the reason for our open houses.

Pine's comment at our front door had illustrated that concern in a very personal way. His comment, plus generous words of appreciation as each group departed, made it clear there would be more coffee, punch, cookies, and bars ahead. Every fall, for new faculty, during Extension conferences or campus work sessions for statewide staff, and at least two other times for all campus faculty, Shirley and I would have the privilege of hosting our colleagues.

Perhaps it was unsaid, but it was Shirley's and my intent that when the time came for us to leave K-State, it would be a rare faculty member who could say, "I've never been in the Presidents' Home."

* * * * *

There were two other groups of people whose importance Shirley and I wanted to acknowledge by hosting in the President's Home. The only problem was our schedule. It was not until the last week of September, early in our second year, that we had two nights that we could have townspeople as our guests. And, the following Sunday afternoon we had a hundred or more retired faculty and spouses in the President's Home. For us, in both cases, it was both meeting new people and renewing acquaintances.

* * * * *

Athletics is a highly emotional business and emotion is not limited to game day or game night. Compared to the decisions and actions by other university people with whom I have worked, it seems that coach's decisions and actions are more likely influenced by emotion, less by objective review of facts and circumstances. Following is but one example.

The New Athletic Director that Didn't Show

March, 1976

I would hire five athletic directors (A.D.s) during my presidency. However, only four would serve in that job.

After I had reassigned Barrett I appointed a committee to seek and screen director nominees and candidates. The committee developed a good list, including two people I knew personally and high on the list. Those two were Tex Winter, a highly successful K-State basketball coach in the early '60s, and Stan Sherriff, football coach and A.D. at the University of Northern Iowa. Another high on the list was Hyndman Wall, a former assistant A.D. at K-State, and then A.D. at, I believe, a university in the Southeast. He had been popular with the K-State fans and was well known in Manhattan. I interviewed all three.

Because A.D. or coaching positions are so public and news travels so fast on the athletic grapevine, especially of an offer declined, we were cautious in our process. We checked references via confidential phone calls, arranged interviews at distant airports or hotels, and, in the case of campus visits, met in private homes. Before a formal offer was made, we wanted to be sure the person chosen would accept.

Though Winter had a very high regard for K-State and Manhattan, he was enjoying another coaching success at Northwestern and just could not get interested in administration. Sherriff was tempted but had taken the lead in construction of a new dome for football on his campus. In the end, he could not bring himself to leave UNI.

Wall was interested. He spent a day or more in Manhattan, including a visit with me and, at the end of an extended session with the screening committee in Snell's home, the committee was satisfied. Wall was satisfied, and told Snell he would accept an offer. Snell called me.

I drove out to Snell's home, met first with the committee and they assured me Wall was the man. I then met with Wall and made the formal offer. He accepted with enthusiasm, said he was sure glad to be coming back to K-State. Of course, Wall's presence in Manhattan had been detected and rumors were flying. A long-time acquaintance of Snell, Wall would stay overnight at the Snell's home and we would arrange a public announcement for the next day.

Early evening, however, Snell called, "We may have a problem. Wall is in my study talking to his wife and this is the third time they've talked since you met with him this afternoon." The apparent issue was the effect of their move on a family relative.

Not long after that, Snell was in our driveway. Wall had not been able to convince his wife about the move by phone. Wall had told Snell he needed to fly home. He would get things settled with his wife and would be back late the next day for an announcement. Snell had loaned him a car to drive to the Kansas City airport for a late flight home.

Wall never returned. Snell had to send his son to Kansas City on the airport shuttle to retrieve his car.

* * * * *

With a new athletic director there would also come another change, incorporation of women's sports into the Department. Two changes at a time would be a heavy load for the athletics staff and for those fans and donors close to the Department.

One Department of Athletics

On Saturday, March 27, 1976, we announced the hiring of Jersey Jermier, an assistant director of athletics at the University of Iowa, as our new A.D. At the same time, we announced that the A.D. and the Department of Athletics would be responsible for both men's and women's sports, effective July 1.

Combining men's and women's sports into one department brought another backlash from a few of the donors, "We'll be d__ed if we'll let any of our money go to that women's basketball program!" Several formed their own fund-raising group; I don't recall the name they gave it. Leaders made it clear their money would still come to the Foundation for athletics, but it would be clearly designated for the men's programs!

I told those who talked to me, among them Norman Brandeberry of Russell, that I saw no problem with that. The amount of state money I budgeted into the Department would not be affected and the A.D. had total freedom to allocate that state money where it was most needed. In fact, their move may have helped; it allowed some of the more vocal to "let off steam" and more donations may have resulted.

When I later formed a search and screening committee to find a replacement for Jermier (his departure described later), I asked Brandeberry to give me three names from his group and I would name one to the committee. I often did that with groups to be represented on a committee; it gave me the freedom to balance a committee for gender, geography, or other factors. Brandeberry sent back word he would give me only one name and it would be Brandeberry! When athletics is involved, emotions run high.

A few years later, after Brandeberry had been appointed to the Board of regents, he invited Shirley and me to Russell for an area alumni dinner. He picked us up at the local airport and our drive into town was fully occupied by his telling about his daughter's success as a member of the local track team and his pride in her athletic achievements.

I nudged Shirley. Was he now a supporter of women's sports?

* * * * *

The management change in Athletics was only Step One in getting the Department's financial house in order. Another step had to be getting rid of several debts, especially unpaid rent to the Foundation for the athletic dorm. That had been one of the debts I had learned about in that June 30, 1975, meeting with Foundation trustees.

Why is the Athletic Dorm Losing Money?[4]

This building seemed an insoluble problem. It was in terrible physical shape and heavily mortgaged. The structure had been built in the late 1960s on KSU Foundation-owned land, financed with both donations and borrowed money.

It had been part of K-State's late 1960s effort to get K-State football out of its perennial hold on the bottom spot in the Big 8 conference.

I could imagine the arguments presented to President McCain. Athletes would have their own training table, with more calories, more protein, and more choices. Coaches could more closely monitor their players' study time. A new facility just for athletes, and with a swimming pool, would give a big boost in recruiting.

The Foundation had been the vehicle. It owned land between Ahearn and the then new football stadium. The Foundation borrowed money to supplement donations and built the building. Rent paid by Athletics would service the mortgage, both principal and interest, and eventually retire the debt. However, athletics was now behind in its rent payments ($6,700 per month).[5] The Foundation was using other money to make the mortgage payments and avoid foreclosure.

Using what records could be found, our finance staff had calculated the dorm was losing about $100,000 per year. In the process, we had learned some of the reasons. Though I am sure coaches would have preferred eating at home with their families, some were taking their meals at the dorm, presumably to monitor student-athlete's behavior, especially study habits. But, records showed no compensating income.

More significant and far more egregious, some non-scholarship athletes were simply housed and fed in the building. Records were inadequate to establish details (and, obviously, not known by me at the time) but the practice was compensating, illegally, for the football scholarship limitation imposed by the NCAA and Big 8 Conference for previous rule violations.

After getting a reasonable picture of Athletics' total financial problems I took a look at the dorm. Though the building was less than nine years old, doors would not close and sturdily-built lounge furniture, desks, and chairs were in bad shape. Carpet was nearly worn through. The kitchen needed work. The building was hardly adequate for student living, let alone a positive for recruitment.

I believe that for every problem there is a solution. For this problem, however, the solution would not be simple.

* * * * *

It may seem to the reader that a state university presidency exists for the primary purpose of dealing with athletics. In this case, it was just that circumstances made athletics the most demanding for my time. And, it does engender interest and fascination. But I was, from time to time, able to focus on a few other significant issues. One was the expected decrease in numbers of Kansas high school graduates.

What do the Demographics Show?

K-State and its sister universities had enjoyed steady enrollment increases during the 1960s and early 1970s as the baby boomers enrolled in college. However, a 1975 projection indicated that the numbers of Kansas high seniors would drop 25 per cent, from 33,249 in 1972 to 24,931 in 1986.[6]

Another study, a bit later, reported 30,723 seniors in 1976 and projected the number would drop to 20,963 in 1991.[6] Projections are based on certain assumptions, likely different in the two cases. However, it was clear that Kansas' state universities would likely see enrollment decreases and K-State should be prepared.

Because the number of state financed faculty was influenced by enrollment, we could expect some loss of faculty positions. We needed to be cautious in making staffing commitments, hiring and granting tenure. Especially, we needed to watch enrollment shifts among colleges and departments.

As a further precaution, in 1978 I named a faculty/administrator committee to develop a financial exigency plan, in case there should ever be a perfect storm, a drop in both enrollment and state tax revenues, requiring termination of some tenured faculty.

* * * * *

With an expected enrollment decline, student recruitment would be increasingly important. Within that total recruitment effort, it became apparent that we needed to put K-State in a more competitive position in attracting high ability students. That would have impact on K-State's long-term reputation.

Where are the National Merit Semifinalists?

In preparing to speak to members of Phi Eta Sigma, a freshman scholarship honorary, in late April of 1976 I had asked for trend data on our entering freshman class, including average ACT scores (American College Tests, which a high proportion of university-bound students take during their senior high school year). What I learned was disturbing.

Whereas the average score for K-State freshmen had been 22.1 in the fall of 1965 and 22.4 in the fall of 1970, for the fall of 1975 the average was 20.9, a dramatic drop![7]

Some high school seniors take the SAT (Scholastic Aptitude Tests) in place of or in addition to the ACT. K-State's SAT score trend line was also not encouraging. Average SAT verbal score for K-State freshmen had dropped from 466 in the fall of 1967 to 434 in the fall of 1975. The average SAT math score had dropped from 492 to 472 in the same time span.[7]

It is well recognized, and logical, that a university's scholastic reputation among high school students is influenced by the university choice and experience of their predecessors, their school's recent graduates. If recent graduates near the top of their class have chosen University X and are having a challenging and positive experience, top students coming along will more likely enroll in that university.

These data had prompted me to ask Student Affairs Vice President Chet Peters, under whom the financial aids office operated, how many National Merit semifinalists we had at K-State. Each year tens of thousands of high school seniors across the U.S. take the National Merit Scholarship Program qualifying examination, competing for major scholarships that are provided by hundreds of corporations and universities. Those scoring highest on the qualifying examination, usually 96th percentile or above, are designated National Merit semifinalists. Universities compete in recruiting these premier students, and a most effective recruitment device is a significant scholarship.

Peters did not have data on numbers, but told me there were likely not many semifinalists at K-State. The University was not a member of the National Merit Program. I asked, "Why not?"

Peters had a reasonable answer, money. Large scholarships are needed to effectively recruit national merit semifinalists. K-State scholarship funds were limited and the University's philosophy was to provide a larger number of limited dollar scholarships. Some national merit scholars might have chosen K-State, but it would be on the basis of the curriculums K-State offered, family loyalty, proximity to their home, or other reason.

I still wanted to know how many National Merit semifinalists were at K-State. Peters' staff would later establish that in the fall of 1977 there were nine, freshmen through senior. That prompted my next question, "Where are the rest of Kansas' semifinalists?" I do not know how many were elsewhere, but 133 were at the University of Kansas and 23 at Wichita State University. The total for the three universities was 165, freshman through senior.[8] (In 2008, according to the annual report of the National Merit Scholarship Corporation, 779 Kansas high school seniors participated in the exam competition and 174 graduates earned the Semifinalist designation.)

Reality was clear; if K-State wanted to aggressively recruit National Merit semifinalists, and earn its rightful place among Kansas and U.S. universities, it would take a lot more scholarship money. We had taken some steps in that direction; we would need to reinforce those and take more.

I was convinced that in order to attract more high ability students, K-State needed to join the National Merit Program and find the money to provide attractive scholarships. For a time, that was another problem. Though our financial aid staff handled the mechanics of administering scholarship funds (as well as loans, work study funds, etc.), scholarship policy and most award decisions were made by a committee of faculty and a K-State Foundation representative. That committee had a rather long standing lack of interest in the National Merit Program, obviously due to the limited dollars, but I also heard expressions that the program might be too elitist for K-State. That I could not accept.

After Peters saw the steps being taken by the Foundation for more aggressive fund-raising (described later), he was on board to join the National Merit Program. He would encourage Financial Aids staff and some key faculty on the committee; I focused on Foundation representative and local banker Al Hostetler. Hostetler had been very supportive on other issues and had become a good friend. Quite conservative in financial affairs and deeply concerned that our scholarship program benefit as many young Kansans as possible, Hostetler was dubious about the National Merit Program. However, whatever was good for K-State in the long run, he wanted to support. In time, when he came to realize the tremendous fund-raising potential of the Foundation (which he served as executive committee chair) he also embraced the idea.

Once Hostetler realized the value to K-State of the National Merit Program, he encouraged other scholarship committee members to support the idea. K-State's joining the program was announced by our Student Assistance Director Mike Novak on July 1, 1977.[9] That fall, as part of a total university effort to attract our share of higher ability students, I wrote a personal letter to each of that year's Kansas semifinalists.[10]

By the fall of 1979, we would have twenty-four National Merit semifinalists at K-State. By 1983 we would have forty-one, and by the fall of 1985 the number was fifty-two, more than five times the number in 1977![11]

How about ACT and SAT scores of entering freshmen? The data in my pocket notebook do not show significant change in SAT scores, but ACT scores in the early 1980s would be back above 21 and would reach 21.4 in 1984.[12]

Where are Kansas' college age National Merit semifinalists at this writing, spring of 2010? When K-State joined the Program, I set a long-term goal of half being on the K-State campus. That goal was obviously unrealistic; a good many of these top students are recruited by major non-Kansas universities such as Harvard, Yale, SMU, or Stanford. However, if half enroll in Kansas institutions and K-State attracts half of those, there might be, from among the 2006, '07, '08 and '09 high school graduating classes, about 174 (25% of 174 x 4 years). I hope so.

* * * * *

The ACT and SAT score averages in the preceding section confirm that most new K-State students are bright. Some are also a bit naïve.

Is Duane There?

It was a rare evening at home, just the two of us, reading. Shirley answered the phone to a breathless question, "Is Duane there?" She handed me the phone with a knowing smile that seemed to say, "Another residence hall freshman or new fraternity pledge."

I took the phone, "This is Duane Acker."

"This is ______. I just got back to my room and there was a note taped to my door to call Duane at 539-2412. The note said it was urgent!"

About that time it registered on the caller that Shirley had answered the phone with, "This is Acker's" and I had used my full name. I might hear an "Oh, oh," then silence.

I jumped into the silence, "Stay on the line, now. This is President Acker and some of your friends are probably just down the hall or around the corner, listening and watching. Let's visit a bit."

The conversation was not long, but I would learn a bit about his classes and what it was like in the dorm or fraternity. And, his friends' fun had been dampened a bit.

Where Did My Time Go?

June 30, 1976

At the end of my first year in the presidency, I asked Mrs. Lindquist to tabulate, from her calendar, how I had spent my time. The information might help me in budgeting my time in the year ahead. Her calculations are summarized in the table on the following page.[13]

Though I was well aware that it had been a busy year, I was surprised at the numbers. Among the meetings and speeches, on campus and off, were twenty-six service clubs, thirty one alumni groups, and eighty advisory, commodity, or interest groups. I was also surprised at the small proportion of time I had spent working directly with deans and vice presidents, though most would have been involved in other of the listed activities. The University of Mid-America, mentioned in the next-to-last entry, was a consortium of largely Big 8 universities offering courses via TV.

How Work Time was Spent, July 1, 1975 – June 30, 1976.

Work Category	Per cent of time	Average hours/ week
Students, including 24 sorority or fraternity events, 11 residence halls, 16 department clubs and 19 classes or seminars	13.5	7.6
Faculty interactions, including 64 visits to departments, branch stations, county offices and other project locations	10.5	5.8
Vice presidents, deans and directors	8.9	5.0
Regents, legislative committees and Kansas executive branch departments	6.4	3.6
Council of Presidents and visits to other Kansas universities	3.7	2.1
Meetings and speeches off campus	17.9	10.1
Meetings and speeches on campus with off-campus groups	9.5	5.4
Office, correspondence and phone	11.3	6.6
Intercollegiate athletics, on campus	4.6	2.6
Out of state, including 6 days with U. of Mid-America, 6 on athletics and 5 at a new presidents' seminar	7.9	4.5
Personal leave	6.2	3.5
Total	100.0	56.8

The data show that the president of a major state university is more likely to find themselves behind a lectern or in a car or plane than behind the desk in his or her office, especially their first year.

Chapter III

The Web

For any business or institution, there is a web of interrelationships and interdependencies, some formal and many informal. Any disruption in the status quo threatens relationships and often the social or business status of people in the web. University athletics is an example.

In 1975, K-State had been at the culmination of a twenty-five-year presidency, with key university actors in place most of the latter years. University information staff, the assistant to the president, and Alumni Association and Foundation staff all had close working relationships with athletics leadership. Local and Topeka sportscasters and sports writers depended on the Department for the latest news on players or schedule, to fill column inches or program time.

There were mutual benefits, access, acquaintance, friendship, choice seats, business volume, identity, and being part of the group. Keck's Steak House, one of Manhattan's best, was a favorite spot for the director to host major donors. A state senator sold promotional items to the Department. Friendships became strong, and practices became traditions. There was good media coverage and, certainly, loyalty to K-State athletics and its leadership. Athletics' loaned car recipient list (it is common for auto dealers to provide their support by loaning cars to university athletics departments) had grown to include some university staff outside the athletics department. One car recipient, I learned, was a key central officer from whom I should have been able to receive unbiased counsel on any issue. These were but examples, understandable in a community of mutual interests.

At the same time, the very existence of such has multiple consequences when there is a change in a key actor or in operating policies. Each member makes a judgment, "Do these changes risk my business, my access, my choice seats, my valued place in the group? If so, is it worthy of protest? Or, can I benefit from the change? Should I protest, support, or just watch?"

During my first year in the presidency, as I initiated changes in the status quo, faced and acted on a series of personnel, financial, operational, and attitude issues in intercollegiate athletics, it was fascinating, and very revealing, to watch the responses of people in the K-State athletics family. I might classify several as the Statesmen, the Protesters, or the Watchers.

The Statesmen

I felt personal appreciation for, and recognized the extraordinary value to K-State of several individuals. Though all were part of the web, strong supporters of K-State athletics, major donors, and friends of coaches and the A.D., their knowledge, core convictions of right and wrong, and willingness to base their posture and words on the facts they knew and their core convictions cause me to call them statesmen.

First was Al Hostletler, major owner and chairman of Manhattan's First National Bank and Chairman of the K-State Foundation executive committee. Hostetler had been the first to raise an objection after Barrett's presentation in that June 30, 1975, meeting. And, he grounded a lot of lightning, fielding calls from concerned fans after Barrett had been reassigned in late December. I understand that Hostetler's response to "What's going on?" in those calls was "Hold your fire; there is a lot that you don't know." Hostetler knew, perhaps even more than I did. Next were two Foundation executive committee colleagues, abstractor Robert Wilson and local attorney Richard Rogers. I know that they, too, fielded calls and main street visits.

The respect with which these three were held and their being "in the know" as members of the Foundation executive committee, plus their support of my several actions, conveyed the message that circumstances had required action.

Cruise Palmer, managing editor of the *Kansas City Star,* and Rick Harman, Kansas City restaurateur, both K-State alums, invited Shirley and me to dinner in Kansas City in early January, 1976. They let us know they understood K-State athletics' management problems and the need for attention. Palmer followed up with further support on several occasions.

Regent John D. Montgomery, publisher of the *Junction City Daily Union.* Though most members of the Board of regents had no connection at all to K-State athletics, I had briefed them fully. To a person, they supported my actions. It was Montgomery, though, who came forward personally, when I was being blasted by sports writers and some fans, with reassurance that I was on the right track. Junction City was close enough and he had enough friends in Manhattan to know some of facts behind the issues.

Former K-State dean of agriculture and vice president, A.D. "Dad" Weber. He likened my reassignment of Barrett, which had come as a surprise to most, to President Ford pardoning Nixon. Had I discussed some of the problems and sounded out a wide circle of people for alternative actions (often done in such circumstances), it would have unleashed enough friends of the status quo that resulting political pressure might have prevented me from taking needed action.

Dr. Bob Snell, chair of the athletic council. He was in a difficult spot as the new chair of athletic council and with a new president on board. However, he played his role perfectly, kept in touch with the athletics department, the A.D., and coaches, relayed information I was unable to get directly, and gave me good and steady counsel. We had many long discussions regarding the seemingly endless and disturbing facts and circumstances.

Jack Goldstein, owner of Manhattan Steel and Pipe Supply, and Fred Bramlage, owner of a Junction City beer distributorship. Both were major donors, key Foundation trustees, and successful business people who would brook no nonsense in financial matters.

There were more that I would like to include. Many not listed were the quiet people, a number of Manhattan professional and business people who were not about to make public their support; there was too much emotion among some of their neighbors, customers, or clients. However, at the cash register, at a reception, in church, or otherwise, they would convey a message of thanks or support.

The Watchers

Publisher Ed Seaton, *Manhattan Mercury*. In the total process, the *Mercury* played a proper role, reported the news and let columnists express their opinions. Though I might have been less than pleased with some of those columnists' opinions, or even the content of some news items, I admired the way that Seaton kept the paper and his staff on point.

Earl Brookover, Garden City cattle feeder, and Don McNeal, Council Grove publisher, both highly successful but modest people. I had been acquainted with both during my first tour at Kansas State and they had been members of the presidential screening committee. They were not the type that would insert themselves in controversial issues, but I felt comfort in knowing their level headedness and their deep interest in K-State. I knew they were watching the process and I felt I had their quiet support.

C. Clyde Jones, who had stepped out of the athletic council chairmanship following Rainsberger's selection. I did not seek out his advice or information at the time and that was my error. My thought toward Jones was the same as my thought toward McCain. Each had no doubt done their best; the problems were now Snell's, as council chair, and mine. I am sure Jones had no desire to be a continuing actor. However, I know that he had to be a most attentive watcher.

Dr. Dan Upson, professor of veterinary medicine. After a committee appointed by McCain recommended to me a few weeks after my arrival that the director of athletics report directly to me rather than to the council, Upson, a committee member, submitted an opposing minority report. When I received both the committee's report and Upson's, I consulted with my Anderson Hall colleagues, long-time central administrators, and approved the majority recommendation. That was a mistake; it took away some insulation of the president. Upson's view was better.

Most of the faculty, deans, and vice presidents. Neither Vice Presidents Beatty nor Chalmers wanted anything to do with athletics. Young (facilities) was not one to seek involvement outside his responsibilities and Peters (student affairs), as the lead person helping women's basketball get underway, had had enough run-ins with the A.D. and men's coaching staff that he felt he would be too biased to get involved. Deans, too, were generally quiet watchers; they had too many things to look after in their own units.

How about the faculty? There were certainly some faculty friendships with Department of Athletics personnel that caused some angst. As a whole, though, I was strongly applauded by faculty, in that administration was, as some said, "finally taking some steps that would bring athletics back into the University, to operate as a part of the University."

The Protesters

To list names might be inappropriate. In time, most of the emotional blasting gave way to such as, "I guess it was needed but why did it have to be so public?" In athletics, nothing stays private very long, and very few things are without emotion.

I recall reading in the *Topeka Capital-Journal* at 7 a.m. the day after Barrett had been reassigned a blast at me by Dr. Richard Spencer, a Scott City veterinarian and alumnus member of the athletic council. My reading was interrupted by the phone. It was Spencer. "I just read my quotes," he said, "I guess I got it off my chest. But I want you to know I'm still on the team and want to help."

At the same time there were several who would not be deterred, and their issues were more than the Barrett reassignment, especially my earlier statements about following the rules and "No slush fund." I was first visited in my office by a state senator. He told me that K-State football could and should be Number one or two in the conference, that "there are a lot of rules that can be interpreted a lot of ways, and one has to interpret them his own way." His message was less than subtle.

The next visit, from a member of a major donor family, was even more to the point. To have a successful football program I would "have to do what other Big 8 presidents have done, look the other way and let coaches have freedom to do their own thing, to recruit any way they can." He followed up with "the alumni are pretty stirred up" and if I did not want a real mess I "better not interfere with recruitment efforts."

In neither of the latter cases did I argue with my visitor. I simply listened, asked if they thought K-State could afford another conference and NCAA probation for violating rules, and thanked them for being candid with me.

I interpreted these visits in two ways: 1) They and others had been helping K-State coaches violate conference and NCAA rules in player recruitment and did not want to quit. 2) They wanted to help me survive as president, by warning me to back off.

Regardless, there was no way that I would change my posture and my position statements to staff or others.

On an alumni group trip in 1984, I recognized one who had been among the most vocal and critical in an early January, 1976, meeting with some rather disturbed booster club members from across the state. In that meeting one of the boosters, apparently frustrated that I was taking a hard line on following the rules had blurted out, "Acker, you just don't understand!" I shot back, "The hell I don't; I've been there!" One evening he recalled the meeting and volunteered that when I shot back he "began to understand what had been going on." He followed up, "That was when I developed respect for you and the steps you were taking."

Though intercollegiate athletics would continue to demand far too much of my time during my first four years (considerable described in the next chapter), the extent and pervasiveness of the problems would allow their resolution to give me, in time, extraordinary satisfactions. My ears had been burned and my hide rubbed raw on more than one occasion (and more would come), but I would not lose sight of where we needed to go and would not lose the determination to get there.

By no means do I suggest that every decision I had made or would make would be the right one, and there had been and would be unfortunate discomfort visited on several key actors. However, each decision had been and would be made with the goals paramount, respectable winning records, follow the rules, and balance the books.

I know that nothing is permanent, that there will always be competitive and emotional pressures in athletics. That is one of the reasons for school, intercollegiate, and professional sports programs! However, as in all of life, competitive and emotional pressures must be held in reasonable bounds; the program or activity must retain credibility.

I would leave the K-State presidency, in time, with extraordinary satisfaction that I had contributed to K-State's strength and credibility in intercollegiate athletics. I would have liked more consistent winning records in all sports. However, each sport would be credible, the women's program would be moving toward equality with the men's, the Department would be following the rules, the mortgage on the athletic dorm, by then Edwards Hall, would be retired, athletes would be dispersed in all residence alternatives, management and monitoring systems would have long been in place, and the financial books would be balanced.

* * * * *

Few elements of a university engender more enthusiasm and fan support, and few give university presidents across the country more public pressures and frustrations, than intercollegiate athletics. The next chapters share, in some detail, some of those pressures and frustrations. To see the enthusiasm and fan support, spend a few nights in Bramlage Coliseum.

Chapter IV

Intercollegiate Athletics

Athletics had demanded much of my attention my first year. In March of 1977 it would demand more. Shirley and I would be glad we had already celebrated our 25th anniversary with an early January trip to New Zealand and Australia.

Coach Hartman Comes Back to Town

Wednesday, March 23, 1977

This was our 25th wedding anniversary day, but there would be little time for private celebration. Shirley and I would be in Minneapolis for our women's first ever post season basketball tournament. Student Affairs Vice President Chet Peters, who deserved credit for the women's program, and his wife would accompany us in a chartered plane to Minneapolis.

There would be a bonus for us. Following the afternoon game and a K-State alumni reception, we could have dinner with our younger daughter, LuAnn, a Minneapolis physical therapist, and her husband before flying home. But events would change our plans.

In recent days my attention and that of many fans had been focused on men's basketball coach Jack Hartman, being courted by his alma mater, Oklahoma State. Although we rarely missed a home game, visited the locker room to commend Hartman and his team after hard fought wins, and otherwise expressed support, he had let it be known he did not feel he was getting enough attention from the administration.[1]

Hartman had been distressed that I had not immediately endorsed his push for a new coliseum to replace twenty-five-year-old Ahearn Field House.

And, the more stringent policies and procedures for purchasing equipment and for travel arrangements implemented by our new A.D., Jersey Jermier, bothered him.

I had approved a significant salary increase for Hartman for the next year. Both Jermier and I had made it clear that we wanted him to stay at Kansas State and I had approved extending his coaching appointment four additional years.[2]

However, early on Tuesday, March 22, Hartman announced he was going to Oklahoma State and the evening *Manhattan Mercury* carried a front page photo of him departing the local airport in a private plane. To me, that photo just did not look right. Hartman's facial expression, visible through the plane window, was not one of enthusiasm or happiness. I commented to Shirley, "Don't be surprised if Jack ends up back in Manhattan."

About 9 p.m. the call came, from Snell. Hartman was back in town. He had flown to Stillwater, met with the OSU team, had come to the reality that Oklahoma State's Gallagher Hall was older and smaller than the field house he had left, and had had second thoughts. He had flown back to Manhattan in the early evening, gone directly to his old office in Ahearn, and called Snell. Both were trying to locate Director Jermier.

My response to Snell was that since Hartman had made a public commitment to Oklahoma State, he should think things through carefully. Perhaps he should go hide for a day and just think. I also emphasized to Snell that, since Hartman had made that commitment to Oklahoma State, we had to be cautious in our actions.

More calls followed, from Snell, then from Snell and Jermier together. Hartman did not need to think. He wanted to stay at Kansas State. He was at his desk in Ahearn and would not leave. Hartman wanted to come over to the house and visit with me.

My response this time was a bit more to the point. I would be pleased to visit with Hartman, but only after he had settled his situation with Oklahoma State and its director of athletics. If Hartman wanted to stay at Kansas State, it would be wonderful! However, he needed to talk out with Jermier the thorny issues that had bothered him, joint use of Ahearn facilities by men and women, perhaps coordinated scheduling of games, purchasing procedures, and whatever else needed to be clarified.

"If Hartman decides, on his own and after those conversations, to decline the job at Oklahoma State, he should inform them," I said. "I should not be involved in any conversation with Hartman until then."

It is perhaps an understatement to say that some fans were publicly distressed with the changes I had made in athletics, including the decision to combine men's and women's sports in a single department (though some of the same people would tell me privately that all the changes had to be made). Hartman was a popular and excellent coach and I could not appear to resist Hartman's return. However, I had had enough of Hartman's public griping about Ahearn Field House and lack of administration support. And, I would not be involved in what might be perceived as an effort to help him renege on a commitment to another university. I made it clear to Jermier that there would be no further adjustment in Hartman's salary for the next year, above the significant amount I had already approved.

One sometimes needs an outside perspective. Early the next morning I called Dr. Robert Parks, a fellow Big 8 president, at Iowa State. I considered Parks one of my long-time mentors and models, from the time he was a new dean of instruction at Iowa State and I was an associate professor and member of our college curriculum committee.

I shared with Parks the background and the current situation with Hartman and asked his advice. Parks was helpful; he advised that with such a winning record and fan support for Hartman, "You can't afford to not take him back."

At 8:30 Jermier and Hartman came to my office and Hartman told me he wanted to stay at Kansas State. I told him I was very pleased with that, if he had informed Oklahoma State of his decision.

He said he had made contact, but a final call needed to be made after the visit with me. That bothered me, but we proceeded. I reaffirmed that I wanted him to stay. He had a successful record as our coach, he followed the rules, and he gave the kind of leadership our student athletes needed and our people respected. We needed him. At the same time, I told him I would insist that henceforth his public statements should be totally positive regarding the University, the athletic facilities, and the administration's support.

Both Jermier and I emphasized the salary for the next year had already been established; there would be no further change, no enticement for him to back out of the Oklahoma State job. He simply had to inform the people at Oklahoma State.

Though I was disappointed and distressed at this total episode, I know that most good coaches are highly emotional people and that Hartman had let his frustrations build out of proportion. Returning to his alma mater had had high appeal, and by that move he would have been saying to Jermier and me, "So, there!" Such is human.

But now he had faced reality. He wanted to stay at Kansas State. He would make the final call to the Oklahoma State A.D., Floyd Gast, coincidentally, his college classmate and personal friend. We talked about the need to make that call immediately, that we needed to schedule a press conference, and that there needed to be a press release to which we could all agree. They left my office for Hartman to make the call.

By 11 o'clock, the time our plane was scheduled to leave for Minneapolis, I had received no confirmation of Hartman's final call to Gast. He had made another call, but it had not been "the final call." Gast had said that if Hartman backed out, his own job might be on the line, and appealed to Hartman to reconsider. At the least, Gast pleaded for time to notify his president and several key Oklahoma State regents.

Hartman felt an obligation to honor that appeal; he had put Gast in a precarious position. I told Jermier that Hartman's presence in Manhattan was probably well known by now and his decision and the call had better get made.

No way could I depart for the women's game in Minneapolis. I told Peters to proceed; he and his wife would represent us at the game and Shirley would arrange for our daughter and husband to join them for the K-State reception.

I walked over to Ahearn and the Athletics Department office, where things were in turmoil. Hartman was thoroughly demoralized, distressed, caught in his own conflict, and almost pleading for help. I told him he had made the decision and that we fully supported him in his decision.

We proceeded to schedule a press conference for 1 p.m., but I was still not certain what the press would be told! Would we be announcing Hartman's continuing as Kansas State's coach? Or would it be confirmation that he was going to Oklahoma State?

I emphasize that Snell and Jermier deserve much credit, not in causing Hartman to make his decision, but in serving as good listening posts while Hartman worked out all his misgivings and embarrassment. He finally made the final call to Gast.

I reminded Hartman of the press release; he needed to write down what he wanted to say. However, he was in no condition to write it. I wrote it, Hartman and Jermier concurred, and we gave it to Sports Information Director Glen Stone to fill in the details and get it reproduced.

Lunch time had come and gone. Hartman, Jermier, and I walked over to the Big 8 Room in the K-State Union for the press conference. The word had spread that Jack was back in town. I learned later that "Jack is back" had appeared on at least one sign in Aggieville. The Big 8 room was full, students, several members of the K-State pep band, several deans and faculty, a number of local supporters, and, of course, sports writers and sportscasters.

My words to the group were only, "I present to you the head basketball coach at Kansas State University, Jack Hartman."

As Hartman stepped to the microphone there was standing applause, demonstrating not only respect for Hartman and his coaching abilities but also their empathy for the embarrassment he had to feel.

Hartman's first words were perfect, "Folks, I committed a turnover." He proceeded to express appreciation for Kansas State and the fact that the administration had stuck by him in a very difficult and embarrassing situation. He apologized for the discomfort and embarrassment he had caused Oklahoma State, and declared he would do the best job he could for Kansas State. His heart belonged to Kansas State and he wanted to remain at Kansas State.

I walked back to my office, called several key athletic supporters to make sure they were informed, and then left the office. I was determined to spend a little time with Shirley on our 25th anniversary. I also wanted to get away from the phone; I had no desire to replay the issue with the media.

Shirley and I got in our little Honda Civic, drove out across the U.S. 177 viaduct and up the Republican River valley road to the southwest. We continued across the interstate, and followed several ridges and creek valleys southeast toward Alta Vista. The Bluestem was greening up and a few early flowers were in bloom. It was a beautiful afternoon in the Flint Hills.

We drove back into Manhattan about 5:30, but I still wanted to avoid the phone. We bought two hamburgers and milk shakes at McDonalds and drove on north to the lookout at the west end of the Tuttle Creek dam. There we enjoyed our 25th anniversary dinner and the lengthening shadows of a March sunset.

* * * * *

While Hartman was being courted by Oklahoma State, his departure for Stillwater, and his return, another drama was playing out.

The Would-be Successor

Late March, 1977

When a head coach announces his departure, any assistant coach that is not to go along will start making phone calls to find another job. A new head coach will likely want to choose his or her own assistants.

Hartman's assistant, Mark Reiner, had been with him only a couple years, but had developed a strong following. He was an excellent recruiter, the players liked and respected him, and he had filled in well during a brief Hartman illness. He would be a popular replacement.

During Hartman's brief absence to Stillwater I had received more than one phone call urging me to immediately name Reiner as our new head coach. Fans were not taking any chances; he might get picked off by some other university. In fact, while Hartman was flying back to Manhattan, some fans had organized a rally at Reiner's home, encouraging him to stay at K-State.

I would have been willing, after checking with a few others, to have approved a recommendation by Jermier to name him head coach. I did send indirect word to him that I wanted him to stay; I could say no more than that.

So here was a popular and capable assistant coach who, for a few hours, saw himself as the likely new K-State head coach. Then, his boss comes back and he is still the assistant.

I give credit to Reiner; he tried to accept the situation and correspondence on file suggests that he had.[3] However, a few weeks later we lost him to another opportunity.

* * * * *

From time to time a U.S. president tries to control the media, and they may succeed to a degree. However I believe that any effort by a university president to control a college newspaper is both unwise and outside the spirit of the journalism discipline that one's university teaches.

Freedom of the Press

Not once in my years as president did I ask or suggest to a colleague that they should ask the *K-State Collegian* not to print an intended item. Only once was I asked to intercede, and this was by Football Coach Ellis Rainsberger, in a 10 p.m. phone call.

It seems a *Collegian* reporter had interviewed some football players and fans about the athletic dorm and relationships among the players and coaches. The resulting article was scheduled to appear in the next day's *Collegian*. Rainsberger was distraught, feared the piece would damage him and the team. Would I call the *Collegian* editor (the student editors would be putting the finishing touches on the next day's issue about that time) and ask that the piece not be printed?

I told Rainsberger I had reservations and would likely decline, but that I would give it a few minutes thought and call him back. I called Max Milbourn, long-time assistant to the president, and he strongly concurred in my judgment.

In reporting back to Rainsberger, I tried to calm him. I told him that my experience with a succession of *Collegian* reporters was that they tried to be accurate and factual, that we needed to have faith in their freedom of inquiry and reporting, and that we also needed to have faith in readers to weigh what they read. Rainsberger was not interested in further philosophy, but there was another reason for my response. Reporting and editing a college paper is part of the teaching/learning process under the guidance of a very able faculty adviser. To interfere with the *Collegian* publishing an article would be like asking a student to discard an assignment before it could be evaluated by the instructor.

The piece appeared, with little embarrassing content.

Inaccuracies and out-of-context statements did appear from time to time in the *Collegian*. However, that is part of the territory for a coach, a president, or anyone else in reach of student reporters, columnists, or editorial writers. This is no different than with commercial media and their career staff.

Whenever I may have felt abused by what was printed I would recall a suggestion from Nebraska Chancellor Jim Zumberge upon my acceptance of the K-State presidency, "Just remember, today's newspapers are used to wrap tomorrow's fish."

* * * * *

"Where there is smoke, there is fire." In the case of Coach Rainsberger, there were several instances of smoke. The first was the financial losses of the Athletic Dorm, most occupants of which were members of a large football squad. Another, next described, triggered investigations that brought down both Rainsberger and his boss.

Goodby, Coach Rainsberger

November, 1977

Early in the third year of my presidency, a Salina alumnus had told me that he had gotten wind of some improper recruiting practices in K-State football, but he could give me no specifics and would not reveal his source. It was not but a few weeks later that actions by Rainsberger triggered a thorough investigation.

I was at a November budget hearing in Topeka when a reporter asked if I had heard of Rainsberger's actions the previous afternoon at Highland Junior College, where our junior varsity football squad had played Highland. I had not. It seems that at a critical time in the game Rainsberger had sent in a red-shirted freshman who had come along just to watch. By that action he had used up a year of that young man's eligibility.

When Rainsberger realized the consequences, he pulled the boy out. He had later gone to the scorer's table insisting that boy had not played and that the record be changed to reflect that. That event, plus the comment by the Salina alumnus, prompted questions, and other information began to flow.

The housing and feeding of non-scholarship players in the athletic dorm was a part of the latter. Rainsberger's days at K-State were over.

Once uncovered, it became clear the pattern of irregularities had gone on for some time. Would I follow my declared posture with the A.D. (a pattern of rule violations not caught and the A.D. has to go)? Jermier had been on the job nearly two years. I also knew he was a long-time friend of Rainsberger and that Rainsberger had suggested him to the A.D. search and screening committee. Had Jermier known of the irregularities? Or, had he just failed to monitor?

Enough alumni knew my posture and determination that I received a few calls of caution. One of our most loyal and generous supporters, Fred Bramlage of Junction City, who would later give us help on establishing a Kansas City office for K-State and provide the lead gift for what would be Bramlage Coliseum, was one. As with most major donors, Bramlage was reticent to interfere, but he was concerned, "Duane, K-State athletics has been in the news enough; do you really want to terminate Jermier and have more?" I responded that I had no choice. The pattern of violations was clear and it would lead to another probation for football; Jermier had the responsibility and knew the consequences. K-State must regain credibility in athletics!

Some time later, generous supporter and Manhattan friend Jack Goldstein told me about a meeting of Manhattan business people Rainsberger had called soon after his arrival, the spring before I had arrived. Rainsberger had asked for, as I recall, $300 from each attendee. He needed the money to help recruit top players.

DeLoss Dodds, K-State grad, former track and cross country coach who had served as interim director before Jermier's arrival and had later had joined the Big 8 office staff, was lured back as A.D. and Jim Dickey was hired as football coach. Dodds and Dickey had a long hill to climb, with continued scholarship limitations for football and continued payments to retire the debt on the athletic dorm.

However, they could enjoy several pluses. With actions recently taken, I felt there was finally acceptance among supporters and all coaches that contributions and coach behavior would be within the rules and that expenditures would be prudent. Fan support for K-State athletics was unshakable.

Dodds was also helped by Jermier's early selection of Con Colbert as finance officer for the Department. Colbert remained with the Department and made many valuable contributions until, late in my time at K-State, he was named A.D. at Pan American University in Texas. Though I hated to see Colbert go, he left with my blessing and I was thrilled to see him have the opportunity to lead a department.

There followed, with Dodds, Colbert, Dickey, Hartman, Akers, and their colleague coaches, what seemed, in many respects, some very good years for K-State's intercollegiate athletics. Not all would come easy. As the reader will see in later sections, there would be a good bit of internal confrontation and stress in order to provide a full complement of women's intercollegiate sports.

* * * * *

On earlier pages I mentioned that I had not asked enough questions after I accepted the presidency and during my early weeks in the job. Had I had more information, would I have made the same decisions and taken the same actions?

In regard to athletics, what I would learn a decade later told me that my early judgments and actions regarding athletics had been right on track. It would also confirm that some of my good Manhattan friends (though no names were mentioned) had been goaded into the type of improper actions they would not have even considered within their own profession or business.

Confirming Information

February 11, 1986

At a dinner party about four months before I left the presidency, Clyde Jones, chair of the athletic council until a few months before I had arrived as president, told Shirley and me a story that paralleled what Jack Goldstein had told me years before (about a cash-raising effort by Rainsberger), and more.[4] He related that when Rainsberger was hired in late 1974 he had been the ninth choice; eight others had turned down the job, understandable, with the program being on probation. The day Rainsberger's name surfaced for consideration Jones was asked to check him out with some of Jones' friends at the University of Illinois, where Rainsberger was or had been an assistant coach. Jones placed the call, but by the time the call was returned that evening, Rainsberger had been hired and the hiring announced!

Jones' friend told him to "cancel the employment," that within three years Rainsberger would have K-State back on probation. That was prophetic; K-State was on probation by the spring of 1978 as the result of Rainsberger's behavior.

I understood why Jones had resigned as chair of the Athletic Council and I admired him for having done so.

Jones echoed Goldstein's message, adding the details that there had been about 100 supporters and that Rainsberger had said he needed $30,000. That would figure about $300 per attendee and about $1,000 per recruit.

By this date it was all history; Rainsberger was long gone and the resulting probation was long over. But Jones had re-confirmed that the attitude toward conference and NCAA regulations and the loose financial culture of the Athletics department had not been limited to internal operations; it had extended well into the community and beyond.

I have often wondered, "Who and how many of my Manhattan and statewide friends were involved? Were there any faculty in the group? Who on campus, other than Rainsberger, knew about that meeting? Did Barrett? Could he not have known? Did any of my vice presidents? If they did know, why didn't they tell me?"

I should also add, "Why didn't I ask more questions? By a series of questions, could I have ferreted out this or other helpful information?"

It is difficult to fault most of those supporters who forked over cash or a check; they wanted to be helpful to K-State. They were good people who wanted a winning team and, hopefully, more fans coming to Manhattan to watch the team. They had, no doubt, been assured "it is necessary," and "this is the way it is done." If so, they had been misled.

Yes, violations seem endemic in intercollegiate athletics. But to claim "everybody does it" is simply an incorrect statement. Most coaches and athletic directors, especially the successful ones, are careful in rule adherence. They exhort their fans to support them legally and they have systems in place to monitor operations. They intend to protect their good reputations.

It is usually the impatient and panicky coaches or coaches and A.D.s who are not able to say "No" to unethical actions that stain intercollegiate athletics. K-State's program had been so stained.

In my words and actions during my first years, I had stepped on a lot of toes without knowing whose toes they were. I am glad that I did not know.

* * * * *

After Rainsberger's departure and with Jermier's tenure as A.D. in jeopardy I was, of course, directly involved in the hiring of a new head football coach. We rather quickly attracted Jim Dickey, who had a solid reputation for abiding by rules as well as good coaching skills, and he put together a batch of good assistant coaches. Dickey and his staff had done well, with limited time, recruiting promising high school seniors for the following fall and were ready for the official start of spring practice, the date and duration specified by NCAA regulations. I felt good about what might be ahead for our football program. But, I was due for another surprise.

The New Coaching Staff in Trouble?

Spring, 1978

A few days before that spring practice starting date I returned to my office from lunch to learn that local media had appeared at a late morning meeting of the athletic council. Media had apparently been tipped off that David Laurie, a council member and member of the Physical Education faculty, would report evidence that Dickey's staff were violating rules by coaching their players ahead of that official spring practice date.[5]

In Ahearn's west gym section, the football squad had been going through routine conditioning steps, perhaps practicing defensive and other moves. Coaches were on the benches, watching; that was totally legal. However, at some point, one or more of the coaches apparently got up off the bench, walked onto the floor, and told or showed some of the players just how do to whatever they were doing. That would be coaching, not allowed before official spring practice.

I should insert here a feature I had observed in more than one university situation, the closer two departments in subject matter or activity, the more competition and even jealousy. As college curriculum committee chair at Iowa State, I had had to negotiate a settlement when the Horticulture Department proposed a new course in turf management. The Agronomy Department had objected, said the course belonged in their department because it involved both grass and soils. And, when my Animal Science Department wanted to re-title an animal reproduction course as Physiology of Reproduction, a veterinary professor claimed his college had exclusive use of the word, physiology.

At one time, intercollegiate athletics at K-State had been within the Physical Education Department. I do not know when the split had occurred but, until the new stadium and football offices had been built, all staff had remained in the same building, Ahearn. There was continuing competition for office space and use of the gymnasium and other facilities. Perhaps most significant, some Physical Education faculty thought intercollegiate sports less than academic, yet most coaches salaries were higher and they certainly got more public attention.

Though inter-department stress existed, I make no judgment as to Laurie's motives; I knew him to be a respected instructor and both Shirley I had admired his hobby work, restoring a Model A Ford. However, the publicity was not what K-State football and a new coaching staff needed. Further, Laurie's motives could not be my immediate concern. Considering that Rainsberger's earlier actions would likely put K-State on another probation, I had Jermier get the coaches together at the football office building and we had a rather short "Come to Jesus" meeting. If there was any chance that there remained in the football offices any winking at rules, or if any of Dickey's staff felt the rules had flexibility, such had to be cut off.

* * * * *

Eighteen months earlier, the athletic dorm had seemed an insoluble problem; this day we would celebrate its new life as Edwards Hall.

Dedication of Edwards Hall

October 17, 1978

On this day we officially dedicated this former athletic dorm, newly-named Edwards Hall, now part of the residence hall system. It was appropriately named for K-State's long-time and former director of residence, Thornton Edwards.

With Football Coach Rainsberger's departure, after a pattern of rule violations, I had made the decision, with considerable campus and Foundation trustee support, that there would no longer be an athletic dorm. Jim Dickey had been hired with that understanding. The building would become a part of the residence hall system and athletes would have the same housing options as other students.

First, though, I had to get the building transferred to state ownership. Could the state accept mortgaged property as a gift?

Fortunately, Governor Bennett had appointed a second K-State alum, Dr. Jack Reeves of Garden City, to the Board of Regents and I led Reeves through the building on his first visit to the campus. It did not take long for Reeves to concur in our judgments. We agreed that if state acceptance of mortgaged property was legal, I would ask the Foundation trustees to transfer title to the state, Reeves would support regent action to accept the property, and I would guarantee to all parties that the Department of Athletics would continue to pay the principal and interest until the mortgage was retired.

From where would we find money to renovate, to bring the building to good condition? I would not consider transferring money from the instruction budget. Two of my most appreciated management team members, Vice President Chet Peters and Student Housing Director Tom Frith, volunteered an option. They told me about a fund set aside to update some residence hall recreation rooms, a project long planned. Frith was willing to put the issue to his residence hall staff and student leaders. They discussed and debated and, in time, reached the judgment, "To help the University, this renovation needs to be done. We'll just put off our recreation room up-dating a year or two."

* * * * *

Never did I believe that I would feel joy and satisfaction heading to a football game in a driving sleet storm. However, while Regent Sandra McMullen and her husband, Joe, several of our staff, and Shirley and I were finding our way across the field and into the protection of the enclosed VIP section of the Shreveport, Louisiana, stadium, that was exactly the case.

The First Bowl Game in 85 Years

December 11, 1982

Along with two planeloads of other K-Staters, certainly including Athletic Council members Bob Snell and Kathy Treadway, and such good donors as Fred Bramlage, plus hundreds who had come by other means, we were in Shreveport, Louisiana, for K-State's first post-season bowl game in eighty-five years of football!

In the football locker room after K-State defeated Colorado in November of 1982, winning an invitation to K-State's first post season bowl game. To my right are Athletic Director Dick Towers and Coach Jim Dickey; to my left is Governor and K-State graduate John Carlin. (Photo courtesy University Archives.)

With the Big 8 competition Dickey had faced, it had taken a few years to get traction. Eventually, he had concluded he simply needed to stockpile talent for a year, red-shirt a batch of skilled recruits, so he could eventually field a team that could hold their own in the Big 8. He and Dodds cautioned me it could mean a couple bad seasons. However, it was clear they had the right management strategy and I assured both Dodds and Dickey I would stand behind them all the way. It worked and, though Dodds had left for the

University of Texas A.D. position, K-State won the right to participate in its first post-season bowl game, the Independence Bowl, in the fall of 1982.

I emphasize two points. 1) Dick Towers, who had replaced Dodds as A.D., deserves much credit for K-State being selected. His support of Dickey and his work with the Independence Bowl selection committee and Big 8 Conference staff were superb and may well have been the deciding factor. 2) Dickey's win record that year was the result of both his stockpiling talent and his willingness to take risks during the games. In my judgment, and echoed by many in the stands, he "let it all hang out," caught opposing teams off guard with unexpected calls a number of critical times. It was a fun season.

Unfortunately, those good years with football on the upswing were interrupted. Fans of those years may each have their judgments; it seemed to me that, perhaps as a result of the Bowl appearance, Dickey became more methodical and cautious and that did not work. Conference wins and game attendance slipped. And, in time, Dickey departed.

* * * * *

Combining men's and women's athletics into a single department had been only a minor step toward equality for women athletes. It may have relieved me of dealing with such issues as which team could use the Ahearn court, but the issues, themselves, remained. They had to be dealt with inside that combined department, as well as with many of the long-time supporters. There was also a related issue. Neither the Big 8 Conference nor the National Collegiate Athletic Association (NCAA) would have anything to do with women's sports!

How About Title IX?

In 1972 Congress had passed legislation to insure equal opportunity for women in all of education. That legislation's Title IX provided guidance for women's athletics. The lever for compliance was that violation of Title IX guidelines could make a university ineligible to receive federal funds of any type. That was a big lever, with federal research grants, contracts, and student loan funds increasingly important and with federal funds helping finance the Agricultural Experiment Station, Cooperative Extension Service, and water resources research.

In this regard, K-State had two positive circumstances at my arrival as president: 1) K-State's Athletic Council carried responsibility for both men's and women's intercollegiate sports and membership included several women, one as Council vice chair and University representative to the fledgling Association for Intercollegiate Athletics for Women (AIAW). 2) Our women's basketball program under Coach Judy Akers had established one of the top winning records in the Big 8 Women's League.

To think that a new athletic director, Jermier, could have quickly resolved all those issues, would have been naive. Feelings were intense and long standing. And, Jermier had not only been new to the position, he had been new to Kansas. Except for Rainsberger, staff and supporters had not known him and he had not known them.

I had learned the significance of that in an earlier experience. At SDSU I had had two successive new heads of the Department of Animal Science, both brought in from outside. The first had stayed only one year. The second brought about some needed changes, but he got blocked on one or two big issues by some staff seniority and industry relationships. After he was lured away by another university, I brought back a native South Dakotan, one who had had a successful SDSU faculty career before leaving for the private sector. He was already known in the state and he knew all the actors and relationships, on campus and off. He therefore had a good sense of how and how fast he could make some needed moves in the Department's program. It had been fascinating to watch.

Departments of Athletics or Animal Science are far different from departments of English, History, or Chemistry. For those latter, the key actors and relationships are virtually all on campus; there is no off-campus political base of involved clientele.

With Jermier's departure we had gone after our former track and cross-country coach, DeLoss Dodds, who had been in the Big 8 Conference office two years, to come back as A.D. Dodds' K-State teams had had excellent records. He had the respect of the staff, was well connected among alumni, and had done a good job as interim director between Barrett and Jermier. Dodds was exactly what we needed, and he came into the job with the clear understanding that moving toward a full women's program was a big part of the task.

By that time I had restructured the Athletic Council, using new by-laws developed by a student-faculty-alumni committee. The Council would be advisory to the A.D. rather than to me.[6] I had asked John Graham, associate dean of the College of Business, to chair the newly structured council. Snell would continue as a council member and faculty representative to the Big 8 and NCAA. Thompson had left for another opportunity and I appointed Beth Unger, then Associate Professor of Computer Science, to the council and faculty representative to AIAW and the Big 8 Women's League.

It was clear that, as Snell had devoted much time to athletics, Unger would likely need to devote more. She and I knew that to achieve the changes needed would take time and determination. But, neither of us knew just how much.

I had spent too much time on athletics my first several years. I felt I now had in place the policy and guidance people I needed for athletic, Dodds, Snell, Unger, and Graham. Graham would later resign from K-State to head the Kansas Farm Bureau Insurance Company and I would name Veryl Switzer, then assistant vice president for student affairs, as chair. With the Council advisory to Dodds rather than to me, I would devote less time to athletics. Consequently I was not aware of just how much of Unger's time was consumed on the many issues that she and the women's program encountered.

Unger later shared with me some of her experiences, including that at times she would be devoting ten to twenty hours a week.[7] The day she accepted the appointment, she said, "I was shown around the facility and met the coaches who had offices in Ahearn (football coaches officed at the stadium). As we approached men's basketball Coach Jack Hartman, Dodds said, 'Jack, I would like you to meet someone' I forwarded my hand to shake and Hartman did the same. DeLoss followed up, 'This is Beth Unger and she is the new AIAW representative.' Jack pulled his hand back, refused to shake my hand."

"We moved on," Beth continued, "but the encounter foretold the challenge of establishing an environment of opportunity for K-State women in intercollegiate athletics."

Though Hartman's reported behavior appears out of bounds in today's environment, the reader should recognize that in the late 1970s he was simply reflecting the "men only" culture of intercollegiate athletics, the culture in which he had professionally developed, the culture he knew.

Years later, well after my time, I know that Hartman gave tremendous help to the women's basketball program, shared his coaching skills, became a strong supporter, and perhaps even coached the women's team on an interim basis. Hartman was a winner. Though he may have resisted strongly the cultural change that was sure to come, when he saw that it had come, he would help make winners in all of K-State basketball.

How long would it take for that cultural change? How long would it take for Dodds, Unger, coaches, University administration, and fans to achieve equal intercollegiate athletics programs for women?

* * * * *

To achieve equal opportunity for women's athletics at K-State would require determination, negotiation, and patience on the part of the women's coaches, players, Dodds, and Unger. Patience sometimes gave way to confrontation, what

Unger described as red-in-the-face "debating" between Akers and Hartman. It was serious business. To call it a parallel to the Civil Rights movement may seem to some a bit strong, but on a micro basis it was amazingly parallel.

The Sit-In

By the fall of 1979 tremendous progress had been made. I find a November, 1979, K-State report to the Kansas legislators who comprised Kansas' 1202 Commission, which monitored Kansas' compliance with Title IX.[8] (Title IX had gotten the legislature's attention; members were not about to let universities risk losing federal funds and be called on to replace those funds with state money!) A part of that report was a list of seventeen changes that had been made since July 1, 1978, to move toward equal treatment and opportunity for K-State women players and coaches. They included adding a women's golf team, a full-time certified trainer for women, office reassignments to integrate coaches of a sport in common office areas, and presidential awards for both male and female athletes.

The line-up is for presentation of the first presidential awards for student athletes, at half time of a K-State basketball game, January, 1979. To my right are Governor John Carlin, Dr. Bob Snell, faculty representative to the Big 8 Conference and NCAA, Dr. Beth Unger, faculty representative to the Association of Intercollegiate Athletics for Women, and the two award recipients, Kristi Short and Floyd Dorsey.

Not all of that had resulted from low-key negotiation and patience. Though there had been a single department for several years, the women had not been allowed to use the men's weight room. Not even confrontations between coaches had opened the door. In frustration, members of the women's basketball team had staged a sit-in. They simply occupied the weight room, just before the men would normally appear, and refused to leave! As at the lunch counter in Selma, it had the needed impact; the women's use of the weight room was worked out. And, that November, 1979, list included "a full-time weight coach was hired to coordinate all weight training."

The women's basketball team continued to play championship ball and Shirley and I attended the women's home games with the same regularity as with the men's. The team had a loyal following (most fans oblivious to the tensions behind the scene) and attendance gradually grew. However, there remained far fewer in the bleachers than the quality of play and competition deserved.

Unger, in time and in discussion with Dodds and members of the Council, would urge a double-header, both teams playing the same night. A trial was finally arranged, but even that required some detailed planning. Because ticket sales were separate, the women would play first, Ahearn would be cleared, and the men's game ticket holders then admitted. Hopefully, some men's fans would show up early and buy tickets for the women's game.

Unger reported that when she arrived, ahead of the women's scheduled game time, things were not going well. The shot clocks were missing. The women had always borrowed the men's shot clock for their home games, but for this night the men had taken their clocks! The game was played, but without the shot clocks.

While all this was going on—and the shot clocks and the weight room sit-in are but examples—another set of frustrations, refusal of the Big 8 conference and NCAA to play any role in women's sports, had to be addressed.

I knew that I would have little leverage on that issue with the Big 8 Conference. My reassignment of the gregarious Barrett and combining women's athletics with men's a few years earlier had made me essentially persona non grata among several of the Conference decision-makers, some of the Big Eight athletic directors, Executive Director Chuck Neinas and perhaps even a few of the faculty representatives.

Though the eight university presidents had the ultimate authority, few were eager to spend their leadership authority on this issue. In fact, when I had told my colleagues at our Big 8 presidents' meeting at the January, 1976, Orange Bowl that I was combining men's and women's sports into a single department, a couple had responded, "Acker, do you really want to take that on?"

It was clear that there had to be one conference for both men's and women's sports (and one national organization for the Big 8 level of competition). But most of the presidents pretty well left Big 8 policy up to the assembled faculty reps and A.D.s. Because I knew that I could not be effective, I was glad to have Unger on board. And, fortunately, there was one Big 8 campus head, University of Missouri-Columbia Chancellor Barbara Uehling, who was willing to take it on.

Uehling's and Unger's experiences with the Big 8 conference duplicated what had been going on within K-State's department. Unger started with K-State's Council, including Snell. Should not the faculty representative to AIAW also attend the Kansas City meetings of the Big 8, along with the A.D.s and the NCAA faculty rep? Pressure was also coming from Uehling and, I am sure, at her direction, from Missouri's NCAA faculty rep.

Fortunately, another spontaneous sit-in, in the Kansas City Big 8 conference room, was not necessary. AIAW representatives' attendance was allowed. However, they were asked to sit in chairs along the wall and were to only observe and answer questions!

Eventually there was reasonable consensus on the logical path, that women's athletic teams had to be governed by the same organization, nationally and at the conference level, as the men's. Confrontations still had to happen. Demands for fairness still had to be made. And, relationships remained strained in many quarters. However, in time, the barriers came down. By the 1981-82 season the NCAA, as well as AIAW, would offer national championship events in several women's sports. And, in 1983 AIAW would cease to exist.

As I review these encounters I cannot but agree to the parallel with the U.S. civil rights movement. What civil rights activists had to go through and what those involved in advancing women's intercollegiate athletics had to go through are amazingly similar.

Being the first in the Big 8 to form a single department, and one of few major universities in the U.S. to do so, this may have been more evident at K-State than elsewhere. Unger, Dodds, and our women coaches no doubt helped pave the way for others.

Though I am proud that K-State was the first Big 8 university to form a single department, by no means do I suggest K-State was the conference leader in all women's programs. Several other Big 8 schools had long had well-financed separate departments of women's athletics and had fielded teams in several sports. K-State had some catching up to do.

With continued efforts by people like Dodds and his successor, Dick Towers, Beth Unger, and her successor, Kathy Treadway, and the several coaches, it would! By 1985, K-State would offer as many intercollegiate sports for women as for men, our women's basketball team would have finished in the top ten in the nation five times,[9] and our women's track team would rank tenth in the country.

* * * * *

Yes, I did get frustrated from time to time, with both the time requirement and the content of the athletics issues with which I had to deal. I would share some of that frustration much later with K-State's well known radio voice, Ralph Titus.

How About No Athletics?

In a 2006 oral history interview with former KKSU radio voice Ralph Titus, he would ask if I would much rather have come to a university that had nothing to do with athletics. I responded that I did not know that was a possibility unless you go to the University of Chicago. Athletics is simply part of the territory for which a university president is responsible.

In those first days and weeks in the presidency I had looked at my total staff and wondered, "Was there someone on the central university staff to whom I could delegate this responsibility, or even a major part of it? Was there a person that I could put between me and athletics to some extent?" Could I have tapped someone else to take charge?

My answer was, "No."

The one whose philosophy was closest to mine was Chet Peters, but he was an anathema to some of the coaches and supporters, certainly to Barrett. Dan Beatty was obviously the logical person from a financial standpoint, but he just would not touch it! Neither Paul Young nor John Chalmers, though both able people, had any logical connection or evidence of concern for what needed to be done.

Max Milbourn's talents were directed more toward building and keeping smooth relationships than wading into what would assuredly be rough waters. It seemed that Ken Thomas was, in essence, co-opted by his apparent close association with Barrett and other athletics staff. I almost had to drag Milbourn into my office to be there when I would talk to Barrett about reassigning him to another job. And Thomas was not much interested in preparing the media release.

Was there someone outside of central administration that I could have drawn in to take charge, to support and undergird Snell, the then new chair of the athletic council? I could think of no one who had both the strength of status and the objectivity needed.

I really had to do it myself.

Chapter V

Political Theatre

No state university president is ever far from some act of political theatre. Whether it was defending to a legislator some of Economics Professor Leonard Schruben's statements on the economics of grain ethanol, urging industry support for a new building, or solving a problem for the son, daughter, or spouse of an influential alumnus, I was often a willing or unwilling actor. In this chapter are a few examples; the first example is of the easy type.

Because of my years as an agriculture dean and director of research and extension programs, I would sometimes be asked to speak at industry conferences. Far more valuable than any oratorical skills, my involvement would lend the status of a land grant university presidency to an issue facing the industry. Following was such a circumstance, and the gist of my message.

Where to Send the Bill

September 26, 1977

In the 1970s, with national attention to the Soviet space-race competition, funding for agricultural research was coming up short. Federal appropriations, largely to and through USDA, and state funds to agricultural experiment stations were not even keeping up with inflation.

A presentation I developed for the American Society of Agricultural Consultants, "Where to Send the Bill for Agricultural Research," seemed to strike a note.[1] I would first provide a bit of history regarding the Morrill, Hatch, and Smith Lever acts. I would then mention USDA's research stations and laboratories, such as the USDA Grain Marketing Laboratory just west of the K-State campus, and the fifty state experiment stations.

Those fifty state experiment stations, as a group, are an especially valuable resource for the country. They insure 1) response to each state's knowledge needs, 2) dispersed attention to all regions and regionally important commodities, 3) competition among scientists, and 4) a structure that allows cooperation among states on high-cost research.

Historically, agricultural research focused on more efficient production of plants and animals. Many assume, therefore, that the farmer or rancher is the primary beneficiary. Not so. Any financial advantage a producer gains from new knowledge is short-lived; their neighbors learn quickly. Once production knowledge is widely held, supply increases and price drops. All of society therefore benefits from the volume, quality, and price. Because there are so many beneficiaries, it seems proper that the bill be paid by all, via tax funds, state and federal appropriations.

My message:

- Send the bill to those who eat. Plentiful volume insures reasonable cost.
- Send the bill to those who want to stay healthy. Food is high quality and nutritious.
- Send the bill to those who handle product. Product volume means more transportation and processing business.
- Send the bill to those who produce inputs, such as fertilizers, herbicides, genetic stock, and machinery.
- Send the bill to those who buy foreign oil or foreign cars, or who like foreign travel. Farm exports help the U.S. trade balance, offset some of the high-volume importation of consumer products.

In summary, the bill should be sent to the American public. It is appropriate that public funds be used for agricultural research. Its beneficiaries should be its patrons.

As an instructor might refine a lecture for the second section of their course or the next semester, one refines a speech for successive audiences. It seemed that "Send the bill to…." caught the interest of and brought exposure to a number of audiences, from county livestock or soil conservation groups to the Newspaper Farm Editors of America.

Of course the message and messenger brought K-State to the fore. Every presentation included several examples of K-State research output and impact, such as drought tolerant soybean varieties and a K-State-developed urea product for ruminant nutrition.

*****

It seems that I would find myself behind a lectern or in a car or plane as much time as behind my desk in Anderson Hall. My faculty and clientele were statewide and several key audiences were beyond the state's borders. Presentations to federal agencies, congressional committees, alumni, and industry groups are part of a land grant university president's territory.

Back on campus it was a rare week that I did not have three to five presentations, a student club, college banquet, or a national group convening on the K-State campus. An oft-told story is of the sign on a campus washroom hand drier, "Press here for a message from your president."

To adequately prepare for these many communication opportunities, I needed help. One of the most valuable hires I made early in my time was that of Jan Woodward, with the title of communication assistant. I told her initially that she was not a speech writer; I had my own way of putting words together. I would identify the three or four points I wanted to make to an audience, she would gather supporting data, K-State illustrations and background information on the audience group, and put together a skeleton from which I would talk almost extemporaneously. As with a classroom lecture, if one really knows their subject, one should not be reading word-for-word from a text.

In a short time, Woodward had listened enough to my extemporaneous presentations that she could put together one almost as I would deliver it. Some conferences needed a written copy for published proceedings. After I had outlined the points, she would put it together. I would underline words or sections, and perhaps insert a few last-minute thoughts for the presentation. She would then take what I had used, polish it up, and send it off for the proceedings.

*****

An achievement for the University can sometimes be accompanied by a few moments of embarrassment. But the goodness of the event usually voids any negative consequence. Such was the case when the wrong spread appeared at the wrong time on a K-State Union luncheon table.

Margarine for the Dairy Dedication

December 13, 1977

On the wall of our farm home is a painting by well-known Kansas City artist J.R. Hamil of the former K-State dairy barns on north Denison Street. It was given to Shirley and me as a welcome-back-to-Kansas gift by Ernest Lindsay, president of Farmland Industries, a regional cooperative then based in Kansas City. (Hamil's father had been a Farmland vice president and I had worked with him, Lindsay, and their colleagues, plus member cooperatives in Kansas, South Dakota, and Nebraska.) When new facilities north of the campus would be completed the cows and calves would move and the abandoned barns would be renovated as service buildings for planned greenhouses, part of the future Throckmorton complex.

On completion of the new dairy facilities, we scheduled a morning dedication ceremony for this date, then a luncheon for involved faculty, administrators, and industry leaders plus, of course, legislators who had led the appropriation efforts.

Behind this project is a story—campus lore—shared with me by Roger Mitchell, who had arrived as vice president for agriculture in early 1975, a short time before I would be named president. During the latter part of a legislative session, likely 1973 or 1974, as decisions were being made on capital appropriations, Representative John Vogel of Lawrence and his House Appropriations Committee colleagues were visiting K-State. They had the University's long-term capital needs list, perhaps including Engineering II (Rathbone), the classroom-office building (Bluemont), and Plant Science (Throckmorton). After touring existing facilities, likely with Max Milbourn, vice presidents, and deans, they had assembled in President McCain's office to share their observations and hear from him. McCain reinforced, of course, the need for each project on the list.

According to the story, Vogel spoke up, in essence, "Mr. President, without new dairy facilities on this list, I'm afraid it won't have much value to the committee." The new dairy facility was soon inserted, near the top. Planning funds were provided by the legislature in 1974 and construction funds of $1.2 million in 1975.[2]

Neither Mitchell nor I was around at that time, but understanding the workings of a state legislature, the proportion of members with farm and ranch related interests, and the political sophistication of agricultural organizations, especially dairy, I have no difficulty accepting the story.

Mitchell and I made a courtesy call at Vogel's farm east of Lawrence a few months after I arrived. That visit was worthwhile. When bids came in for the project in mid-winter, 1975-76, we were $300,000 short. With Vogel's continued leadership, the legislature accommodated that shortage with an emergency appropriation.

Though I think of a dairy herd on the edge of a land grant campus as a positive—people love animals and the cows and young calves attract and fascinate—I would be pleased to see the cows gone from the Denison site. I would not be chided at church by across-Denison Street neighbors about the aroma and the flies, as I had been a decade earlier.

Back to the dedication. It had been a prideful morning for all, certainly for Department Head Charlie Norton and his dairy faculty and farm staff, but also for Max Milbourn, who had been a key actor with legislators. At we gathered in the Bluemont Room for the luncheon I was especially pleased to see the Union staff had pitchers of milk and plates of cheese on the table. Soon after we were seated, however, I heard an "Oh,oh" from Representative Ambrose Dempsey, a dairy producer from northeastern Kansas. He reached into the dish in front of us and held up a neatly packaged individual serving of margarine!

* * * * *

Next to athletics, perhaps the topic that demanded large amounts of my attention and emotional energy was what could be done about the burned out Nichols Gym shell. Following is the second act of my involvement in what would be a near eighteen-year saga. (Act One, What About the Castle, appeared as part of Chapter II.)

The Castle: Raze or Stabilize?[3]

January, 1979

During the 1979 legislative session Senate Ways and Means Chair Wint Winter of Ottawa caught me in the hall of the capitol building and told me he would like to help us "cure the Nichols problem." Winter had been one of several KU graduates who had gone out of their way to welcome me back to Kansas. He and his wife had hosted a reception in their Ottawa home after a meeting I had had with the Franklin County Extension Director Robert Bozworth and his Extension Council, late summer of 1975.

Winter said the legislature would provide $125,000 to either raze the Nichols ruin and clear the site or preserve the shell. This could help bring the issue to a head! I appreciated Winter's concern and offer of help.

The 1978 Kansas legislature had tried to help. Senator Ross Doyen, a K-State alum, had introduced and achieved passage of a bill to authorize plans for Nichols reconstruction, with the understanding that half of the construction funds would come from private sources.

I thought that might hold promise; perhaps Nichols could become an art center! We included both Nichols reconstruction and an art center in a fund-raising feasibility study that was scheduled. (See also "The Wish List" in Chapter VIII.) However, the response for each was disappointing, so there had been no basis to seek follow-up construction funds in our formal request to the Board of Regents for this 1979 legislative session.

The day after Winter's offer I assembled members of my Administrative Council (vice presidents and deans), my Consultative Council (including faculty and student leadership), and the Long-range Planning Committee, the latter including planning staff and a number of faculty. I relayed Winter's offer and asked their advice. There was vigorous discussion and debate. The larger number supported razing the ruin and clearing the site, some expressing strong conviction and long-time frustration.

On the other side, though smaller in number, were those who said that no matter what, the shell could not be torn down! Some even suggested the shell should remain untouched forever, at least for that someday when funds might be found to rebuild. A few had said nothing, so I asked each person in the room to state their choice—preserve as a ruin, tear it down, or do nothing. About 65 per cent said, "Tear it down." About 25 per cent opted for preserving it as a ruin; the balance either offered no opinion or suggested doing nothing.

After dinner that evening I walked over to the structure and around it several times, weighing what I had heard and potential consequences, plus an idea that had emerged in the afternoon session. That idea was to preserve Nichols' main entrance, the pylons on each side, and the entrance ramp, but raze the balance of the ruin, then build a drive behind the pylons from Mid-campus Drive to the southwest corner of McCain Auditorium. There would be sufficient space at McCain for a turn-around and a few handicap parking spaces. Such a need was obvious, and I had received pressure for such from townspeople who frequented McCain. Maybe solving the McCain access would offset the ire of those who wanted the total Nichols shell retained.

The next morning I walked the Nichols-McCain site again, then called Winter. I told him we wanted the $125,000, and that we would use it to preserve Nichols' main entrance, the pylons, and the ramp, and to design and build the drive to McCain.

His response, "Fine; I'll see that you get the money." By noon his committee and the full Senate had unanimously approved the appropriation and forwarded consideration to the House. Mid-morning I drove to Emporia to speak at a southeast area Extension staff luncheon, relieved that this thorny Nichols issue would be settled.

During lunch I was called to the phone. Student Affairs Vice President Chet Peters was on the line, "A 'Save the Castle' group of students has gathered outside Anderson to protest your decision on Nichols. Would you meet with them at 4 o'clock? The leaders want to organize a rally."

At 4 o'clock I was back on campus and on the south steps of Anderson with the "Save the Castle" student leaders and a loud speaker, but only forty to fifty students were on hand. The rally leader turned to me, "Would it be O.K. to delay the rally? Tickets for a rock concert went on sale at 4 and most of our supporters are in the ticket line."

I told him it was their party and that I would be glad to meet at any time. As I turned to go back into Anderson I heard a couple boos from the group. I grabbed the microphone, told the group what their leader had asked for, and that I would meet and answer questions at any time.

As the leader announced the rally delay until 5 o'clock, two young women from the crowd followed me into Anderson and my office. They apparently wanted to tell me personally why they disagreed with my recommendation to the legislature. One, though, could hardly contain herself. "I'm so excited!" she said, "The protest, I mean. There were several protests while my sister was here and I was afraid I'd go all the way through K-State and there would never be one!"

By 5:15 there were perhaps 300 at Anderson's south steps, mostly students but also some faculty. I described the alternatives I had been presented, my earlier pledge to resolve the long-standing issue of Nichols, the input and advice I had sought from a wide sector of the campus, and the rationale for my recommendation. The crowd was respectful and listened well, but was not to be deterred. "Save the Castle" leadership and Student Body President Greg Musil urged the students to caravan to Topeka the next day to lobby Kansas House members to vote down the appropriation. The caravan would assemble early morning at the football stadium parking lot.[4]

Through the next day we received complimentary reports from Topeka on our students' behavior. They were well organized, approached representatives respectfully and constructively, and pressed hard for the appropriation's defeat. I was frustrated, of course, that Nichols' resolution might escape us, but could not help but be proud of our students' reported behavior. I also had several phone visits with local State Representatives John Stites and Ivan Sand. They had also had calls from some Manhattan townspeople opposed to the appropriation.

I appealed to Stites and Sand to support the appropriation, to not leave me out on a limb. I had responded to a specific request from the Senate appropriations chair, had obtained input from a broad group of the right people, and had made a difficult but necessary decision. Eleven years had elapsed since the 1968 fire; the state (university and legislature) should demonstrate it is capable of resolving an issue within eleven years!

Late afternoon Shirley and I flew to Larned for an alumni meeting, still expecting House approval. When we returned, about 11, Barry Flinchbaugh, who I had brought in from an Extension public policy position to succeed

Milbourn as my link to the legislature, was waiting in his car at our front porch. He had bad news. Some House members were angry with Kansas State for putting them in a difficult position. Though they felt my recommendation was a good one, they were under intense pressure to vote against it. House leadership was requesting that I withdraw my recommendation.

I felt the House members' anger was misplaced. My colleagues and I had fully considered the options offered. I had made a decision and was willing to take the heat. Now, rather than simply vote down the appropriation, House leadership was asking that I reverse myself and withdraw the recommendation.

My response to Flinchbaugh was blunt, "Nuts! If they don't want to support it, tell them to vote it down. That is what they are elected for." But, he persisted, "They've watched the process and understand. They don't want to vote against a president on such a visible issue; yet, they don't want to be blamed for tearing down a landmark. If you don't withdraw, there may be hell to pay for some other things we need this session."

After a few minutes venting frustration, I told Flinchbaugh to call the deans and vice presidents at 6:30 the next morning for a 7:30 meeting in our conference room.

To the assembled group Flinchbaugh and I laid out the situation and I asked for their advice. Though some wanted Nichols retained, the group was near unanimous in wanting the issue finally resolved. It had gone on far too long! In the end, though, there was general consensus it would best serve K-State for me to withdraw my recommendation. However, I should tell legislative leadership we would depend on them to find the solution.

I called Sand,[5] a loyal university supporter and valuable communicator in this process, and told him I was withdrawing my recommendation. His response, "Thank God," confirmed Flinchbaugh's concern of the night before. I went on to say, "Ivan, I'm done with this issue. It is now in the hands of you and your colleagues." His response: "That's fair enough." (So ended Act Two of this multi-year saga. Act Three, "Nichols Hall, from the Castle," appears later in this chapter.)

* * * * *

K-State and its sister institutions had enjoyed steady enrollment increases through the 1960s and early 1970s as the baby boomers were coming to college. However, the increases would soon be over and K-State and sister institutions would see an enrollment decline. We had taken some internal preparatory steps, and we also needed to alert the local business community.

The Chamber and Projected Enrollment

December 5, 1980

Projections in 1975 indicated that numbers of high school seniors would drop nearly 25 per cent from 1972 to 1986.[6] The Western Interstate Commission on Higher Education (WICHE), had later projected Kansas high school graduates would drop from 29,397 in the spring of 1981 to a low of 24,372 in the spring of 1986. Numbers would, in time, go back up to a projected 28,639 in the spring to 1999.[7]

State appropriations were based, in part, on enrollment, so I had named a faculty/administrator committee in 1978 to develop a financial exigency plan, just in case there should ever be a perfect storm, a drop in both enrollment and state tax revenues, requiring termination of some tenured faculty. I had told our faculty senate, "Our best projections suggest that, while we probably have already peaked in enrollment, the size of the decrease will not be significant until 1982. It probably will be quite substantial between 1982 and 1986 and then will level off or even turn slightly upward."[8]

However, K-State's enrollment in the late 1970s had not yet peaked. Sharp increases in College of Engineering enrollment, from 1,842 in 1977 to 2,819 in the fall of 1981, kept our reported enrollment on an upward trend.[9] Much credit for that goes to Dean Don Rathbone and his outstanding faculty. The peak would not be until the fall of 1981. During the 1970s there was considerable apartment construction in Manhattan, but it had not kept pace with demand and residence halls were packed. In fact, one year Shirley opened the third floor of the President's Home to several young women until space would be available in residence halls later in the fall.

K-State's first enrollment decrease, slightly less than 500 students, would be in the fall of 1982.

On this day, December 5, 1980, several of my staff and I were participating in a Manhattan Chamber of Commerce retreat held in a Kansas City motel. The retreat focus was, most appropriately, K-State's projected enrollment decrease, a major concern to Manhattan businesses and apartment owners. How could the decrease be minimized?

I appreciated this focus by the Chamber, and its aggressive support of our recruitment efforts. The Chamber provided funds to help with university career days and open houses for prospective students, including shuttle buses to and from campus. Chamber staff worked with alumni to bring students from Wichita and Kansas City, and even provided funds for some staff recruitment trips to St. Louis schools. These efforts had helped keep enrollment increasing. But I also had to be sure Chamber members faced reality regarding the future.

Regent's budget officer Tom Rawson (later to become a K-State vice president) had projected fall enrollment for each regent university and I shared with the retreat group his K-State projections. They are shown in the accompanying table.[10] FTE pertains to full-time-equivalent, fifteen credits per student for undergraduate curriculums and a smaller number for veterinary medicine and graduate students.

Projected Enrollment at K-State.

Fall	Head count	FTE
1981	17,784	17,126
1982	17,259	16,620
1983	16,945	16,318
1984	16,234	15,633
1985	15,722	15,146
1986	15,316	14,749

For Chamber members, business people, realtors and apartment owners, this was not a happy picture. Nor was it for me and my colleagues. However, based on demographic data, it was expected reality.

I described to those present a series of University and individual college efforts directed to minimizing the decrease. Home Economics, Architecture and Design, and Arts and Sciences had each assigned a staff member for coordinating recruitment. Home Economics had added a men's career day. Engineering was sending honors and professional society students to recruit at their own and surrounding high schools. Agriculture's student ambassadors were contacting home area counselors, teachers, and prospective students, and Arts and Sciences had launched a two-way telephone hook-up with high school honors students.

Continuing Education was adding more evening and late afternoon classes, and had developed a Phoenix program to encourage those who had interrupted college to return and pursue their degrees. Both Admissions and Affirmative Action offices were recruiting minority students in visits to high schools and urban community centers. Our Aids and Awards office was awarding scholarships earlier to insure that more top students chose K-State. We had joined the National Merit Scholarship Program (details elsewhere, Page 48) and our Foundation and colleges were hard at work attracting money for these and other scholarships.

We also had to overcome an unfortunate and ill-advised 1980 Board of Regents policy action, regionalizing the state for off-campus courses in other than unique disciplines. K-State and Ft. Hays State were assigned generally that portion of Kansas west of Topeka.[11] Our College of Education was forced to back out of a Kansas City graduate program in education administration, and that cost the University both head count and FTE. The College tried to compensate, attract more students by adding courses in our unique specialty, adult and occupational education.

Engineering and Journalism focused on internships in the Kansas City area. We charged a new dean of Architecture and Design, Mark Lapping, to develop a thirty-week Kansas City internship program. With the help of Athletic Director Dick Towers, Alumni Association Director Larry Weigel, and Foundation Trustee Fred Bramlage, we also established a joint athletics-admissions staff position there to increase K-State visibility. By the fall of 1985 we expected to have at least 1800 students from Johnson County at K-State, prompting a suggestion to a Kansas City alumni audience that we might, in time, call the area KSU-East.[12]

Would those declining enrollment projections presented to the chamber members, and well known by K-State faculty, prove to be accurate? Or, would the collective efforts of our K-State campus and Extension faculty, college leadership, admissions staff, Alumni Association, Foundation, and the Manhattan Chamber somehow minimize the decline? Two later sections speak to that question. One discloses a problem with early data; the other will answer the question.

* * * * *

Campus enrollment would touch a number of Manhattan business people; the next issue touched just one, a local banker. And, he would not be happy about it!

They Towed Whose Car?

It was about 4 o'clock that Facilities Vice President Gene Cross rushed into my office. "You need to know before you get a phone call," he said, "our security people just towed Al Hostetler's car from a handicap designated stall!"

Though many of these stalls remain unoccupied most of the time, they had to be kept free for the handicapped. Cross had told his security staff that no one was immune from the law or university parking regulations. Violators' cars should be ticketed or towed. But towing was a judgment call and Hostetler's car would not be my first choice for towing.

Hostetler was the primary owner and chairman of Manhattan's First

National Bank, a loyal university supporter, and Executive Committee chair of the K-State Foundation Board of Trustees. He and his wife had become our closest non-university friends. They were considerably older than Shirley and me, but so supportive and loyal that I could talk to them privately about any issue. Beyond that, Al had a well-known—he would laugh about it too—short fuse.

I had encountered that short fuse in my first contact with Hostetler, June of 1962, when we had arrived in Manhattan for my associate dean post. We had purchased a house under construction at 2802 Oregon Lane, needed a loan, and I was making the rounds of banks and savings and loan associations. At the First National Bank, Al Hostetler, then president, was the man to see.

As I walked in he was having an intense conversation with an apparent borrower, the exchange loud enough that I could not avoid hearing. The borrower was in the used car business and had publicly announced he was going out of business before telling his banker. Hostetler was not happy.

The man left, I walked up to the counter, introduced myself, and told Hostetler my purpose. Based on quotes I had received from other lenders, I asked if his bank would consider a loan at 5 ¼ per cent interest. Hostetler's response was quick and blunt—perhaps some adrenaline was still flowing from his previous conversation—and in the form of a question, "Why should we give you a loan at 5 ¼ per cent?"

I confess that getting a question in response to a question does not set well with me; our visit did not last long and we arranged our loan at another bank.

I had never asked Hostetler if he remembered that visit, probably our only time we had met during my earlier time in Manhattan. When we returned in late June, 1975, Hostetler had been the key figure in my first encounter with K-State's financial problems in athletics. And, as I set out to handle those difficult and public problems in athletics, Hostetler was a rock. I know that he grounded a lot of lightning from concerned athletic supporters across the state.

Back to the towed car. I am sure Hostetler would not have parked in a handicap stall if there had been another space available, and he was probably on campus helping do the University's work. He was on our University Scholarship Committee, likely on his way to a committee meeting, and did not want to be late.

I turned and placed a call to him. Fortunately, he was back in his office and had had time to cool down. "I was wrong," he said. "I would sure have appreciated someone tracking me down, but I did deserve to be towed."

Perhaps Hostetler's fuse was short, but it had burned out quickly. He was still a rock.

* * * * *

An unanticipated joy in the K-State presidency was establishing a close personal relationship with former Governor and 1936 Republican presidential nominee, Alf Landon. K-State had initiated a lecture series named in his honor in the 1967 and, because of the caliber of speakers attracted, the series had become nationally recognized. The series was financed by a group of Landon patrons, private citizens who paid $300 annually to attend the three to five lectures each year and associated luncheons with the lecturers. This time I had called Landon with a question.

Reserved Seats for Governor Landon[13]

September 7, 1982

I enjoyed many visits with Governor Landon, either by phone or he would join me for lunch at the Topeka Club atop the Merchants National Bank. He would often call midmorning on Sunday, ready to talk about a university or political issue of the day. A few Sundays, Shirley and I would be a few minutes late for the 11 o'clock church service.

Landon would just want to talk, perhaps try out an idea and get a response. Though approaching ninety-five, his interests were broad and his analysis of issues always logical. Both fiscal conservatives, we tended to agree on most issues. He also liked to needle a bit, with humor and seeking a comeback, especially if K-State football or some other K-State item was in the news.

On this day I had placed the call. My first years in the presidency, he was yet in his mid-eighties and never missed a series lecture. He would be on stage with the guest lecturer, the student body president, faculty chair of the lecture series, Landon Patron Chairman Robert Wilson, and me. Landon always got a warm response from the crowd when he was introduced and waved his purple tie.

Advancing age and a few health problems had prevented him attending some of the recent lectures. However, with President Ronald Reagan coming the following Thursday for a lecture and to celebrate Landon's 95th birthday, I wanted to be sure he was able and planning to be with us.

"You bet I'll be there; I'm looking forward to it," he had responded.

I then told him I wanted him to bring along any family and friends he would like and I would have front row seats reserved.

"Don't reserve more than two or three," he said, "You know, at this age one doesn't have many friends left."

I followed up. "I want to reserve plenty. We don't have this kind of celebration every day and I don't want you to leave anyone out that you would like to have."

He was quick on this response, too, "I know what you're thinking, that I might not be around for my 100th" And here came the needle, "I'll be around. I don't know whether you will be. If K-State doesn't win more football games, you won't!"

Neither of us would be on hand for Landon's 100th birthday. I left K-State for Washington about four years later, stopping to visit Landon and his wife in their Topeka home my last day in the state. And, Landon died a few months short of his 100th birthday.

* * * * *

Reserving seats for Landon's family and friends was the easy part of preparing for Reagan's visit. The most difficult was choosing a gift for the President.

The Right Gift for President Reagan[14]

September 8, 1982

To have President Reagan at K-State for a lecture and to honor Governor Landon's 95th birthday, September 9, would be a coup. K-State would receive national media coverage. We were grateful for the efforts of Landon's daughter, Senator Nancy Kassebaum, in getting this event on the President's schedule.

When the President is to come to town, the Secret Service is in charge — of any arrangement for which they want to be in charge! Security of the President is first priority. Ahearn Field House would accommodate the expected crowd and Facilities Vice President Gene Cross would coordinate with the Secret Service to see that all arrangements were in order.

As the date approached, one issue had been yet unsettled, and I had brought it up with some campus leaders who happened to be in my office, "What gift should the University give the President?" Student Affairs Vice President Chet Peters suggested a purple saddle blanket with a K-State logo; this would be appropriate because both Landon and Reagan liked to ride. Student Body President Bill Rogenmoser liked the idea, but former Faculty Senate Chair Heinz Bulmahn was taken aback, "A saddle blanket!?" To him, a saddle blanket just did not seem academic.

I continued to solicit ideas; the Secret Service would need to approve and we had to consider possible campus reaction. One never knows what will become a campus cause célèbre. Among suggestions: A pewter plate engraved with Anderson Hall, a popular item among alumni, a football jersey, and a large-scale glass replica of the White House, made in his spare time by our Chemistry Department glass blower, Mr. Ono.

There was a problem with each. The pewter plate would not show up on TV. As for the football jersey, K-State had just finished a lengthy NCAA probation and was not yet known as a football powerhouse (an invitation to the first post season bowl game in its 85 years was to come later that fall). The glass replica of the White House was too large, too heavy, and too fragile for a stage presentation.

Another of Ono's creations was then suggested, a Klein bottle. A Klein bottle is a physical representation of the mathematical concept of infinity. Ono would cut holes in the side and the bottom of a long-neck flask. Then he would heat and bend the neck down, into and through the side hole, and fuse the neck rim to the edges of the bottom hole. There would be no end to the flask's structure; it would be infinite.

Faculty leaders thought the Klein bottle a great idea. It would highlight the scientific and academic focus of the University! And, student leaders were satisfied. When one can achieve faculty enthusiasm plus student and administration willingness, one may have a winner! We would check it out with the Secret Service.

The Klein bottle was rejected by the Secret Service! It could break, injure the President. Also a media person from the president's advance staff had arrived. "Even worse," he had said, "on TV it would look like a glass bedpan!"

By the time we got this complete reaction, time was short. I had to risk faculty disdain and ask Mike Johnson, then my legislative assistant, to find two purple saddle blankets, one for Reagan and one for Landon. Our Clothing and Textiles Department staff could sew on the K-State logo. The Secret Service and the President's Washington-based speech writers (advance staff was in constant contact with Washington) thought the saddle blankets were great! They were safe, large enough to be seen on TV, and represented the mutual interest of Landon and Reagan. It seemed that most would be satisfied.

With all the horses and saddle shops in Kansas, finding two purple saddle blankets should be a piece of cake. Johnson soon reported back, however, that he had called every saddle shop he knew of and they had plenty of saddle blankets, but no purple! He had even called a shop at Chimayo, New Mexico, and would keep searching.

We needed to have the pewter plates ready as back up. Jan Woodward got two from the Alumni office and had them tied with a purple ribbon.

About 10 0'clock the morning before the lecture day our athletic trainer came into the office with a football jersey. It had a large "1" on the front and

Reagan's name on the back. He asked if I would be willing to give it to the President during his visit. I thanked him for his initiative and took the jersey, but explained that we already had a gift in mind, saddle blankets.

"Saddle blankets?" he responded, with obvious dismay. I did not take time to mention the back-up pewter plates.

The President's speech writer then heard about the pewter plates and he was indignant! "We already have the saddle blankets written into the speech. The President loves it!"

Johnson kept searching for purple saddle blankets, and the textiles staff was ready to attach the K-State logo in case he found some. And, we got a call from the Chemistry Department still pushing for the White House replica.

By the time I left the office for dinner, Johnson had still not found purple saddle blankets, so it would have to be the pewter plates. We would just accept the speech writer's unhappiness.

I was getting into bed when I got a call from Cross. The Secret Service had gotten into the act on the pewter plates; I assumed the speech writer had enlisted their help. The Secret Service man had suggested, "If there can't be saddle blankets, how about football jerseys for both Landon and Reagan?"

My patience was wearing thin. We had already by-passed the football jersey idea. I told Cross, "Tell your Secret Service man that if we are limited to football jerseys, there will not be a gift!"

That shook loose a compromise. Secret Service agreed to let us present the pewter plates if I would do everything in my power to get two football jerseys.

It was nearly 11 p.m. I called Associate Athletic Director Con Colbert. Colbert was the type that one is lucky to have in an organization, always ready to help. I mentioned the football jersey the trainer had brought in and "Is there any way you could get me two matching jerseys for tomorrow morning, one for Reagan and one for Landon?"

I got the expected 11 p.m. response, "Just what did you say?"

I explained the situation; Colbert then understood and was ready to help. But he was also ready to negotiate! "I haven't been able to get tickets for Reagan's lecture. If I deliver to you two jerseys, one with Number 95 and Landon's name and one with the Number 1 and Reagan's name, will you get my daughter and me into the lecture?"

"Con, you've got a deal!" I said, and I went to bed.

At 8:30 the next morning Colbert was at Ahearn Field House with two perfectly matched jerseys, with the numbers and names sewn on, and I gave him his tickets.

Photos of Reagan and Landon holding the football jerseys were featured in the next issues of both TIME and U.S. News and World Report. They were also carried by a multitude of daily papers and most TV networks that evening or the next day.

President Ronald Reagan and Governor Alf Landon displaying their K-State football jerseys following Reagan's Landon Lecture, Rebuilding America. September 9, 1982. Reagan's K-State visit was arranged to coincide with and recognize Landon's 95th birthday. To Landon's right are his daughter, Senator Nancy Landon Kassebaum, and Senator Bob Dole. (Photo courtesy of University Archives.)

Epilogue: Johnson lived in Abilene. On a Saturday night a few weeks later his daughter returned to the house, "Dad, weren't you looking for some purple saddle blankets a few weeks ago? They have a stack on sale down at Ritter's Western Wear!"

* * * * *

My recollections shift now from the President's staff to the Governor's spouse. I had been pulled out of a Topeka regents' meeting to take a call from Mrs. Karen Carlin, the governor's new wife. She needed help.

The 4-H Style Show and the Governor's new Wife[15]

May 16, 1983

She had married Governor John Carlin in early '83 or late '82 and, with her two children, ages eleven and fourteen, had moved from the Lawrence area, Douglas County, to Cedar Crest, the governor's mansion on the northwest side of Topeka, in Shawnee County. Her children had been 4-H members in Douglas County and wanted to transfer to a Shawnee County club. That should have been simple enough, but she had encountered problems and was calling for help.

One or both of the children wanted to participate in the Shawnee County 4-H Fair style show the first week of August, but Shawnee County 4-H rules required that one be a club member in the county for at least ninety days prior to the fair. The ninety-day date had already passed.

I suggested a solution: "Since the children are still members of a Douglas County club, why not have them participate in the Douglas County Fair style show this year, and shift to Shawnee County for next year?"

"Oh, we can't do that," she explained, "The Douglas County Fair is July 21-28. Those are the dates of the National Governor's Conference and we want the children to go with us." She was persistent.

I told Mrs. Carlin I would check it out with our 4-H staff, but cautioned that to by-pass rules established within the county could risk some embarrassment to her and a highly respected governor.

When there is a local 4-H problem, whom do you call, the state 4-H leader or local staff? My answer is "Local!" I called Herb Bulk, long-time Shawnee County Extension director. I knew Bulk well; he was a steady hand.

I described the problem and asked for Bulk's judgment as to its seriousness and whether he thought anything could or should be done. He described the county's standard club size and existing policies. He also said that the club Mrs. Carlin wanted her children to join required that a parent accompany the child to the first three club meetings after being admitted to membership.

Though Bulk did not say so, it was likely that he had already have been confronted with the problem and was therefore not surprised to be getting a call from the director of extension, the dean, or me. He would investigate further.

Monday morning, Bulk called back. It was apparent he and his staff had put in a good many week-end hours on the issue, largely with individual club leaders. He assured me that all recognized the political sensitivity and would do their best to protect the governor and his family. One of the club leaders would be contacting Mrs. Carlin and would be both frank and as helpful as possible in trying to accommodate her children in their club.

I did not ask Bulk for details; I had no desire to know. I thanked him and his staff for their effort, and then called Mrs. Carlin. I told her that our Shawnee county staff had done the best they could, that she would be receiving a call from one of the local club leaders, and that I hoped satisfactory arrangements would get worked out.

I heard nothing more.

* * * * *

At least once a year I would get a call from the governor's office relaying a citizen concern. In one case, a supplier of rodeo stock had appealed to the governor because our student rodeo club had chosen a different vendor for the spring rodeo. We simply checked with the club adviser to confirm that reasonable procedures had been followed, relayed that to the governor's staff, and they could respond to the complainant. We never received pressure from either Governor Bennett or Governor Carlin.

This concern came direct.

Who Gets the Sales Commission?

The call to me was from a Nutra-Life saleswoman and she was not happy. After repeated efforts, she had finally sold some Nutra-Life product to our football program, only to be told by another Nutra-Life representative that he should get half the sales commission. He had reportedly told her that he was a large donor to K-State's athletic program, knew the president well, and the president had indicated this would be proper. (I had found that being quoted, erroneously or with no basis at all, was one of the risks of the presidency. Consequently, both Shirley and I had learned to be exceedingly cautious in conversations.)

Early in my tenure I had insisted that the Department of Athletics seek bids for services and supplies. A review of Athletics' finances had discovered that, though some supporters provided goods and services even below cost (a department rationale for avoiding the bidding process), a few had taken severe advantage of the Department.

With bidding, a booster can still bid below cost, get the bid, and thereby help the Department. Of course I had concurred that the Department should insure that donors have opportunity to bid and that their bids receive thorough consideration.

I recognized the name given to me and he was an appreciated donor. However, I had no reason to know our football team might be using Nutra-Life; I did not even know what the product was. If Nutra-Life would help the team and the Department bought it at a competitive price, I would be all for it.

I assured my caller that my office would check into it and get back to her. I gave her name and phone number to Mike Johnson; he would follow up with Athletics' business office. In a short time Johnson confirmed to the caller that, yes, some Nutra-Life had been purchased by the Department, but who got the sales commission was Nutra-Life's problem.

* * * * *

Perhaps I had known Charlie Hostetler too long and too well. No doubt he deserved it, but did I really say it?

Charlie, Go to H___!

Saturday, August 22, 1981

Charlie Hostetler and I had been members of the Manhattan Jaycees in the 1960s, during my time as associate dean. I had enjoyed that group, worked on projects with a number of young Manhattan business people, including Charlie, then a junior staff member in Robert and Barbara Wilson's abstract company.

By the early 1980s, Charlie had moved over to the First National Bank and replaced his father as chairman. And, key to this story, he was at this time Board Chair of the Manhattan Chamber of Commerce.

This evening, at Charlie's insistence, I had agreed to interrupt a long-planned evening of cards with friends, Alan and Janice Lee, in our campus home (the Lee brothers, Alan and Robert, had built our home on Oregon Lane in 1962) and walk down to Aggieville for a few minutes where the Chamber was hosting a welcome back watermelon feed for K-State students. I had first resisted committing to go, feeling this was a Chamber party and the University president's welcome to students should be limited to a different setting. However, I wanted to maintain good relationships with the Chamber, so had agreed.

About 7:30 I laid down my cards, excused myself from our guests and walked down to a parking lot south of the Aggieville theatre. I was to be on hand when Hostetler spoke briefly to the crowd. It would not take long.

As I turned to leave, Charlie grabbed me and wanted to talk about campus parking for some K-State athletes. Those students who had gathered for the Chamber welcome had moved on to the local pubs or a movie. Only Mike Hauser, Manhattan's young Chamber executive officer, Charlie, and I remained.

I was well acquainted with the issue. One of our coaches had wanted reserved parking stalls adjacent to the campus dining hall so his players would not need to walk a couple blocks across campus after practice to their evening training table. Few things are as sensitive on a campus as reserved parking stalls and I had supported Vice President Peters' decision that reserved stalls for the athletes were unwarranted.

The issue was settled, as far as I was concerned. It was none of Hostetler's business, and I did not appreciate coaches using local business people to carry water to me, or a local business person volunteering for the task. I responded to Hostetler that if the coach wanted to appeal the decision, the coach and the athletic director were welcome to come to my office and we would discuss it.

But Hostetler would not quit, and made a comment sharply critical of

Peters. As the administrative sponsor and supporter of women's basketball nearly a decade earlier, Peters had been the target of some sniping by a few men's sports enthusiasts. However, of my Anderson Hall colleagues, Peters was probably the most thoughtful and considerate of any issue that came before him. A shot at Peters in this case was unnecessary.

Hostetler kept pressing. I was even more pointed in my response, in essence, "Charlie, this is a matter between the coach and those of us on campus, there is no place for you in the matter." By this time, Hauser had disappeared. He wanted no part in this conversation!

I turned to leave; I needed to get back to our guests. However, Charlie would not give up, grabbed my arm and pressed again on the issue. I had had enough. I made a parting comment and walked away.

Though my memory of the encounter is vivid and I know what I was thinking as I turned to leave, I have no documentation as to what I said. If I said those words to Hostetler, though unquestionably deserved, it was probably not wise. My first few months in the job I had drawn a line in the sand on the handling of Department of Athletics' money with one of the town's bankers. Now I had drawn a deeper line, on all issues, with a second.

There would be evident repercussions, even long after I had left the presidency. As head of a local bank and, in time, gaining an appointment to the Kansas Board of Regents, Charlie would have a continuing forum.

* * * * *

As I watch universities and boards of regents in the 2000s, I see more encouragement of presidential entrepreneurship. With rising costs and failure of state appropriations to match those costs, I note that regents will tend to support about any university judgment that will either add or preserve dollars. Universities are encouraged to add or delete programs, recruit students from wherever they may be, and pursue about any financially sound effort consistent with the University's mission. Not so in the early 1980s in Kansas! The following illustrates.

Consultants and the Doctor of Education

April 4, 1984

This was not the best day to be hosting consultants the Board office has brought in to study state university colleges of education. I had read in the morning *Topeka Capital-Journal* that state treasury revenues were $18 million below estimate and, by unfortunate coincidence, the House-Senate conference committee would this day make their final decisions on higher education appropriations for the 1984-85 fiscal year. We had a one per cent faculty salary increase and a $330,000 supplemental for increased utility costs riding on their judgment. And, as the reader will see in a later item, I had a personnel item that needed addressing.

This business of using consultants to advise the Board on duplicative programs had frustrated all the campuses, for two reasons: 1) A one-day consultant visit is hardly sufficient to make valid judgments, in this case, on K-State's College of Education. 2) It shifts a part of campus management to board staff; the Board's executive officer would present consultant recommendations to the Board, along with his own opinions. Presidents would be essentially cut out of the decision-making process. The only plus was that Board Chair Jim Pickert, who represented the Board in this visit, was one of the most sincere and considerate persons with whom I had worked. He would keep things on an even keel.

I joined Pickert, Board Executive Officer Stan Koplik, Provost Owen Koeppe, the two consultants, and the consultants' two assistants in Anderson Hall's conference room. The leader of the consultant team was a tall and somber former education dean from New York, whose very greeting conveyed that his style was intimidation. Fortunately, his partner was an affable, retired Big 10 university president, who would disarm apprehensive Education Dean David Byrne and involved department heads with self deprecating anecdotes. He had a way of using question lead-ins that would extract the information and perspectives that a good consultant needs to gain. "Perhaps this will be constructive," I thought.

The leader, the former dean from New York, turned things over to their two assistants. Those two were a contrasting pair. The first, a young, curly-haired New Yorker said little. He seemed awed by the open spaces of Kansas and the open behavior of our faculty. He may also have been surprised that these Plains people wore the same suits and neckties and watched the same network TV news as New Yorkers. He listened, with interest!

His co-worker, though, was more eager to impress Pickert and Koplik, the latter having hired the group. He quoted data, sometimes erroneously, from a College of Education staff paper, refuted a suggestion that he had misread the data, and concluded the College was in terrible shape. He then drilled Provost Koeppe with, "What have you done about it?" This was all before Pickert had his first cup of coffee.

It was a long morning, with little discussion that was constructive to improving a college of education. Hiring these consultants was part of the Board's response to legislative concern about program duplication among the universities. The consultants would provide some cover for judgments the Board would make, likely the closing of some programs within several of the education colleges. The Board would not want to face the wrath of any university alumni organization by closing a college of education.

We devoted most of the day to the process, and bid the consultants goodbye with the offer to forward any further data they might need for their work.

In the end, a Board decision would be for K-State to close down its Ph.D. program in Education and to offer only the Doctor of Education. The Education Ph.D. would be limited to the University of Kansas. This understandably offended some of our Education faculty. They had worked hard to initiate the Ph.D. years earlier and to strengthen the related courses and research experience. The Doctor of Education is considered by some academics as second tier, generally requiring less independent research.

Once the Board decision was made, however, my posture and message to our Education faculty was, and needed to be, that if they promoted the Doctor of Education degree and built enrollment, there should develop even more loyalty to K-State among Kansas K-12 schools. More educators who aspire to become a school principal or superintendent pursue the Doctor of Education degree than pursue the Ph.D. Those who earn the Ph.D. are more likely headed to college or university positions.

By the way, we did get that salary increase money and the supplemental appropriation for utilities.

* * * * *

That fall the governor's wife had another problem and I was pulled out of another regents' meeting.

Cutting the Trees at Cedar Crest[16]

September 24, 1984

To improve the appearance of Cedar Crest, the governors' mansion and grounds just off I-70 on Topeka's northwest side, Mrs. Carlin had decided that the trees lining a vacated drive extending south from the mansion should be removed. They were largely short-life Siberian Elm and appeared rather ragged. There were broken limbs and a few dead or dying trees.

Environmental sensitivities had made cutting down any tree, especially on public property, politically risky. However, Mrs. Carlin had planned well; she had asked K-State Extension Forester Jim Nighswonger to prepare a plan for at least an equal number of trees to be planted on Cedar Crest grounds. Unfortunately, the plan was to be delivered to Mrs. Carlin the following Monday, and a public relations emergency had developed today.

Penitentiary prisoners had been arranged to cut down the trees next week, but had shown up this morning and started felling the trees. Things were going along well until a tree fell on a prisoner. Topeka Emergency Services had been called to the scene and that had alerted the media.

Television and newspaper reporters and cameramen had descended on Cedar Crest to cover the accident, and then reporters started asking Mrs. Carlin, "Why are you cutting down all the trees?" Mrs. Carlin told the reporters there was a plan to replace the trees, but she did not have the plan!

She had called Nighswonger's office but he was in southwestern Kansas on another Extension assignment. Was there any way I could track down the plan?

I called Nighswonger's office and learned that, since the plan involved state property, it had been forwarded to the state architect's office in Topeka for approval. Good news! I reached Norman Wilson in the state architect's office. He had seen the plan, said it was entirely satisfactory, and he would get a copy rushed out to Cedar Crest.

Mrs. Carlin could satisfy the media that there would be no net loss of trees at Cedar Crest.

* * * * *

Several times a week I would work out some of my frustrations and give my cardio-vascular system a good surge on the racquetball court. In later years it would usually be late afternoon with local steel company executive Dennis Mullin at a private racquet club on the west edge of Manhattan. Sometimes it would be with AIB President Bill Hoover or former student body president, then local attorney and future U.S. Senator, Sam Brownback. Emphasizing the difference in age, I sometimes tell my politically acquainted friends I regularly whipped Brownback on the court. I do not need to mention that Brownback had one knee in a cast or at least heavily bandaged at the time.

I could also get a work-out on our Iowa farm, 240 miles away. There was always some roadside brush to cut.

A Spare Axe Handle[17]

October, 1984

Shirley and I would leave this Thursday evening for a much-needed three-day week-end at our Iowa farm. The past two weeks had been especially full. There had been a two-day regents' meeting in Wichita. That was followed by Homecoming activities, including the parade, a luncheon for invited guests, the game, and a follow-up reception for donors. Even Sunday had been committed; I had spent most of mid-day with a governor's rural education group in the K-State Union.

I had met with the faculty senate on tenure policy and the Foundation executive committee regarding high bids on the coliseum and the need to raise more private money. I had spoken at an alumni meeting in Hutchinson and a service club in Salina, and had met with Regent System presidents and chief academic officers in McPherson. Shirley and I had had dinner one evening at the Tau Kappa Epsilon fraternity and a group of FarmHouse Fraternity pledges had stopped by my office to visit.

I had also talked with Athletic Council members Bob Snell and Beth Unger regarding some issues with women's basketball, Vice President George Miller about his reorganization plans in the facilities division, with the deans as a group on budget issues, and with a Human Ecology faculty member who had a good suggestion for campus beautification. And there had been a two-hour seminar with deans and department heads on student attrition and retention.

My only breaks had been racquetball games with Tom Arthur and Dave Fiser, the latter at 4 o-clock on Sunday, and a haircut at 4 on Tuesday.

Then, early this afternoon, just before I was to begin an orientation session with several new department heads, the regents' office called for more information on our 1985-86 fiscal year budget request. Though I had fully briefed board members, with a copy to board staff, it seemed the latter felt it their duty to keep my administrative people fully occupied.

I was looking forward to the week-end, and working off my frustrations cutting brush. As I was about to leave the office, my staff stepped in with an axe handle, festooned with a big, red ribbon! There was a story behind the axe handle.

In the fall of 1982, I had made considerable progress clearing brush along a fence-row at the farm and was finishing it up over the Christmas Holidays. Both my axe and hatchet had served me for more than fifteen years. They had been sharpened many times and had a few chips, but the handles were the originals.

My assistant, Mike Johnson, called to tell me that Governor Carlin was ready to appoint former KU Chancellor Archie Dykes, then CEO of a Topeka-based insurance company, to the Board of Regents. Dykes was extremely capable. However, as chancellor he had dealt with the Board and legislature on the principle of a zero sum game, what KU can get, other universities do not get. A team member working for the System of six universities he was not.

An hour later came a call from Carlin seeking my reaction to his consideration of Dykes. Though I did not hold back in my response to Carlin, I was quite sure the decision had already been made.

That afternoon I probably cut more brush than I had the two previous days. And, in the process, I had fractured the axe handle. On my return to the campus, my emotions relieved and with some humor, I had shared that fact with my staff.

Considering the recent ten day's agenda, my staff thought a spare axe handle might come in handy.

* * * * *

In some respects, this next item was a re-play of the Bluemont/Throckmorton case ("Who Changed K-State's Building Priorities," Page 36). Money for two major structures would also come at the same time, but only after much political pressure from both inside and outside the University.

Two More Buildings

March, 1985

New laboratories for chemistry and biochemistry were sorely needed. Neither the space nor air exchange capacity in Willard Hall was adequate for the increased numbers of students or to protect students and staff from chemical fumes. The project had been at the top of the University priority list for several years.

Weber Hall's meat processing lab did not meet current federal meat inspection regulations. That fact, the volume of research animals going through that lab, and growth in student enrollment had made both renovation of the lab and an addition to Weber a critical need.

Circumstances for political support paralleled the Bluemont/Throckmorton situation. Every university has a chemistry building. How many Kansas voters, other than perhaps a few high school chemistry teachers or parents whose sons or daughters had complained about the chemistry lab fumes, could get excited about a new chemistry building for K-State? How many would tell their state representative or senator it was high priority? How many would seek out and tell the governor?

In contrast, among Kansas' universities, only K-State had an animal science department and meat laboratory. The Kansas livestock industry was strong, well organized, and continually involved in the political process. Whether or not a K-State graduate, anyone with a cow herd, swine herd, sheep flock, or feedlot, plus any horse owner who had a link to our outstanding extension staff, had an appreciation for and some loyalty to K-State's Department of Animal Science. These people understood the need; they would not be bashful in writing the governor or twisting the arm of their state legislator.

Mike Johnson and I had repeatedly toured regents and legislators through Willard Hall, with department heads Ken Klabunde and David Cox pointing out the structural limitations. Even Shirley, hosting the spouses when legislators made a campus visit, would route them through Willard on their way to the Union for lunch.

Leaders of the Kansas Livestock Association had arranged similar tours of Weber and most would have a legislator in tow. Johnson and I would be there, along with Department Head Don Good and staff, plus Dean John Dunbar, to express my support and appreciation for their interest.

I had worked in a meat lab as a student, taught meat processing two years in partially completed, high-risk facilities at Oklahoma State, and nearly every one of my research animals had been processed, and product tested and measured, in meat labs at Oklahoma State or Iowa State. I knew well the need.

The odds of K-State getting appropriations for two major projects at the same time were low, so the livestock leaders pressed me to move the chemistry/biochemistry building out of first place on K-State's priority list and replace it with the Weber project. Industry leaders thought that with an animal scientist in the president's office, this shift should be a slam dunk!

However, I had also completed ten chemistry courses, had a graduate minor in biochemistry, and had inhaled my share of sulfuric acid and nitrous oxide fumes. I understood that problem. And, I understood the value of being consistent in legislative request priorities.

The livestock industry leadership intensified the pressure. If I would put the Weber project at the top of the University list, they would virtually guarantee that the governor and legislature would provide the money in the upcoming 1985 legislative session. Dean Dunbar's Agricultural Advisory Council picked up the chant, told me in strong terms, "That meat lab just can't wait!"

As I visited with that Council in its November, 1984, meeting, some members' comments on the Weber priority were so blunt and aggressive that Area Extension Director Phil Finley of Colby who, among other staff, had been sitting along the wall, later wrote me a personal note commending me for retaining my "calm and dignified" manner.[18]

At the same time, several of my administrative colleagues and faculty concerned about the chemistry facilities were carefully watching this process and they got nervous. One kept in my ear, "If you make Weber top priority, you'll lose faculty support on the other side of the campus."

To me, the issue was clear. If I could keep the priorities intact, chemistry/biochemistry first and Weber second, we just might get money for both.

My continued unwillingness to make the priority change prompted a few livestock industry leaders to claim that the K-State president had no interest in supporting that industry and its needs. That was ridiculous, but I know it motivated some to press harder on the governor or their legislator. I did not appreciate their claim, but I was glad for the motivation it prompted.

Because the Kansas legislature had so many requests for high-cost capital projects, the House and Senate had formed a Joint Building Committee to set priorities within dollars available. That committee had proven its worth, both in credible work and in reduced pressure on members of the two houses. Its recommendations were invariably endorsed by both houses.

By coincidence, this Committee would finalize their recommendations to the two houses late in the day that Kansas agricultural groups would host a legislators' dinner at the Topeka Ramada Inn. Shirley and I drove to Topeka for that dinner and we had just taken our seats when I saw Committee Member Keith Farrar, a western Kansas farmer, walk in. I rose to greet Farrar as he made a bee-line toward me. Before I could say a word, he said, with a smile and wink, "Acker, we gave you one you didn't want, so we decided to also give you one you did want!"

Fantastic! Two more at one time!

Farrar's words, "one you didn't want," along with the smile and wink, confirmed that he and some other committee members had been told that Acker was an obstacle for the Weber project. The Committee's approval of both projects made it clear that members knew well K-State's needs. It also confirmed their respect for our holding tight to our established priorities.

Though I am proud of both completed structures, when I walk along Mid Campus Drive past chemistry/biochemistry and look closely, I see some shreds of my hide in the mortar.

* * * * *

In my early years as president, we had investigated the potential for renovating Ahearn Field House to accommodate larger crowds. The infeasibility of that, and evidence that a new coliseum was the only project that would attract private funds, had put us on the road to both the coliseum and a hoped-for tradition of private giving to K-State. However, our architect's cost estimate for the coliseum was too low, the planned capacity had to be reduced, and additional funds had to be solicited. Also, a former legislator who was by now on the Board of regents was not enthused.

The Lone Vote Against Bramlage Coliseum[19]

June 27, 1985

Regent Wendell Lady motioned me to follow him out of the room just as a Board Facilities Committee meeting was getting underway.

Lady, a K-State graduate and a senior member of Kansas City's Black and

Veatch Engineering, was a key member of the Kansas House appropriations committee my first year back at K-State. On appropriations issues, he was not an easy member to convince. But he had my respect; I observed him to be always prepared, fair, and above board in his dealings.

In time, Lady became speaker of the House, then a candidate (unsuccessful) for governor. At a K-State football game, November, 1979, after John Carlin had won the gubernatorial election, I had recommended Lady to him for a regent post.

As in the legislature, and in contrast to some of his regent colleagues, Lady gave his alma mater no quarter. He supported or opposed in accord with his judgment as to an issue's worthiness. As to a new coliseum at K-State, I would learn, Lady was opposed.

No capital project is easy, but every step for the coliseum had been difficult. It was not the universal first choice among some alumni and most faculty for a privately funded project. Yet, many of the K-State family wanted it and I saw it as the vehicle for a much-needed fund-raising experience for our Foundation. Lady, yet in the legislature when it had been first proposed, had likely worried that some state money would be sought. As a regent, he had expressed reservations.

It had been after one of Lady's comments that fellow K-State grad and regent member George Wingert, recognizing the pressure for the coliseum from athletic boosters and many alumni, had sympathized, "Acker, you're damned if you do and damned if you don't."

The coliseum would be totally financed by private funds from generous donors. For some K-State grads, giving money to their state university had been a new idea. But, after Mr. Bramlage had made a major commitment and a couple others, Earl Brookover of Garden City and Jack Goldstein of Manhattan, had come through with pledges of a half million dollars each, our campaign committee had raised a total of more than six million dollars..

Though six million had been the estimated cost, with continued inflation and a staff wish list that kept getting longer, the structure's design and planned capacity had been revised several times. We had asked some donors to increase their commitments, and they had. We were ready for regent approval to seek bids for construction. If bids came in within dollars committed, it might be possible to break ground yet this fall. We had pressed at every step and Board Facilities Officer Warren Corman had been most helpful.

Today's facilities committee agenda included "Discussion of K-State's planned coliseum." When I had seen that phrasing on the agenda a few days earlier, I had asked my facilities staff, who were handling the issue with Corman, why the item did not say "*Approval* of K-State's planned coliseum." They had explained that, since the state architect had asked for some minor refinements in specifications, formal Board approval could not be at this meeting. After the refinements were completed and the state architect approved, formal Board approval would be handled in a regent conference call. Corman had said such was normal.

Our information staff had prepared a bid-seeking announcement for release after that planned regent conference call. The release would let enthused alumni and donors know that the coliseum was really going to be built, and would alert potential bidders. Unfortunately, one of our information staff had erred, and had included that item in a mailing early this week with other media releases.

I had been disturbed to see the piece in this morning's *Topeka Capital-Journal*, and some regents would be, if they had seen it. I would explain the error as I briefed the committee on design details and the approval sequence that Corman had outlined. Unfortunately, Corman was absent this day, attending a conference in Arizona.

Lady had seen the release in the morning paper and was not happy. I explained the error to Lady, but he had another problem, that the committee agenda showed "Discussion" instead of "Approval." I also explained that.

Lady was not satisfied, and called Regent Executive Director Koplik out of the meeting. Lady told Koplik he wanted "Approval of the coliseum" on the committee agenda so he could vote against it. (After committee action, items would go the next day's full Board agenda.)

Koplik professed ignorance of the total issue (prudent for an executive director caught in a problem) but, noting Lady's intensity, took the position that plans must not be complete, there should be *no* consideration by the committee, and bid solicitation should be delayed. The next opportunity for Board action would be late July.

I was not about to buy that, and insisted that Koplik call Corman. However, rather than place the call in our presence, Koplik went into his office and closed the door. He came back out in rather short order to tell us Corman had said the plans were not ready for approval by the state architect. There was no need for any committee consideration until the late July meeting.

Koplik had made Lady content and both returned to the committee session.

I smelled a rat, and the odor was pungent. I asked Corman's secretary to place another call to him. I told Corman that either he or K-State was being sold down the river. I recited what had occurred and the rationale he had given my facilities staff.

Corman immediately confirmed, "Yes, the drawings are in order. The state architect is pleased with them. Yes, a few refinements are yet needed and they'll be approved by the state architect. Yes, I did suggest only project discussion on the committee agenda, and formal approval later on a Board conference call agenda."

"Warren," I said, "Would you say the same thing to Regent Lady that you just said to me?"

"Sure," he said.

I headed for the committee meeting, asked Lady to step out to talk directly with Corman. Though understandably impatient, Lady followed me out and I handed him the phone. His end of the conversation was largely, "Oh, is that right?" "Is that right?" and then, "This is a heck of a way to do business." But, I could tell he was getting the truth, the valid message. Finally, he concluded, "Well, we'll put it (formal approval) on the Board agenda this month because I want it to be publicly discussed and I want to have a chance to vote against it!"

Formal approval of architectural plans for Bramlage Coliseum was added to the next day's full Board agenda. A motion for approval, subject to final approval of refinements by the state architect, yielded six votes in favor, Lady opposed. Two relatively new board members, unacquainted with the project, abstained.

I would not be around to participate in the Bramlage Coliseum dedication. Several years later, however, back on campus after several years handling food and agriculture programs for the U.S. Agency for International Development, Shirley and I hosted Mr. and Mrs. Bramlage for dinner, then followed them as one of the Coliseum staff proudly showed us its features.

As we walked through the building, I saw far more than the arena, offices, and team locker rooms. I saw the consequence of K-State's first successful multi-million dollar private fund-raising effort. It was an effort of which all K-Staters should be proud. It was also an effort that I hoped and expected would be dwarfed by successive K-State capital campaigns.

* * * * *

Monthly regent meetings are part of the territory for a president. However, the two-day meetings, usually a Council of Presidents meeting the first morning, Board committee meetings that afternoon and the next morning, and a two-hour formal Board meeting the second afternoon, were not my favorite way to spend my time. I confess I more enjoyed handling K-State issues that needed attention, or selling K-State, than sitting and listening to lengthy considerations and discussions.

One Ulcer or Two[20]

June 27, 1985

Shirley and I were at a retirement dinner at the Topeka Country Club for Tom Creech, president of the Kansas Technical Institute, Salina. It was Thursday night of the monthly Thursday/Friday board meeting, an opportunity for board members, staff, and presidents, plus their spouses, to socialize.

To me this was a special night, for two reasons. The first was that I had told the Board members during the afternoon that the next year would be my last as president. Though I had committed to myself that I would stay no more than ten years in the presidency, this next year would make eleven. The Board needed a year to identify a new president.

The second reason was that Creech was a K-State graduate, had done an excellent job, and the Institute had a close relationships with our College of Engineering. I was certain that in time the Institute would become a formal part of K-State. Perhaps because of that close relationship, I would have the privilege of offering best wishes from the System presidents to Creech on his retirement.

It had been a tense afternoon in the Board committee meetings. It is interesting how things move so smoothly at some meetings and others are filled with sniping. I had observed that it was usually one unfortunate issue, perhaps a building project where bids had come in too high, a staff problem at the Medical Center, or some faculty member having tested the limits of academic freedom, that might set a negative tone for the total two-day meeting. Combine that with an out-of-sorts board member or one who, for some reason, is strongly opposed to a project (such as Lady and the coliseum), and the two days were less than pleasant.

Regardless of the tone of the afternoon meeting, I planned to enjoy the evening and verbal jostling with a couple of my colleagues. At one point, Ft. Hays President Jerry Tomanek told Creech and me, "With you two departing, I'll be the old man among the presidents." I injected, "Jerry, you've always been the old man." Though Tomanek has been president fewer years than me, he was older.

I moved over to engage Regent Pat Caruthers, a vice president at a downtown Kansas City, Kansas, Community College, "How goes it this evening?" I knew there had been some changes at her institution that had not set well with her; perhaps I could get her onto a positive topic.

Her response would not lighten my evening, or hers, "I've been feeling lousy all day. I've had one beer and ordered another, but my ulcer is bothering me."

I turned to KU Chancellor Gene Budig, with whom I enjoyed working, "You're not having a beer tonight?" He was empty-handed.

"No," he said, "I feel terrible; my ulcer is bothering.

"You've got an ulcer!?" I was surprised; Budig always appeared calm and in control.

"I've had both an ulcer and colitis for a long time."

Caruthers joined in, "I've got two ulcers, stomach and duodenum."

I wondered, "How many ulcers are there in this room?" Maybe they are the reason today's committee meetings were so tense. Or, are the ulcers acting up tonight *because* those meetings were so tense?

Regardless, after another year, these Board meetings would not be my problem. I would enjoy the evening and do my part to make it enjoyable for Tom Creech.

* * * * *

Many of the thirty members of the Kansas Board of Regents with whom I worked were extremely helpful to me and what I tried to achieve for K-State and the System. High on my list are Emporia realtor and Emporia State graduate Jim Pickert, KU graduates Sandra McMullen of Hutchinson, Dr. James Basham of Ft. Scott, and John D. and John G. Montgomery of Junction City, and K-State graduates Jack Reeves of Garden City, George Wingert of Ottawa, Prudence Hutton of Newton, Frank Lowman of Hays, Richard Reinhardt of Erie, Norman Brandeberry of Russell, and Bernard Franklin of Kansas City.

I can not but express appreciation to all who devoted their time to this service and I am sure that all acted and voted according to their convictions and "how they saw the world." I assumed all would go to Heaven. Yet, when the opportunity came for me to comment on that issue, I could not resist.

Regents in Heaven?[20]

Friday, June 28, 1985

It was the second morning of this two-day Board meeting and two regents, Larry Jones of Wichita and Norman Brandeberry of Russell, had joined me at a breakfast table in Topeka's Holiday Inn. The previous day I had told the Board that I would adhere to my self-imposed limit on serving as president and would resign effective June 30, 1986.

While waiting for our order, Brandeberry asked, "Did you guys get back to sleep last night?"

I didn't know what he was referring to and asked.

"After the 2 o'clock fire alarm," said Brandeberry, "and being out in the parking lot in your pajamas."

"I didn't hear any alarm!" I said. I had had a good eight hours of uninterrupted sleep.

Jones was quick and turned to me, "You were caught in the fire, you died, and you are now in Heaven!"

Having announced my planned resignation, I had reason to *feel* in Heaven. I would have only one more year of inter-university competitiveness and monthly Board meetings. I could not resist!

"This can't be heaven; there are two regents here!"

* * * * *

An earlier section described a 1980 Manhattan Chamber of Commerce retreat where I had briefed members on the projected decrease in K-State enrollment, based on decreasing sizes of Kansas high school graduating classes. The Chamber and University had worked to stem the decrease. Here is what resulted.

Did K-State Beat the Projections?
September, 1985 (and 1986)

Short answer: Yes, through my last fall in the presidency. And, data for the fall of 1986, a couple months after I left the presidency, would confirm the "Yes." Whereas a head count of 15,316 had been projected in 1980 for the fall of 1986, the actual 20th day head count was more than 2,000 students above that, 17,452! Whereas 14,749 FTE had been projected, the actual FTE exceeded that figure by more than 1,100. The FTE was 15,851.[21]

Projected and reported head count and FTE enrollment for the projection years are in the following table.[21,22]

Projected and Reported Enrollment at K-State.

	Head count		FTE	
Fall	**Projected**	**Reported**	**Projected**	**Reported**
1981	17,784	19,982	17,126	18,298
1982	17,259	19,497	16,620	17,979
1983	16,945	18,470	16,318	17,209
1984	16,234	18,092	15,633	16,637
1985	15,722	17,570	15,146	15,996
1986	15,316	17,452	14,749	15,851

By no means was the six-year enrollment decrease in the Head count Reported column inconsequential. The decade-long decrease in Kansas high school graduates, a 17 per cent drop, was real and it had significant impact on K-State enrollment. (The reader is cautioned that the Reported 1981 enrollment, then a record high, was likely an inflated figure. The true figure was likely less than 19,500. See the section, "Data Dilemma," in Chapter VI, Leadership and Management.)

However, the totality of the K-State staff, Manhattan Chamber, and alumni effort had helped stem the decrease. K-State's faculty, college leadership, admissions, Alumni, Foundation, and other staff, along with the Manhattan Chamber and K-State's good reputation, deserve much credit. All helped hold K-State's enrollment, and the numbers of customers for Manhattan area businesses and apartments, at levels higher than had been anticipated.

It is also clear, from detailed study of these and other data, that student retention was a big part of the positive figures.

No decrease in potential business volume is good news to a business community. No decrease in numbers of university students or faculty is good news to apartment owners or realtors. It is no secret, nor was in unexpected, that there was criticism and some second-guessing from the local community regarding the University's student recruitment efforts (described in an earlier section, The Chamber and Projected Enrollment).We were also criticized for making the enrollment projections public and preparing for them with a financial exigency plan. One local business person was rather blunt, "You guys just made it a self-fulfilling prophesy!"

Perhaps we could have sent more faculty to visit personally with high school guidance counselors and prospective students, or taken some faculty or graduate assistant salary funds to hire more recruiters to do those things. Of course, every other Kansas college and university had also ramped up recruitment.

Some Manhattan residents, and even some faculty, will be surprised that enrollment projections for the first half of the 1980s were *significantly exceeded* and that the 1985 and 1986 figures were both about 17,500. I, too, was puzzled when I read in an April 2009 K-State publication reference to a 1986 enrollment figure of 16,000.[23]

I do know that, though we had fully alerted Chamber members to the anticipated decline, we failed to keep them informed that the collective University and Chamber efforts were beating the projections every year. Regardless, I cannot but be proud of how our staff came to the fore during this period of declining numbers of high school graduates and of the good support we had from the Manhattan Chamber of Commerce.

*****

Here is Act Three of the Nichols saga. Though the issue had consumed more of my and others' time, the burned out hulk of Nichols Gym was now the rebuilt and very functional Nichols Hall.

Nichols Hall, from The Castle[3]

March 22, 1986

This evening the K-State Foundation Presidents' Club helped celebrate newly reconstructed Nichols Hall, occupied by the Departments of Speech and Computer Science and also providing storage space for some of our library's near million volumes. Shirley and I, and many of our guests, in tux and gown, were driven up in a horse-drawn carriage to the heavy wooden doors through which ROTC horse-drawn caissons rolled in earlier generations. After a K-State Union-catered dinner in Nichols' atrium and balconies and a brief celebratory program, we would move to Nichols' Theatre in the Round for a student performance of Brigadoon.

Shirley and I had just stepped down from that horse-drawn carriage and were ready to greet members of the K-State President's Club, March 22, 1986, to help celebrate the reconstruction of Nichols Hall. What could be done about Nichols' burned-out shell had consumed at least a few hours or days during every one of my 11 years in the presidency.

This celebration had been seventeen years coming, the eventual result of a 1968 arson fire that had left Nichols Gymnasium a burned-out shell. A formal dedication of the building, involving students, faculty, and other key people, had occurred the previous November.

The reader will recall that I had been given two options by the 1979 chair of the Senate Ways and Means committee, had made a recommendation, and, at the request of legislative leadership, had withdrawn my recommendation. I had then told our Manhattan delegation "it was in their hands."

Following that, the legislature had passed a resolution that provided for a five-member committee to recommend to the 1980 legislature the fate of Nichols. Committee membership would include the president of the K-State faculty senate, the president of the student body (Greg Musil), K-State's senior planning officer (Vice President Gene Cross), and appointees of the Senate president and House speaker. I was thrilled that Representative Robert Arbuthnot, a loyal K-State graduate, would chair the committee. Another loyal K-State alum, Senator Merrill Werts of Junction City, represented the Senate and Robert Dahl, Head of our Architectural Engineering and Construction Science Department, represented the faculty senate president.

Nichols should then be on the road to resolution! But, there would be more twists and turns in the road!

Largely because Nichols had never been on the University's five- and ten-year construction plans, and an early Foundation study had yielded no hope for significant private money, the appointed committee decided against reconstruction of the total structure. Rather, they recommended that Nichols' basement be renovated to accommodate our need for 10,000 square feet of accessible library storage, and that the superstructure be stabilized and the interior landscaped, perhaps as a site for outdoor concerts. I was not pleased with that, but the legislature had charted the course, the committee had made its judgment, and the 1980 legislature would receive their report.

Coincidentally, high on the K-State and Regents' capital improvement list was renovation of Holton and Dickens Halls, to meet safety codes and to accommodate three departments then in poor facilities, Speech, Statistics, and Computer Science. In the middle of the 1980 session, Senator and K-State graduate Gus Bogina, then chair of the legislature's joint house/senate building committee, expressed reservations about both the Nichols committee report and the high square-foot cost of renovating relatively small Holton and Dickens.

Bogina was thorough, did his homework, and was willing to analyze a complex situation. We had several conversations. What eventually emerged from Bogina's joint building committee was a plan to shift the money planned for Holton and Dickens to total reconstruction of Nichols, the latter to accommodate Speech, Statistics, and Computer Science, as well as the library storage.

Fortunately our conversations with Bogina were going on while the regents were in session in Topeka. I briefed K-State grad Frank Lowman, chair of the regents' building committee, and got his concurrence. Within twenty-four hours there was total consensus and we were confident that, with the total legislature's respect for Bogina, the plan would get through both legislative houses.

A few problems were yet to be solved, or rationalized. Five million dollars had been planned for Dickens and Holton, but Nichols had been projected to cost seven million. Fortunately, estimates are estimates! The Nichols estimate got revised.

The next problems: That K-State would get more additional space than planned bothered a few legislators loyal to other universities. And, leaving Dickens and Holton untouched, both antiquated in safety features, bothered some legislators. That last item got largely taken care of by the fact that another new classroom office building was on our five-year plan; K-State was given authorization to raze Dickens. Now, preliminary planning money could be provided for the total reconstruction of Nichols.

Fortunately, the word, authorization, in regard to razing Dickens Hall, has a valuable nuance; it could mean "Do it," or "Do it if you wish." That nuance let me feel comfortable in responding to a granddaughter of the late Professor Dickens with assurance that his namesake building would remain a part of K-State. I was certain that legislative interest in razing the building would eventually evaporate. In fact, the Department of Computer Science was rapidly growing and by the time detailed planning of Nichols was underway, it became apparent it would not hold all three departments. Statistics would remain assigned to Dickens.

Though I would have my fingers crossed through the next several legislative sessions, as final planning money and construction funds were considered, it was a relatively easy process from then on. The legislature had been as eager to get this project finished as was I. Both of us had taken enough heat.

Tonight, with President's Club members, we would celebrate.

Follow-up Thoughts

February, 2009

Major Omaha building contractor Robert Lueder, with whom I served on the board of the Kansas City Federal Reserve Bank, came to the K-State campus to tell our Construction Science faculty and students about his contractor experiences. He used as a presentation sub-title, "The Good, the Bad, and the Ugly." He said that he owed his audience a total perspective, the full reality of the industry to which those students were headed.

Though I do not think of any of these recorded anecdotes as ugly, they do include positives and negatives, satisfactions and disappointments, and the humor and stresses that one in state university leadership experiences. And, I owe my readers a total perspective, the full reality of a state university presidency.

For Shirley and me, there were far more positives than negatives. We cherished the evenings in our home with stimulating and interesting guests, most every one a part of the political theatre in which we were immersed. The several members of the Kansas House and Senate appropriations committees and the joint building committee are examples. Here were some of Kansas' most influential public officials, taking time from their businesses or professions to serve with limited pay not only in the legislative chambers and committee rooms, but to also spend a late afternoon and evening driving to and from Manhattan to see first hand and visit about some of K-State's needs.

There is no satisfactory measure of the contribution that Shirley made to these being positive experiences for our guests. For both legislators and others, with our student helper, she would plan and prepare the meal, bake cookies and bars, or fix a fruit pizza for a mid-morning event. (In later years, enhanced Foundation funds allowed hiring some catering from the K-State Union.)

Also on the positive side, I mention the President's Club barbecue luncheons in our back yard prior to a football game, initiated in the late 1970s as we worked and staffed to ramp up private fund raising. These had gotten off to a difficult start, at least in planning discussions with Foundation staff and some of my office colleagues.

State law had precluded serving alcohol on state property and that was fine with Shirley and me. Neither of our parents had served alcohol (they had neither the desire nor the funds) and my undergraduate fraternity, FarmHouse, allowed no alcohol in the fraternity house. The first university president with whom I had become rather well acquainted, Oklahoma State's Dr. Oliver Willham, had a well-understood philosophy, "Since alcohol is not allowed in our residence halls, we won't use it for entertaining in the President's Home."

However, a visit by President Ford to Topeka in the late 1970s had prompted a legislative exception for serving alcohol, in "the governor's mansion and state university presidents' homes." My colleagues emphasized that many President's Club members would be offended, or at least feel less generously hosted, if drinks were not offered prior to the barbecue.

The first year we held to the no alcohol policy, and were commended by one or two of the Club members. (I would respond that they were my Methodist friends.) However, there were relayed several Club members' feelings that the hospitality was less than adequate, or not in tune with the times. Consequently, we gave in to the apparent need; for later years a cash bar was provided for the Club barbecue.

I should add a related issue, which I considered trivial but that bothered my early legislative assistant, Barry Flinchbaugh. I usually held a Diet Coke at the many cocktail parties or receptions to which Shirley and I were invited. Flinchbaugh had apparently heard someone comment that "the new president must be so straight-laced that he won't even drink with us." And, after I had reassigned Athletic Director Barrett, one of the sports columnists quoted a K-State fan unhappy with my action, "Never trust a man that drinks a Coke at a cocktail party!"

Flinchbaugh told me one evening as we went into a Topeka reception, "At least order a Seven-up instead of a Coke; they'll think it is a gin and tonic."

Chapter VI

Leadership and Management

Members of the K-State leadership team at my arrival as president are listed and characterized in Chapter I, The Summer of Discovery. Changes in leadership structure, team membership, and university programs occurred over time, and management issues needed to be addressed. This chapter describes some of those changes, how certain issues were handled, and some of my related musings and experiences.

Incentives are important in leadership and management and that issue is first addressed, using two examples, international programs and research.

Incentives and Budget Policy

July, 1976

It was important that K-State have more international experiences. Our graduates would live and work in the global economy and society, so they needed exposure to faculty—as many as possible—with international experiences. Faculty can read, but living and working in a foreign setting can result in a higher level of global understanding and cultural sensitivity. Such experience can also build respect for the wisdom and creativity that exist in all countries. Where but in the tribal societies of Africa and the populous centuries-old cultures of Asia, both income-short and food-short, could K-State faculty both contribute more and learn more?

K-State had a student exchange program in Germany, several faculty handled summer study abroad programs, and there was considerable agriculture and veterinary faculty experience in India and Nigeria. There was faculty and administrator interest in more developing country programs financed by the U.S. Agency for International Development (AID), but faculty and administrator enthusiasm had been somewhat muted by a tradition of central University administration capturing virtually all the institution overhead funds that the AID contracts yielded. Little of that money was making its way back to the colleges, Veterinary Medicine and Agriculture, and their departments. Yet, it was their faculty who provided the expertise, perhaps interrupted their own research programs, and, in many cases, made the family sacrifices of overseas travel and living.

Co-incidentally, the same problem existed in federally and privately financed research, and there were both opportunity and need for more such funds. Little, often less than 10 per cent, of institutional overhead money found its way back to the originating and operating unit.

This problem had been easy to solve. I asked for a review of where expenses associated with the Nigeria and India contracts had occurred. With that information, and considering the importance of providing incentives, I established that 40 per cent of the institutional overhead for any international *or research* contract would go directly to the originating department and 5 per cent to the parent college or research unit.[1] Each college dean would have some prerogative, of course, to set or modify the details within their college.

I further established that no state instruction or research funds would be taken back by central administration on the basis that a department or college obtained such contracts or grants. Any state salary money saved by moving some faculty or staff FTE to the contract or grant would remain with the Department or college, to be used as the unit head saw fit. That would apply both within the fiscal year and to subsequent fiscal year budgets.

In short order, K-State staff, led by International Agricultural Programs Director Vern Larson and Agriculture Vice President Roger Mitchell, had made K-State available to AID for institution-developing programs in the Philippines and later, via a consortium of several Midwestern land grant universities, in Botswana. And, federal research grants and contracts steadily increased. Faculty, with the encouragement of Graduate School Dean Robert Kruh and Associate Dean John Noonan, became more aggressive in seeking such funds.

Coincidentally, we made another change in budget policy, to incentivize efficiency judgments by department heads. As associate dean at K-State, I had moved away from the previous years' proportions as the basis for allocating instructional FTE to departments.

Each department had to accommodate three functions with their instruction budget, administration, classroom and lab instruction, and academic advising. For thirty undergraduate advisees I had allocated 0.1 instructional FTE. For handling graduate advisees I used a more narrow ratio, perhaps 0.1 FTE for five or ten advisees. The balance of FTE was allocated according to relative instructional work load (largely student credits) and the relative administrative tasks (time required to supervise instruction faculty and facilities).

This allocation system sent the message that academic advising was important. It also incentivized a department to consolidate courses or course sections wherever feasible, avoiding large numbers of low-enrollment classes. I asked that K-State's instruction funds be allocated to colleges and departments accordingly (with some adjustment based on the relative dollars needed for program strength and quality).

Budget policy sends a message.

* * * * *

Achieving needed change or the approval of an idea is influenced by how proposals are presented to the deciding party. For approval of new curriculums or degrees at K-State, the final decision-makers were the members of the Kansas Board of Regents. Proposal preparation, in the end, is a management function.

The Master of Fine Arts[2]

March 17, 1978

During my earlier time at K-State, there seemed considerable KU paranoia. A few administrators and faculty were too often looking down the river at KU and making comparisons, "How come they get everything?"

Located between Topeka and metropolitan Kansas City, and with a number of legislators being KU law graduates, KU often had dominance on university-related legislative issues. Composition of the 1975 Board of Regents had not helped. But, paranoia is a waste of emotions.

Too often, I found, campus expressions about programs or facilities had been couched in KU-comparison terms, "We need that also." K-State's recent seeking of regent approval for a new master of fine arts degree was an example.

Chalmers had returned rather frustrated from a Council of Academic Officers meeting. Some Council members had questioned K-State's proposal for that new degree, expressing unwillingness to endorse it for Board consideration. It had been rejected once before by the Board and now it was in risk of being rejected again. He was complaining about that and KU.

Finally I said, "John, show me that proposal." I took it home that night and read through it. It was written in a way that basically implied, "KU has one; we should have one." KU may not have been specifically mentioned, but that was the tone, perhaps with such words as "The degree is necessary for this university's visual arts program to also be well recognized." I do not recall the exact words nor do I have a copy of the proposal.

I called Jerry Mattox, head of the Art Department, "Jerry, send me the formal definition of the degree, Master of Fine Arts." I had seen several different art degree titles mentioned in the proposal narrative. As I recall, there was a Master of Arts in Art, a Master of Education in Art, and perhaps others.

Mattox soon got back to me, "What we are proposing is the one that develops commercial illustrators. That is the definition in the art literature of this particular degree, the Master of Fine Arts in Art."

A few days later, recently-appointed Regent Jack Reeves and I were flying to Wichita. Reeves was a veterinarian from Garden City and a K-State graduate, and his family ran a large cattle feeding operation. I said to Reeves, "I have a proposal I want to make to the Board of Regents." I told him what it was and added, "This is the practitioner's degree."

His response was quick, "Sure sounds reasonable to me." When we next got the proposal on the Board agenda, revised in wording, it did not take long to get it approved.

After that Board meeting I walked over and had coffee with the Art Department faculty. I told them, "I want you to appreciate that in the final wording of the proposal and for Board discussion, it was Kansas State University talking; it was not the shadow of KU talking!"

* * * * *

Though a university is considered an agent of change for its students and statewide clientele, change *within* a university is not easy. Organizational change usually results in someone gaining or losing territory, prerogative, space, duties, and/or title. Personal pride is at risk. University people are prideful people, perhaps to a greater extent than the average of society.

Seamless: Teaching, Research, and Extension

July 1, 1978

During my time as associate dean I had watched Dean Glenn Beck and Cooperative Extension Service (CES) Director Harold Jones complete the integration of extension specialists within departments in the College of Agriculture. Specialists had been housed with their teaching and research counterparts, but their salaries, travel expense, and supplies were handled in the CES director's office and they had reported administratively to Dr. Jerry Amstein, head of agricultural specialists.

It had not been easy for Beck to accomplish. Amstein was departing for K-State's India project and CES Director Jones was on board with the concept, but long-time CES Associate Director Paul Griffith was not. Griffith handled CES budget and personnel matters and claimed USDA regulations made it improper, if not illegal, for department heads to handle CES funds. Beck's eventual solution was simple, exchange some FTE tenths of time between a senior extension specialist and the Department head. That made each department head an agent of the CES director, and their handling CES funds assuredly legal. A second consequence, also positive, was that some extension specialists would be paid in part by agricultural experiment station (AES) funds, and so were expected to be involved in research.

There had remained some loose ends, the agricultural engineering and home economics extension staff, neither group housed with their research and teaching colleagues. They remained in the Extension building, Umberger Hall.

Agricultural Engineering had been addressed when Bill Johnson had been hired as department head in 1970; one of his charges had been to integrate extension specialists, physically and budget-wise, in his department. But, on my return to K-State, Home Economics extension specialists were yet in Umberger.

On July1, 1978, with leadership and good will on the part of Vice President for Agriculture Roger Mitchell, Home Economics Dean Ruth Hoeflin, and CES Director John Dunbar, the integration of Extension staff was complete; *all* Home Economics faculty were physically and administratively in Justin Hall.

A year earlier I had sought state funds to expand in the College of Business an extension type program, initially financed by a Small Business Administration grant.[3] Although I had not been successful in that effort, my long-term goal was to see K-State provide research and statewide extension education faculty and programs in virtually every teaching discipline. That might be achieved long after I would leave the presidency.

* * * * *

It is not uncommon for people long in their jobs, whether in a business or the public sector, to believe that how things have been done is the only way they can or should be done. The following is a condensed version of an un-dated piece I found in my files, apparently dictated at a time of frustration early in my presidency.

Offense and Defense in Administration[4]

I see a parallel between members of a football team and members of an administrative team. There is, however and unfortunately, a contrast in how team members function.

I think of university administrators as members of the offensive team. The goal is at "the other end of the field," a joint program with community colleges, an appropriation, a more effective academic advising system, or perhaps a reduction in course numbers and course preparation workload. One member of the team may call the signals, another carry the ball. Some will run interference, some will shout encouragement. One may play safety, protect the play from unforeseen contingencies. All will cheer when the ball gets to the goal line, the appropriation, the efficient process, or the new program.

The unfortunate contrast is that on some occasions an administrative team member gets confused, thinks his or her role is to play defense. Can you imagine a football blocker sticking out his foot to trip the ball carrier? Can you imagine a pass receiver taking time to reconsider whether he should proceed to the goal line? Can you imagine the center turning to the quarterback and yelling, "Just hold the ball!"?

Too often, among administrative team members, we see and hear, "We tried that once and it didn't work." "It is not in the policy manual." "We only write reimbursement checks on Tuesday." "It may work there, but it won't here." "We don't have the software." "Faculty won't like it." "What we have is working."

There is also a time element. A college game lasts sixty minutes. Most weeks I have about sixty hours to get things done. Time spent outmaneuvering or wearing down the blocker takes time I could have spent "moving the ball forward" on that or other issues.

Why do these roadblocks happen? Of course, some proposals may be bad ideas. Maybe the blocker was bothered that he or she was not asked for advice before the idea was advanced. Maybe he or she considers the idea an invasion of their territory. Maybe the blocker just likes to play defense, likes to be the gate-keeper.

I have a lot of respect for a good defensive team. In fact, in my modest high school baseball career, I had far more fun and success on the hot corner, third base, than at the plate.

In administration, my fun and satisfaction comes from playing offense—initiating programs, finding efficiencies, solving problems, getting buildings funded, and then getting those funded buildings designed and built. That should be the source of fun and satisfaction for all members of an administrative team. How can I help team members see the satisfaction from offensive success?

I recall a positive example, a person who could have been a blocker, but who helped his successor move the ball. During my time at SDSU, our new and young director of admissions and records, Jim Pedersen, gathered his staff together to discuss an aggressive change in student recruitment. Among the staff was his semi-retired predecessor, Dave Doner. After Jim laid out his idea, there was a period of silence. In time, the group heard Doner's blunt words, "We tried that once and it didn't work." However, there was a twinkle in Doner's eye and he continued, "But I still believe it's a great idea and I think we should go for it!"

How can one get all members of a team one has inherited to focus on offense, or at least to stay out of the way of those who concentrate on moving the ball?

I should tell them about Dave Doner."

* * * * *

K-State's annual budget included tens of millions of state dollars. Expenditure approval was dispersed among the University's many units. In addition to expenditure accounts for state dollars, there were several hundred "revolving fund" accounts (also called activity accounts), which handled income and expenditures for such as residence hall operations, conference fees and expense, or crop lines produced for release to growers. I had confidence in K-state staff and approval systems, but problems can develop.

An Internal Auditor and Why

July 1, 1979

It was logical that this observation had come from a banker, "Considering the dollars that flow through each university, I am surprised there has been no mention of internal financial audits." Wichita banker Jordan Haines had been on the Kansas Board of Regents less than a year and I had observed that his questions and comments were always on target.

I understood Haines' concerns. Where there are money and people, temptations are ever present. Examples from my twenty-plus years on several campuses came to mind, including a university account paying for fertilizer delivered to both a university farm and the manager's own farm and a second-tier finance officer who quietly resigned amid rumors of misappropriated funds.

Bank boards on which I had served received periodic internal audit reports. A bank's reputation and its very solvency depend on confirmed accuracy. A university should be a model of accuracy and integrity.

Haines' comment got my attention. I knew that I had capable and sincere financial staff, Finance Vice President Dan Beatty, Comptroller Ralph Perry, and Budget Director Ted Dodge, and I trusted them completely. However, I had discovered some long-time traditions, especially in the handling of Foundation and revolving fund accounts, which bothered me. For some accounts, there was no apparent expenditure approval beyond the person whose program the account served. And, in both athletics and continuing education, there had been accusations and some evidence of abuse.

I recognized that no auditor is superhuman, and no system is foolproof. However, should there be a sizeable impropriety or a series of improprieties, and K-State had no internal audit system, the University would be vulnerable.

There was another reason, perhaps self protective on my part. What if I should err in submitting a travel reimbursement claim or a bill for entertainment that state regulations did not allow? Would that get caught internally and returned? Or might a post audit in Topeka bring some embarrassment to me and the University. A state university is both a public entity and, from time to time, a political target. Media look for news wherever it may be.

I therefore established an internal auditor position, reporting to Vice President Beatty, but I would get a direct copy of every audit report. Half of the auditor's time would be devoted to adequacy of and adherence to prudent financial policies and processes. The other half would be available to any dean, director, or department head for any financial accounts related to their units. The latter reflected my belief that line officers should have the prerogative and responsibility to manage and monitor their operations.

In looking back, I may have erred in limiting the internal audit role to financial items. Universities are staffed by able and competitive people, and competition for pride or recognition can get out of bounds. More than once I have learned of inflated publication records and degrees listed on a resume but not earned.

In recent years an internal university audit function has been demanded by law or federal regulations in several areas, such as research on human subjects and laboratory animal welfare. It seems to me that the inspector general position in federal agencies, with that person free to audit a wide range of functions, from finance to program efficiency and impact, is a model for consideration in a major university.

* * * * *

Perhaps the most difficult personnel problem I encountered as president involved the leadership of our agricultural programs. This was my own sector of experience and involved four people I had long known and respected. In the end, there seemed but one workable solution.

One Leader for Agriculture[5]

May 8, 1980

Vice President for Agriculture Roger Mitchell, the top officer, had been hired and arrived a few months before I was named. Continuing in their positions were College Dean Carroll Hess (instruction), Experiment Station Director Floyd Smith (who had been acting vice president during Beck's extended leave), and Cooperative Extension Director Robert Bohannan. Each of the latter three positions had long carried full authority to make program decisions and allocate funds (including federal funds for the AES and CES) within their units.

Most faculty positions were joint teaching-research or research-extension, so department heads had to negotiate among the three, Hess, Smith, and/or Bohannon, on new appointments, salary, and promotions and, in some cases, for operating funds. In essence, department heads reported to three people. Mitchell had a title but not the budget, so held little operating authority, even to settle disagreements among the three. Frustration was apparent in all parties, especially the department heads.

In time, Bohannan returned to a faculty position in Agronomy and was replaced as director by John Dunbar, who was recruited from Purdue. Stresses continued and, in time, became more severe.

All officers were experienced, conscientious, and with sincere motives. But, with strong personalities, considerable seniority in second-level positions, and each person having some constituency, several attempts at solution had failed. I had offered to pull all budgets, instruction, AES, and CES, into my office, and then delegate them back to Mitchell. He declined, apparently feeling that he could eventually forge his team into a cooperative mode. Frustrations, both on campus and off, continued and Mitchell eventually concluded he needed to remove two of the three, Smith and Hess, from their posts.

With the risk of a prolonged legal challenge which that move triggered, I named a small committee of top faculty, industry leaders, and students and asked for their advice. The committee included Dr. Erle Bartley, professor of Dairy Science, John "Junior" Armstrong, president of the Kansas Farm Bureau, and Rolland "Red" Parr, a leader in the state's livestock industry. All three were tops in their field and of unquestioned integrity. I also named two students, an undergraduate and a graduate, and the president of the faculty senate.

It did not take long for them to consider the issues and options, and to give me succinct advice, "There has to be one boss in the agriculture programs; do what you need to do to achieve that."

In some land grant universities the top agricultural officer carried three titles, dean of the college, director of AES, and director of CES, obviously vesting full budget authority in that officer. Three lieutenants would carry the titles, respectively, associate dean, associate director of AES, and associate director of CES. Transition to that seemed to me the most logical way to achieve one leader.

The legal basis for challenging removal from a position is usually that the person has been "removed without cause." If we simply eliminated the existing positions, and created four new positions as described above, none of the four could be considered to have been "removed" from their position.

I consulted with each of the four principals, Mitchell, Smith, Dunbar, and Hess, and outlined my plan. That plan included that I would name a search and screening committee for the dean and director position and, subsequently, for each of the associate positions. Each of the four existing officers held a tenured professorship in an academic department and, if not selected for one of the new positions, would move to that professorship. No one would risk their continued employment and no one would have been "removed from office."

Though I know that each understandably felt abused by the chain of events and stress in which they had been involved, each understood that for the benefit of the total agricultural programs, substantive and quick action was necessary. Each, in time, gave me their concurrence.

The issue and its solution were not limited to the College of Agriculture. The AES funded research in virtually every college of the University and there had been some fear in other colleges that the change would risk that funding. I settled that concern by committing that the per cent of AES dollars then allocated to each of those colleges would not change for the next three fiscal years. (After that, as with departments in the College of Agriculture, funding would properly be dependent on the merit of proposed research.)

When a later screening committee provided new Provost Owen Koeppe and me a list of six names for the top position, dean and director, Mitchell was not on the list. Committee members told us that, though they held him in high regard, they felt that under the circumstance a new top officer was needed.

After listening to each screening committee member's comments on the six finalists, Koeppe and I quickly settled on two of the six, Dunbar and Walter Woods, then head of Animal Science at Purdue. Our judgment was that "Dunbar is here; he knows all the internal and external political forces. Woods is younger and he would probably take the program further."

In the end, Koeppe and I decided, "For the time being, let's settle things down with someone who is on board." We chose Dunbar. He had been somewhat less involved in the stresses, and would fill the dean and director role until his retirement about four years later. Woods would then be recruited to replace Dunbar.

Though all involved had been through a rough time, each of the officers landed on his feet. Mitchell was invited back to the University of Missouri, from which he had come, as Agronomy department head. Within months, he was named dean at Missouri and had an excellent career in that role. Hess took an assignment in the United Arab Emirates, so productive that it was extended. Smith renewed his well-deserved reputation in soil fertility research, just at a time when increases in crop genetic yield potential called for reassessment of fertility levels.

Department heads henceforth had one boss. For faculty and clientele: "Case closed." All could focus on program leadership.

Could such a circumstance and career-affecting consequence have been avoided? Yes, I believe it could, and I offer the following illustration of how: Suppose one is to hire a new dean (or other top officer), with one or more associates in place. Do not just hire a new dean, but address the issue of the total administrative team. Before that new dean is recruited or selected, a president and/or provost should make it clear to the associates that they should expect the new dean to have considerable privilege in determining the subsequent administrative structure and pattern of delegation. The situation parallels that for a new president with a provost and vice presidents in place. A new top officer has to have some prerogative in team structure and operations. Once that prerogative is exercised, administration can be more productive and rewarding to all parties.

* * * * *

K-State's problem in agricultural leadership had not been uncommon in land grant universities, and there are reasons. I use a later experience with Oregon State University as a base to cite several similar situations. Together they yield some lessons in general university structure and management.

A Parallel at Oregon State

Summer, 1982

The call had come from Dr. Robert MacVicar, who had been my instructor in a Chemistry of Vitamins course and a member of my doctoral committee at Oklahoma State University. Now, though, MacVicar was president of Oregon State University and he sought my help. If I agreed, I would join long-time

Ohio State Dean Roy Kottman (who had been adviser to our animal science department club when I enrolled as a freshman at Iowa State) and retired Wisconsin Dean Glenn Pound in reviewing the administrative structure and operations of Oregon State's agricultural programs.

Oregon State's relatively new dean of agriculture, Dr. Ernie Briskey, had apparently suggested me. Though I had known Briskey since we had presented papers at meat research conferences during graduate school days, we had not talked since encountering each other at a Buenos Aires reception twenty years earlier. He knew I had dealt with a situation paralleling that in which he was now involved.

The situation? The directors of Oregon State's AES and CES had been in their jobs for some time when Briskey was brought in as the new dean. The two directors had not seemed especially interested in Briskey's suggestions or advice after he had taken a look at Oregon agriculture's potential and needs. Department heads felt caught in the middle. Sound familiar?

Kottman, Pound, and I would spend two full days asking questions and listening to every key person, especially the department heads. We then recommended some actions to MacVicar. And, I would be asked to return two or three months later to help Oregon State staff fine tune some of the steps MacVicar would take.

I was well aware of similar stresses at other land grant campuses. I believe teaching, research, and extension in a college or department should be a seamless continuum with a common vision for the discipline and for serving the related industry. I also believe that most faculty should be involved in two or all three of the functions. Unfortunately, those in the management chain sometimes do not all have the same vision and may function independent of each other.

The fact that most of each state's AES and CES money came through USDA contributed to the problem, at K-State and elsewhere. USDA memorandums of agreement with the universities provided that each of these units be headed by a director, named by the University president and approved by USDA.

USDA funds were to be disbursed by the respective director or designee and new AES projects using such funds had to be approved by Washington staff. For Extension, there was even a requirement that the words, Cooperative Extension Service, be prominent in letterhead used by CES staff. A director who wanted to ignore a supervisory dean or vice president's guidance might pull out some USDA regulation, and protest that one just can not have two bosses, USDA regulations and the dean. That problem did not exist in the case of instruction; virtually all money was state money.

SDSU had had the problem years before my time and a similar problem had developed at Oklahoma State in the early 1960s. North Dakota State also had a reasonably similar circumstance in the 1970s.

The statewide personal and political linkages that agriculture deans, directors, and department heads have or do not have are also factors in this not uncommon administrative stress. In southern states, where universities seem even more subject to political pressures, separateness among research, extension, and campus instruction has often been what I considered extreme. I recall finding two departments of animal science at the University of Georgia when I visited there early in my career. One handled teaching and research; the second, a Department of Animal Science Extension, was even in a separate building. Of course that Animal Science Extension department reported only to a director of Extension. The dean of agriculture was apparently not involved.

There were also "departments" of Animal Science at two off-campus research stations across Georgia. It took the University of Georgia several decades and, in time, a new dean with long-time statewide political friendships developed while a department head, plus a strong president, to pull all elements of instruction, research, and extension together in the College of Agriculture and in subject matter departments.

In the early 2000s I would help review agricultural research programs at Auburn, Alabama's 1862 land grant university. A major sore point for the dean and department heads was that the director of extension was administratively independent and there was little coordination. Part of the reason in that case was a federal court ruling that required a single director for the extension programs of two universities, Auburn and the state's 1890 land grant university, Alabama A&M.

Having worked in five land grant universities and participated in many regional instruction, AES, and CES meetings and workshops, I knew rather well most of the actors in these several situations. All were capable and good people; many were long-time friends. But when territory concerns and worship of control override good will and respect for one's administrative colleagues, the result is undue stress for nearly all involved. In the cases described, it is the department heads, the people I consider a university's most important administrators/managers, who are in the crossfire. They recruit and guide faculty, they initiate faculty reward (compliments as well as salary recommendations), and they allocate space and budget, all so the faculty can best serve the students and statewide clientele.

I do not believe the location of the CES and AES director title is always the key; rather, it is clear and well understood job descriptions, good will, and respect for each other. At Nebraska, where I served as vice chancellor for agriculture and natural resources, the dean of the college and directors of AES and CES reported to me. We officed in the same building, saw each other daily, and also met on a formal basis weekly for a couple hours, including lunch. My predecessor, then carrying the title of dean, had set the pattern. He coordinated, represented the college with the campus chancellor's office and with the statewide industry. The others signed or delegated signatures for expenditures and worked with department heads in coordinating programs.

On arrival, with the vice chancellor title, responsibility for two additional units, and another office in the chancellor's suite two miles away, I took two actions to insure continued clarity of roles and division of labor: 1) I formalized an organization chart that showed, and I verbally underlined, that department heads, each responsible for their departments' instruction, research, and extension, reported to me. I would, with input from my dean/director colleagues, do their annual evaluations and recommend their salary adjustments. 2) I institutionalized the Institute as an entity by naming the senior budget officer in the group as Assistant to the Vice Chancellor for Finance. He was responsible for financial procedures and monitoring for all funds for all the units, regardless of fund source.

What was the outcome at Oregon State? Our interviews confirmed the evident problem and the evident need for "one boss," but we could only recommend and suggest. Any decisions would need to be made by President MacVicar, including marching orders for involved administrators and/or personnel reassignment.

The reader who may be in a management role may find worthwhile lessons in these several experiences.

* * * * *

Back to K-State's central administration in Anderson Hall. About the time that the personnel stresses in agricultural leadership became public, the fall of 1979, John Chalmers told me of his intent to leave the academic affairs position by the end of the fiscal year (a year earlier than the normal age sixty-five departure from administration) and move to a nine-month appointment as a professor of economics.

A Provost and Why

July 1, 1980

With the clarity that hindsight provides, it is evident that I should have made this change, from the Vice Presidency for Academic Affairs to a new Provost position, in early April of 1975, soon after being named president and before assuming the position. There are several reasons.

1. The president of a major university needs a senior officer to assist in program leadership and coordination of large and diverse colleges with teaching, research, and statewide extension education responsibilities. The vice presidency for academic affairs was seen by many as such an office. However, the person in that office, Chalmers, evidenced little interest in or enthusiasm for the statewide role of K-State. I thought that, as president, I could compensate for that. However, my other duties prevented my compensation being adequate in the University's daily functioning.
2. The division of labor between the academic and agriculture vice presidents was fuzzy. When the academic vice presidency had been established in 1963, it carried no responsibility for the AES or CES. The dean of agriculture (title changed to vice president in 1966) was responsible for all aspects of the AES and CES, and for budget and staffing of the College of Agriculture. Over time, with the academic affairs officer adjacent to the president in Anderson Hall, vs. the dean/vice president for agriculture a quarter mile away in Waters Hall, this differentiation had eroded.
3. From the beginning, occupants of that academic vice president office had evidenced little regard for the wide range of academic skills among K-State's entering students. The focus seemed to be on the highly able and the all-too-common philosophy that all new students should enroll in their standard curriculum and either sink or swim. From my experiences at Oklahoma State and Iowa State, which admitted, as K-State did, any graduate of an accredited high school in the state, my philosophy was to assess the ability of each student, then devise that student's credit load and course selection in accord with his or her ability. The highly able should be challenged to the most rigorous academic experience. Those less able should have, especially their first two semesters, a credit load and course mix that would provide each an *opportunity* to succeed.
4. Making the change immediately would have avoided some frustration and uncertainty on the part of college deans. Should they follow the president's philosophy? Or, as members of the deans' council, chaired by Chalmers, and in routine academic matters with him, follow his?
5. The change would have saved Chalmers some frustrations. It is difficult for one to function with comfort when they know that

their guiding philosophies differ from those of the person to whom they report. To what extent should he constrain or limit his actions from his own philosophy? Though his frustrations erupted from time to time, such as at a principal/counselor conference on our campus and perhaps in a letter about community colleges that found its way into the media, he generally handled them with constraint or in private.

6. I would have sought more counsel and would have had more support from one chosen, in part, for their exhibited enthusiasm for a land grant university's statewide mission. For the best judgments and actions, a president needs considerable counsel and, when a judgment is made, support for that judgment.

Why had I not made the change at the beginning? There were several reasons. Chalmers was a highly able person with strong academic credentials and administrative skills. He appeared to have good relationships with the deans, except for agriculture. In regard to the agriculture relationship, I had even been warned by Regent Executive Officer Max Bickford, "Don't get caught up in that feud!" Having been in the agriculture dean's office ten years earlier, I was reticent to address that feud by replacing Chalmers, the non-agriculture officer involved. I was optimistic that with the new vice president for agriculture, Roger Mitchell, the feud could end. I was wrong.

Why not after the first year? In my first days in office and continuing for months, a more public problem, finances and management in intercollegiate athletics, had demanded my attention. Having made a necessary but controversial personnel change there, I was not eager to make another major change, especially where the issues were less quantitative and documentable.

With the arrival of Koeppe as provost, key operating issues were clarified. I quote from comments to an August 1980 faculty meeting, that Koeppe became "the chief program and academic officer" of the University.[6] That clearly included agricultural programs. I also stated that, "I will sign off on appointment of administrative personnel; Provost Koeppe on all faculty appointments," that "the deans will report to Provost Koeppe," but "for discussion and development of policies, goals, and direction, I will chair the meeting and Provost Koeppe will serve as vice chair."

A council of deans meeting in the early 1980s, after Owen Koeppe was named provost. To my left are Koeppe, College of Agriculture Interim Dean David Mugler, Graduate School Dean Bob Kruh, Human Ecology Dean Barbara Stowe, and LaVerne Lindsay, Continuing Education. To my right are Engineering Dean Don Rathbone, Arts and Sciences Dean Bill Stamey, Dean of Libraries Brice Hobrock, and Assistant Provost Bill Feyerharm. Faces not visible would be Education Dean David Byrne, Business Dean Bob Lynn and Veterinary Dean Don Trotter. (Photo courtesy University Archives and Royal Purple.)

Was the change to a provost position related to changing the agriculture vice presidency back to the title of dean? No. A provost position is senior and a vice president for agriculture could have reported to it. That they happened at the same time is coincidental.

* * * * *

I find in my files a handwritten piece entitled "Games Universities Play," undated and apparently written at another time of some frustration.

Games Universities Play[7]

Some games on the list are played within the University; a few by university leaders as they present their case to the public. Each one listed includes some elaboration.

1. "I would start that new program you suggest if you can provide some additional money for it." When an industry leader, governor, legislator, or top university officer suggests that a new program be initiated in response to some new need, perhaps even an industry crisis, this is a too-typical response. The response means one of several possible truths: a) the suggested program is lower priority than any program we now have, b) I agree on the need, and it

is higher priority that some of our current projects, but I do not have the courage to close down those other projects and shift the money, c) that proposed program is really a silly idea; it would be of no value, or d) I have wanted to add two faculty and some new lab equipment for some time, and if you can get the legislature or president to fund the program, we will sure take it on!

2. "We need to get this proposed Ph.D. program approved in order to attract top faculty." That statement triggers some discomforting thoughts: a) If you do not now have top faculty, how could you conscientiously start the program and recruit students for it? b) Have less than top faculty put this Ph.D. program proposal together? c) Have the dean and president agreed that this new program is a priority and have they committed funds for the department to attract those needed faculty?
3. "If I combine courses or course sections, or drop a course, the administration will take away a faculty position." I had encountered this my first year as associate dean at K-State. The statement told me that whoever was making the position allocations was using the wrong criteria. The criteria should include numbers of students or student credits. A department head should have the incentive to implement efficiencies, and be rewarded for doing so.
4. Misleading enrollment information. Enrollment reporting is a legitimate part of marketing a university, so one may be tempted to select figures that show the most growth. Are the data head count or FTE (full-time equivalent)? One institution publicized a large enrollment growth, but neglected to point out that the later figures included the enrollment of another institution that had, in the meantime, merged into the university.
5. "That NCAA (or conference) probation is unfair! We will appeal!" Fans may want to hear that declaration from the university, but such a statement disappoints. I have yet to learn of an NCAA or conference probation action that was taken without thorough consideration of convincing information. I have a much higher regard for the university and its leadership that says, "When we joined the conference and NCAA we agreed to abide by their rules. We'll take our punishment, discipline those responsible, and work to regain our good reputation."
6. "Get it done, but don't bother me with the details." Or "Don't tell me how you do it; just recruit top players and win games!" I recall interviewing an assistant football coach one Sunday evening in

> the town of a Southwest Conference powerhouse. We had a head coach vacancy and this young man had been recommended. Our first forty-five minutes, discussing coaching and scheduling philosophy, was all on the positive side. I was impressed and asked just how eager he was to be a head coach. His response let me know in a subtle, but very clear, way that he could and would do *whatever* was needed to recruit players that would win. He would get it done if I just gave him the signal. We kept looking, and found Jim Dickey. Dickey did not need or want the signal, just support. And he took us to our first bowl game.

* * * * *

One is fortunate if he or she can go through a several-decade management career and not be severely disappointed by apparent actions of a colleague. If one learns of disappointing actions after the colleague has moved on or retired, one is left with a dilemma. What action can or should be taken?

Data Dilemma

September, 1983

Regent policy required that the official fall enrollment for each university, both head count and full-time equivalent (FTE), was to be the count on the 20th day of classes. That would take into account late enrollees and exclude those few new freshmen who had quickly decided the University was not for them. The FTE was based on fifteen credits per undergraduate student and a lesser number for graduate or veterinary students.

As FTE enrollment had increased in the 1960s and 1970s, the legislature had steadily provided money for some new faculty positions for the following year. To university staff and administrators, as well as some alumni, head count enrollment increases were as high conference rankings were to sports enthusiasts—they gave bragging rights.

The previous fall, 1982, K-State's head count enrollment had dropped nearly 500 students and, though the Manhattan business and apartment owners had been briefed to expect a decrease (See "The Chamber and Projected Enrollment," Page 87), they were voicing concerns.

In this setting came Koeppe with a problem. In preparing to sign off on K-State's 20th day enrollment report to the Board of Regents office, he had for the first time learned that our enrollment tabulations may have violated that 20th day policy! In forwarding the reports in prior years, Koeppe had had no reason to question the tabulations. However, as Dr. Don Hoyt, whose Institutional Research staff assembled the data, handed this report to Koeppe he had mentioned that enrollment numbers for off-campus courses scheduled to start later in the fall were only estimates.

That had raised a red flag to Koeppe! This was a 20th day report! Especially at Ft. Riley, because of troop movements or army training schedules, some classes would begin in October or November. If our previous fall semester reports had included estimates for those late fall courses, K-State would have been submitting inflated figures!

I would learn later a second part of the problem, the apparently inflated figures, was that some students would enroll in both campus classes (data assembled by the Registrar's office) and continuing education classes (data assembled by that unit), both underway on the 20th day. Those students could be counted twice for the reported head count figure.[8]

Koeppe was not comfortable with sending inflated figures. And he knew enough of my posture on such an issue that he should alert me pronto.

Hoyt's Institutional Research Office was well respected. It provided data requested by college or University administrators in the form it was requested. Rationalizing any request with regent policy was not Hoyt's affair. However, I could only wonder why he had not alerted Koeppe to inclusion of enrollment numbers for late-start courses in 1980, his first year as provost. Koeppe was also wondering.

The question now: What 1983 fall enrollment should K-State report? There was only one answer, 20th day head count and FTE!

Koeppe and I also wondered: For how long has there been undue inflation in our fall enrollment figures? Should we inform the Board office that past years' submitted enrollment data may have been unduly high? Had K-State been given new faculty positions based on improper data?

Our 1983 report would make this fall's enrollment drop appear extra large and cause more angst among local business people than reality would warrant. Should we let some of them know why the large reported drop?

Unfortunately, without going back through previous years' input data, we did not know the magnitude of earlier over-reporting. However, data in the following table, calculated from data in an earlier section, "Did K-State Beat the Projections," provide a clue. Note the magnitude of the reported decrease for the fall of 1983 compared to those for earlier and later years.

Enrollment Decreases

Fall	Head count	FTE
1982	484	319
1983	1,027	770
1984	378	572
1985	512	641
1986	118	145

The large drop shown for the fall of 1983 suggests that the magnitude of over-reporting in earlier years may have been 500 or more head count and 150 or more FTE. The wide head count/FTE ratio, 500/150, is not illogical, considering that most of the enrollees in those late fall courses at Fort Riley or otherwise in Continuing Education would likely be taking only one or a few courses. (These data also suggest that K-State's actual head count had never reached the high of 19,982 reported for the fall of 1981. The true fall 1981 figure was likely less than 19,500.)

Further questions haunted me. Why had I not been informed of this issue during my eight years in the presidency? Or, could the inclusion of late fall enrollment have been initiated sometime during my presidency, rationalized by one of my trusted colleagues to keep K-State's reported enrollment trend continuing upward and more faculty positions coming? Should we mount an investigation, find out when the practice began and why? Who and how many former administrators might be publicly embarrassed? And, to what extent would K-State be publicly embarrassed?

Until I had spent a few months as a university president, I had believed that any considered thought or action was either ethical or not ethical and that it should be easy to follow the ethical path. Here was another case, however—K-State athletics had been the first—where the seemingly most ethical action, investigation and full public disclosure, could cause undeserved harm to one or more persons, some now retired, and certainly to the University for which I was responsible. It would also put valuable Institution Research staff in what I felt would be an unfair situation, facing conflicting loyalties to previous and current administrators. We initiated no investigation.

The reader may disagree with that judgment. Some may also wonder, "Why did you not just let the enrollment tabulations continue as in the past?" We certainly could have avoided some of the community heat that came from the unduly large enrollment drop publicly reported for the fall of 1983.

However, neither Koeppe nor I could feel comfortable allowing the continued submission of inflated data.

We let it be, for the time, undisclosed history. K-State's fall, 1983, enrollment would simply show an unduly large decrease, and we would absorb the heat that came.

* * * * *

Two earlier items described conflicts between first and second level administrators in agricultural programs, including K-State. With more externally funded research and extension-type entities, parallel problems can emerge in other colleges. Though we caught it in time, the risk of such had appeared in our College of Business.

A Parallel in the Business College?

September 24, 1983

This evening Shirley and I would host the College of Business International Trade Institute advisory committee, along with Dean Robert Lynn, Institute Director Ray Coleman, and other staff, for a roast pig barbecue on our back lawn, then head to the K-State-Wyoming football game. I felt especially good; we had avoided a problem.

When the idea of an International Trade Institute in the College of Business had been advanced by Coleman, Lynn and I had flown to brief several regents. Such an institute would add an international dimension to an important and growing college. I wanted to enlist regent support for legislative funding. That funding was achieved, with considerable enthusiasm on the part of legislators. Because this was a new program, the funds were appropriated to the University as a separate line item. Lynn appointed Coleman as institute director.

An early and very proper step by Coleman was to form an external advisory committee. With the help of Lynn and me, Coleman put together a top group, virtually all leading Kansas manufacturers of exported products. It was not long, though, until I learned that the Institute agenda, though constructive and aggressive, was not necessarily meshing with or complementing the total College of Business agenda. As with research and extension programs, it was basic that international activities be integrated with student instruction. But, Lynn had not been directly involved as the Institute agenda had been developed.

There is a fine line between an advisory committee and a policy board. I tend to lean heavily on input and judgments from advisory committees; they tell us what our clientele expect from the University. We need to consider their advice, and follow it where feasible. However, since the line officer, department head or dean, is responsible for total program leadership and coordination in the college or department, such line officer needs to be an ex-officio member of any advisory committee.

We had missed a step. The committee should have been appointed by Lynn or, at the least, Lynn should have been specifically listed as an ex-officio member. I made a phone call to the committee chairman, had a concurring visit with Coleman, and Lynn then had had a seat—as dean, a significant seat—at the table in the advisory committee meeting.

As more and more outside funded institutes, with large dollar budgets and sizeable staff, develop on university campuses, I would see risks of more parallel situations. Most major universities now receive a high proportion of operating funds via major grants and contracts from diverse federal and a few state agencies, sometimes a million dollars or more to a senior faculty. Or, the dollars may come as an earmark by Congress, with money directed to a specific topic in a named university or group of universities, but to be administered through a federal agency. Each of those agencies has its own rules for expenditures and reporting.

Institute or project director loyalty can easily move to the external funding source, and risk departure from university policy, priorities, and administrative guidance. The result can be friction, inconsistency in personnel policies, and lack of coordination. How does a department head, dean, or president fulfill his or her responsibility to lead, minimize jealousies, assign space, and insure abidance with state or university personnel policies (salary, titles, and even vacation time) when massive sums have been directed to a distinct university unit? How does one maintain the good will, cooperation, and respect for administrative colleagues' management responsibilities? How does one keep egos in check?

My suggestion is a gentle or firm reminder by the president that these funds come, in large part, because the faculty member or the unit is part of the University. Further, as with any university unit, no administrative or leadership title is permanent. It can be given or removed. A faculty member may hold academic tenure in their subject matter department, but there is no protective tenure in an administrative or project leadership post. The one who appoints can remove. As in the case of CES and AES directors, the president, with recommendation by the dean or other, appoints.

* * * * *

In physics we learn that for every action there is a reaction. In management, I suggest there is a parallel rule: For every action there is an unintended consequence. And, that unintended consequence can show up later.

Delayed Consequences?

After we completed the new administrative team in agriculture I erred in agreeing to one deviation from the title arrangement that I had laid out. It may well have contributed to some problems after I had left.

When Dunbar was named dean and director, his heir apparent for taking over the daily duties of coordinating CES programs was Dunbar's then current associate director, Fred Sobring. Sobring had come to K-State as associate director of Extension after Dunbar had been hired as CES director about four years earlier. With the top officer being dean and director, Sobring would become the CES operating officer, but with no title change.

Dunbar had made a forceful argument that Sobring should be given the full director title. "After all," he said, "how can we promote a person to a broader job with more responsibility and not make a title change?" I had no problem with Sobring assuming the broader operating officer role; I knew he would do well in it. However, to give him the director title was a deviation from what I had mapped out to address the total agriculture leadership problem, and I was reticent to agree.

Dunbar came back with a second argument. He had chosen Sobring, Sobring's loyalty was to him. There would be no problem in Dunbar maintaining full coordination of Extension with research and instruction.

Finally, I agreed to Dunbar relinquishing the Extension director title to Sobring. That was a mistake. Dunbar retired in 1985 and was replaced by Walter Woods. Just as the full director titles being in the second tier positions had been a problem on Mitchell's arrival as vice president, would the CES director title being elsewhere be a problem for Woods, now or sometime after my departure, or for another dean years later?

Considering the history of K-State's structure and depending on personalities and the issues of the day, budget and program coordination of CES with instruction and research could again bring some pain.

* * * * *

One of Murphy's laws: Administration tends to increase. Two problems result: 1) A new administrative office requires money to operate, money also needed for teachers or staff to clean the classrooms. 2) A president has another person with whom to deal. Two circumstances gave me a chance to reduce the number of K-State vice presidents.

From Two Vice Presidents to One[9]

April 4, 1984

When Paul Young left the facilities vice presidency to return to the Mathematics department, I visited with Finance Vice President Dan Beatty about also taking on facilities. A single vice president for finance and facilities is common in major universities. However, Beatty responded as he had to handling athletics' finances; he would have nothing to do with it!

I proceeded to seek a new person to replace Young and settled on Gene Cross, whose resume and recommendations indicated he was an outstanding manager who could delegate well and demand top performance. My instructions to Cross were simple: Keep the campus, in all respects, clean and green, implement a tight management system, maintain a schedule of needed maintenance and renovations, and get quality work done on time. Yes, I did add, "Let the ivy grow."

Cross quickly demonstrated he could carry out my charges. One of the first good steps was hiring Larry Wilson, a K-State graduate, as campus and landscape planner. Wilson would prove to be a big help in our effort to make the campus more attractive. Cross established a schedule of maintenance and renovation projects, and approved projects were getting done in the time allotted. He was an obvious student of management principles, including delegation.

In time, though, I discovered his delegation tended to be complete and unbridled, without his monitoring or review. His instructions to staff were unduly strict and without qualifying cautions. These were causing me some problems.

The Board office had asked Cross for a cost estimate for a coal-fired power plant, recommended by a consultant before my time. I later got a call from the Board office that there were obvious errors in the estimate. Components did not add up to the dollar totals.

Cross and I had an immediate conversation, I cautioned him that neither he nor the University could afford such errors. (For other reasons, the proposed coal-fired plant would eventually be rejected by the legislature.)

I got feedback one day that some faculty in one of our buildings were incensed that class assignments, job announcements, and other materials had been cleaned off hallway bulletin boards and discarded. Faculty bulletin boards are rather sacred. But Cross' instructions to keep buildings spotless must have included or implied bulletin boards and his staff had followed instructions to the letter and, perhaps, beyond.

Then there had been a late night confrontation—almost an altercation—with a young physics professor who had wheeled his bicycle into his office.

Bike racks were provided outside campus buildings and, for safety, there should be no bikes in building hallways. However, because of recent bike thefts from outdoor racks, the professor, planning to work late, had prudently wheeled his bike into his office. This was obviously logical and defensible, but wheeling it through the hallway was "against policy!"

A few weeks earlier, one of my assistants had walked by just as the local towing company was lifting the rear end of another Buick (after the Hostetler case) from a campus "No Parking" zone. Perhaps a note on the windshield for this first-time offender would have been more prudent.

I had told Cross, both in response to each case and in his formal evaluations, that he had to pay attention to detail in the material that crossed his desk and also grant his campus staff the privilege of making judgments in their work. But, my admonitions were not having the needed impact.

Kansas was then a dry state, with generally no alcohol permitted on state property, and security staff did a good job keeping alcohol from entering the stands at football games. For years, however, there had been generous use in tailgating by alumni and boosters behind the non-student stands (common in every university with which I was familiar). Without warning to me or others, Cross had apparently instructed security staff the day before a conference game to enforce the law! They had gone down the tailgate line that Saturday, bluntly telling party hosts to dump their alcohol or they would be arrested.

I first learned of this at a boosters' reception following the game. Though the boosters should have been overjoyed by our four-point victory over Iowa State, several were not happy! Perhaps the security staff could have suggested the tailgate hosts at least keep their alcohol in plastic pitchers.

Then, the previous Friday, my legislative assistant, Mike Johnson, told me that a square foot and cost estimate for the Weber Hall addition and renovation of the meat laboratory, sent by Cross to key members of the legislature's joint building committee, was not defensible.

Most academic buildings need 150 square feet of building space for every 100 square feet of net assignable (classroom, office or lab) space, a 1.5 to 1 ratio. The extra 50 square feet represents hallways, restrooms, and stairs. However, a meat laboratory has few hallways or stairs. An animal holding room connects to the kill floor, which connects directly to both a waste handling room and coolers, and the latter directly to cutting rooms.

Building committee members knew meat lab features; we had toured them through both Iowa State's new meat lab and our existing lab. But our planning staff had used the 1.5:1 ratio; the total square feet and calculated cost were unduly large. Cross had not checked the work for logic before sending it on.

Neither embarrassment from earlier events nor feedback from me had brought needed change. Friday's meat lab arithmetic told me a firm probationary letter to Cross was in order.

Today was Cross' annual performance review. I had begun drafting the evaluation letter on Tuesday. I wanted to be certain that it recognized and commended the good things that he had done—that I had hired him to do. At the same time, I had to make it abundantly clear that if he could not or would not exercise prudence in facilities policy and carefully review materials for accuracy and logic, he would be a happier person (and I might last longer as president) if he looked for a job that was more in keeping with his demonstrated skills. Early this morning I had reviewed and refined the letter; later, after those education consultants and Regent Pickert had left, he and I discussed its content.

Cross resigned a few months later, and moved to a similar job at Columbia University in New York City. He left on good terms, thanked me for the opportunity to work at K-State and I commended him for building a good structure in our facilities operation. Finance Vice President Beatty had scheduled his retirement for June 30, so I combined the two jobs and hired George Miller as vice president for finance and facilities.

* * * * *

When one makes or approves an organization change within a university, one likes to be confident it is the right decision. Once a change is made, it is not easy to undo. I confess this change left a lingering concern.

A Mistake?

May, 1984

Both Arts and Sciences Dean Bill Stamey and Agriculture Dean John Dunbar were recommending that I approve separating their jointly administered and large Department of Economics, housed in Waters Hall, into two units. The Department's extension, research, and courses in agricultural economics, including the agricultural business curriculum, are part of the agriculture budget (including CES and AES funds). The balance of the Department is part of the Arts and Sciences budget.

In searching for a new department head for the existing department, the two deans told me they could not find a high caliber person that either fit the broad department or was willing to take on such a responsibility. They had concluded the only way to go was to make a clean organizational break and seek a head for each of two resulting departments.

I had serious concerns, perhaps articulated most succinctly by comments my long-time colleague, John Nordin, had made when he was leaving a comparable and larger Iowa State department to become K-State's Economics department head two decades earlier. We had worked together closely, Nordin as chair and I as secretary of Iowa State's College of Agriculture curriculum committee.

When I had expressed regret that he was leaving Iowa State, Nordin told me that K-State's combined department, like at Ames, was a key attractant. He expressed it this way, "The economists keep the agricultural economists honest to economic principles and the agricultural economists keep the economists' feet on the ground."

As farm and ranch enterprises become larger, more highly capitalized, and more involved with input and marketing contracts, global trade, and external capital sources, I see more need for adherence to universal economic and business concepts. Agricultural enterprises must also move toward generally accepted accounting principles (GAAP) and away from traditional farm-designed bookkeeping systems.

Graduates in the Agricultural Economics or Agricultural Business curriculums will interact with economists and MBAs (graduates of Master of Business Administration programs) and they will need to be able to talk the same language and use the same systems.

Perhaps as important, agriculture was not the only applied economics in the existing department. Transportation economics, labor economics, and trade economics are all applications of economic principles and concepts. Is there not merit in keeping the several applied economics sectors together?

In short, would the separation be a good thing, long-term, for the academic integrity of the courses, extension work, and research in agricultural economics? Would separating the more state-wide focused agricultural economics faculty lead in time to the resulting economics department faculty being less attuned to the needs of their Kansas students and Kansas' society?

Is this proposed change really a long-time plus for the University, or just an immediate convenience in the department head selection process? Though I have reservations about the separation, I respect Stamey's and Dunbar's judgments. Stamey thinks academically first; Dunbar thinks politically first. Both perspectives are important in a public university.

We discussed these issues at length. Stamey and Dunbar pointed out that both departments would remain in Waters Hall and that nothing would prevent faculty working closely together; there could be joint faculty appointments. Faculty could even drink coffee together! A faculty coffee room is often the best place for good debate or for finding joint research interests. And, I acknowledged that I had sometimes seen more cooperation between faculty in two departments or colleges than between certain faculty within a department.

I approved their recommendation and I had no doubt Stamey and Dunbar would identify capable and effective department heads for each unit. But Nordin's comment still lingered in my mind.

* * * * *

Veterinary Medicine is a high-cost curriculum. Though every state needs veterinarians and its capable young people who aspire to the profession should have opportunity to prepare for it, many states lack a veterinary college. Over the years, there have been a number of interstate agreements to accommodate the latter states' need. In early 1985, there appeared at K-State an opportunity to develop what I thought would be a model program of two-state cooperation.

A Kansas-Nebraska Veterinary College 1985

Major credit for this mutually beneficial effort that would continue for about twenty productive years goes to then Veterinary College Dean Jim Coffman. The details would be rather quickly hammered out and would be approved in February of 1986 by both the Kansas and University of Nebraska boards of regents (and at least informally by legislative leaders in both states).[10] I also credit Regents Richard Reinhardt and John G. Montgomery for their close attention to this effort, including a meeting with their Nebraska counterparts.

In almost every university position I have held, I have been involved in the preparation of veterinarians. The first introductory animal science class I taught at Oklahoma State University included two young women from Texas. Though Texas A&M had a college of veterinary medicine, that university was not yet co-ed. Texas women who wanted to pursue veterinary medicine came to Oklahoma State.

At Iowa State several Nebraskans were among my pre-vet advisees and were enrolled in my introductory animal science and nutrition courses. Some would later be enrolled in the applied animal nutrition/ration formulation course I taught to juniors in the Veterinary College.

As associate dean at K-State I had worked closely with Veterinary Dean E.E. Leasure, Associate Dean Lee Railsback, and the Veterinary College department heads in developing and promoting the pre-veterinary curriculum in the College of Agriculture. That curriculum helped our student recruiting efforts and college enrollment.

At SDSU my office handled a modest budget to pay the out-of-state fees for South Dakota students enrolled in the Veterinary College at Kansas State or Iowa State. While doing their pre-vet work at SDSU, several worked part-time in our Veterinary Science Department diagnostic laboratory.

My most intense effort was as Nebraska's vice chancellor. Nebraska's long-time agreement with Iowa State no longer existed and there came a strong push by the state's livestock industry to establish a college of veterinary medicine at UN-Lincoln. Though Nebraska's board of regents, president, and UNL chancellor were going all-out to support the state's agricultural industry, they had strong reservations about a college of veterinary medicine. State money for higher education was just too scarce. I concurred, not only for that reason but also because Nebraska's animal population would warrant only a limited-enrollment college. Cost per student would be extraordinarily high.

Fortunately, most of Nebraska's practicing veterinarians concurred in the University's posture. However, the University needed to address the issue. We took two steps: 1) Our faculty worked with the state veterinarians' association (NVMA) in preparing a bulletin that outlined the pros and cons of a Nebraska school, with supporting data on cost and animal population. 2) I sought a new Nebraska contract with several existing colleges. I spent a day each at Missouri, Minnesota, Colorado State, Iowa State, Kansas State, and Oklahoma State. Though all veterinary deans, several of them long-time acquaintances, were hospitable and empathetic to Nebraska's needs, their numbers of high quality in-state applicants plus, in a few cases, their existing contracts with other states, simply precluded their giving serious consideration to a contract for Nebraskans.

A few years after my move back to K-State the Nebraska livestock industry re-ignited their call for a Nebraska college and convinced the Nebraska unicameral to commit some funds—on the condition that federal money could be found to complete the financing. Western Nebraska Congresswoman Virginia Smith, a good friend from my Nebraska days, led the effort in Washington. She suggested that the animal numbers at the USDA Meat Animal Research Center (MARC) near Clay Center, Nebraska, would be ideal for clinical year experiences for Nebraska students as well as students from nearby professional colleges. She sought help from neighboring state members of Congress to support an appropriation for dormitories and training facilities at MARC.

I had empathy for my Nebraska friends, understood her logic, and agreed regarding the potential value of MARC. However, when Kansas' senior Senator Bob Dole expressed concern and asked my advice, my own assessment caused me to fully agree that federal money would be better used elsewhere than for a new college (and Nebraska's money would be better used on existing programs at UNL).

In the meantime, K-State had fulfilled its commitment to increase its college class size upon completion of totally new facilities in the late 1970s. Further, both at K-State and nationwide, because of reductions in numbers of high school graduates and other factors, application numbers had declined. There was also a side issue for our K-State veterinary students, important and not easily addressed; there were limited swine, poultry, and dairy animal numbers in close proximity to Manhattan for our students' clinical experiences.

Therefore, when Coffman reported to me in early 1985 that one of my Nebraska successors, Vice Chancellor Roy Arnold, had contacted him about a joint Kansas-Nebraska college, I told him, "Go for it!" The potential for K-State students to gain clinical experience at MARC, a part of the idea, would be a big plus.[11]

The process, however, was not as simple as these few paragraphs imply. Mississippi State University also sought (unsuccessfully) the Nebraska relationship, offering, at one point, one million dollars less cost to Nebraska than our K-State cost projections. With two universities, two boards of regents, and representatives of two legislatures involved, and their necessary concurrence on details, I remain amazed at how quickly and smoothly this Kansas-Nebraska arrangement came to pass.

Epilogue: At this writing, early 2010, my personal involvement with veterinary medicine continues, and not only as a local veterinarian's client. I serve on the advisory committee of Iowa State's Department of Large Animal and Clinical Medicine. Several years ago Iowa State Dean John Thomson told me—and I was disappointed to learn—that the Kansas-Nebraska College had come to an end. (I was to learn that actions by the Nebraska Unicameral was the major reason.) Thomson was in negotiations with Nebraska leadership regarding a new joint venture. Iowa State's President Greg Geoffroy had responded to Thomson as I had to Coffman in early 1985, "Go for it!"

That agreement has been finalized and Nebraska funds have allowed adding faculty to accommodate the increased workload of Nebraskans coming to Iowa State for their junior and senior years.

* * * * *

I insert a comment made by one who helped edit this material when she reached about this point in her work, "It seems to me that it would have been depressing to be slogging through all those personnel and political issues."

My response, "On the contrary, it was those very challenges that helped make the president's job fun—at least most days." In many respects a university presidency is like being a football quarterback in a hard-fought game. There might be some incomplete passes and one might get sacked a few times, but the completed passes, long runs by teammates, and scores on the board more than compensate. Or, as suggested in a conversation shared later, a presidency might be comparable to the thrill of riding—and the challenge of staying on—a newly broke mare.

Experiences beyond the campus added to our fun.

Chapter VII
The Campus Beyond

Some may visualize a university as partly shaded walkways that connect vine-covered buildings, with students two or three abreast rushing to their next class and a few young men and women studying or visiting under the trees. Some may include in their vision a chemistry lab, complete with beakers and pipettes scattered on black-painted benches, fume hoods in the background. More recent campus visitors might see a chemistry lab featuring a battery of electronic equipment that instantaneously measures a substance's individual elements or compounds.

Those more familiar with a land grant university would also see, across the street from those vine-covered buildings, a bookstore, a sports shop, and a couple pubs. Beyond the opposite side of the campus they would see crops and soils research plots, animal buildings, and grazing land for livestock and ecological studies. They would also see university cars leaving campus with Extension faculty headed to education sessions arranged by one or more of the University's area or county Extension offices, or to judge at a county fair. Or, that car might include a professor and his or her graduate research assistant on their way to a distant research station to measure the yield of, in the case of Kansas, pecans or wheat, or perhaps the effect of summer heat on ornamentals. A land grant university is far more than a campus.

As each state legislature accepted the provisions of the Morrill Act of 1862, which provided federal land that could be sold to help finance establishment of a land grant college, it also decided where such would be located. The town that won this new enterprise would have convinced the legislators that it could provide not only land for academic buildings, but also farmland where students could be taught the latest in crop and animal production.

Manhattan offered its state legislature Bluemont Central College, a small Methodist school in financial difficulty a couple miles northwest of the town, plus a tract of land between there and the city. The latter is where K-State eventually developed.

The Hatch Act of 1887 provided federal funds to help establish in each state a formal entity, an agricultural experiment station (AES). Agricultural professors would hold campus field days and also travel by train or other means to outstate locations for speeches and farm tours sponsored by farmer clubs or local leaders. This work was, in time, sharply enhanced by the Smith-Lever Act of 1914. That act provided federal funds, to be matched by states and participating counties, for a Cooperative Extension Service (CES) headquartered at each land grant university.

This statewide role of K-State rubbed off on many of the University's disciplines; citizens' expectations of K-State were not limited to agriculture. By the mid 1970s K-State had an extensive list of off-campus courses, mostly night classes within reasonable driving distance of the campus, including Ft. Riley. In addition, the College of Education had responded to professional educators in the Kansas City area by offering graduate level courses there.

Though I had many rewarding days with county and area Extension staff at branch research stations and with university clients across the state—including a day with my Education faculty in Kansas City—few lend themselves to this collection of presidential anecdotes and experiences. This tells me that things were going well in those statewide functions. Personnel or other problems were being well handled. Few issues demanded presidential involvement. In contrast, several of K-State's global involvements and a couple property issues near the campus, did.

Two events not otherwise described on the following pages do stand out in my recollections. The first was an evening at our agricultural research station on the south edge of Hays, where Superintendent Bill Duitsman and his successor (after Duitsman had been named state Secretary of Agriculture), Bill Phillips, would host a dinner for staff after their April field day. That field day always drew a big crowd and I rarely missed.

After the dinner at Superintendent Duitsman's home, a Friday night in April of 1976, beef scientist John Brethour invited me across the station grounds to his office. There he showed me how his small computer would not only formulate cattle rations but also simulate other aspects of feedlot and cow herd management. My SDSU and Nebraska staff had used computers for work with producers, but Brethour had moved beyond what they had been doing. A second fascination for me was that, with Dan Beatty having told me his personal approval was required for any departmental computer purchase, and not likely given, just how had Brethour managed to acquire his? When I asked Brethour, he only smiled. (Station superintendents and department heads can be very creative when technology advances confront university bureaucracy!)

With my increased awareness of advances in computer technology, via Brethour and other faculty, university policy on computer purchases got changed, to parallel that for other equipment purchases.

The second was a July of 1980 dedication of a new center for our southeastern Kansas agricultural research programs and staff. Though we had excellent facilities at Colby, Garden City, and Hays, our work and staff in southeastern Kansas were scattered at Mound Valley, Chetopa, and other sites, all in outmoded facilities. Vice president Mitchell and I toured Board members to these various locations one evening during a two-day regents meeting at Pittsburg in 1976, and got their support for a new arrangement. Soon we had a $450,000 state appropriation to renovate a building at the Parsons State Hospital grounds for K-State's Southeast Kansas Center.[1]

In geographic terms, the balance of this chapter covers a wide spectrum, from the campus edge west to China and the Philippines, and from the campus edge east to Nigeria and Botswana. We start with the campus edge.

A Buffer for the Herds and Flocks

Fall, 1976

The thought had struck me the previous fall, during my early morning jog beyond the north edge of the campus.[2] We would soon be dedicating a new dairy production facility in that area, but it and the adjacent swine, poultry, and beef feeding units could soon be at risk of residential encroachment. Flint Hills grazing land beyond those facilities, with potential as building sites, was not owned by the University.

My primary focus was the 270-acre tract directly across the road north from the beef feeding unit. It was owned by the Hepler sisters and leased to the University for livestock grazing. Most of it provided a fantastic view of the campus, Manhattan, the Blue and Republican Valleys, and the Flint Hills beyond. A portion of the land, the slopes facing north, provided a similar view of Tuttle Creek Lake. And, a few of the peaks afforded both, an almost 360-degree panorama. What an attractive area for a housing development! Were I a developer, I would be camping on those Hepler sisters' doorstep.

Campus growth in the 1950s and early '60s had forced relocating these animal operations from the campus to this location. In fact, I had been involved in the mid-1960s in selecting the site. It was close enough to the campus for easy access by students and faculty, yet campus growth would not soon force another move. The land, already owned by the University, was used for feed production and relatively little acreage would be covered by buildings. We considered it an ideal location.

However, in the intervening years Manhattan had experienced tremendous residential growth. Essentially bound on the south and east by the Kansas and Blue Rivers, virtually all the growth had been, and would be, to the north and west.

There were a number of single-family homes, sororities, and the Jardine Terrace apartments across Denison Street from the K-State dairy barn and milking herd. Though some enjoyed the evident farm atmosphere, we had had some complaints. More than once, during my earlier time at K-State, I had had my ears chewed at Sunday church by one who lived directly across the street from the barn. She did not like the occasional "cow smell," or the flies that she attributed to the herd. It did not matter that the barn and the cows had been there for at least two decades before she and her husband bought the land, built their house, and sold off a good many building lots.

That and other experiences had caused me to form a basic rule in regard to siting or protecting a university's animal facilities: It may take time, but when there is a conflict between people and animals, people will eventually win.

There seemed no immediate problem. I had been assured by several that the Hepler sisters had no interest in selling the land; they were happy with having the University as a tenant and seeing the contented cows and calves on the land they loved. But, circumstances change and when they did, or soon thereafter, several million dollars of investment in those animal units would be at some risk. In time, another relocation of animal facilities might be forced; there would be both dollar cost and loss of the convenient campus proximity. The University simply had to acquire that land!

The K-State Foundation would be my vehicle. I briefed the trustees' executive committee and proposed that they seek to purchase the land; the Agricultural Experiment Station would pay sufficient rent to fully reimburse the Foundation for both principal and interest. When fully reimbursed, the Foundation would gift the land to the University.

It was during 1976 that circumstances did change; one of the Hepler sisters died and the K-State Foundation purchased the land at a public auction. For an investment of just under $250,000,[3] K-State's multi-million dollar livestock and poultry facilities would be more fully buffered from residential encroachment.

* * * * *

Our change in budget policy, to credit 40 per cent of international program or research contract overhead money to the originating department, plus five per cent to the parent college, had the intended effect; activity in these areas increased. Though it was not the only reason for K-State negotiating a contract for work with two universities and the Ministry of Agriculture in the Philippines, it was a factor. Department heads and faculty were more enthusiastic and faculty participation had been quickly arranged.

K-State in the Philippines

January, 1977

Several K-State faculty had been dispatched to Central Luzon State University (CLSU), the Philippines, during the latter part of 1976 and it seemed important that I be as acquainted with their tasks and circumstances as I might be with campus programs. I therefore arranged for Shirley and me a four-day stop in the Philippines during a trip we had long planned to New Zealand and Australia to celebrate our up-coming twenty-fifth wedding anniversary. It was in early January, 1977, before the Kansas legislature got seriously underway.[4]

My first purpose was to establish acquaintance with AID and Ministry of Agriculture officials, with whom our Manila-based staff would work directly, and our U.S. ambassador. It was important that we confirm both their expectations of this new project and their support. There were four foci to the project: (1) Graduates of the University of the Philippines, Los Banos (UP), and CLSU would come to K-State for master's degree course work, and then complete their thesis on their home campus. (2) Strengthen national agricultural policy and data input to that policy via the Ministry of Agriculture, Manila, (3) Technology development for food production and processing, from fish and livestock to farm and vegetable crops, all at or near CLSU. (4) Strengthen Extension programs, from production through processing.

Three senior K-State faculty, Agricultural Engineer George Larson, Agronomist Ernest Mader, and Animal Scientist Burl Koch, and their spouses were at CLSU. Shirley and I were eager to see both their working conditions and their housing accommodations. All were good. With these K-Staters and CLSU staff, we visited campus classrooms and offices as well as research and teaching facilities.[1]

We also learned of several problems our staff were experiencing, such as the difficulty in getting personal autos into the country, the potential jealousies from the low salaries of CSLU faculty relative to our K-State staff, and the lack of proximity to shopping facilities.

Our next stop was the University of the Philippines at Los Banos, with which our Manila-based agricultural policy staff would also be working. Shirley and I had a bonus there, being greeted by my one-time Iowa State graduate student, Dr. Jose Eusebio (whose nephew was later a student at K-State). Eusebio had two jobs, leader of swine research and assistant to the chancellor for research.

Eusebio gave us a second bonus. His family operated a tailor shop near the University campus and, in short order, he brought me a made-to-measure barong I could wear to a dinner hosted by the University chancellor for several department heads, five K-State alums, and Shirley and me.

We had a second day in the UP vicinity, visiting poultry, fruit, and cattle farms, including extensive visits with the operators. This gave us a more full understanding of the industry potential and tasks that Philippine universities and the Ministry faced.

AID policies had changed from the time of K-State's earlier contracts involving India and Nigeria. Rather than a direct AID contract with K-State, that agency provided grant and loan funds to the Philippine government and our contract was with that government. That added administrative complications, sometimes diverse motivations and expectations, and certainly another layer of decision-makers. We were especially fortunate in the administrative experience of our successive team leaders, Dean Carroll Hess and former K-State AES Director Peairs Wilson (who had been Hawaii's dean of agriculture in the interim).

With so many parties involved—two Philippine universities and a ministry, a U.S. federal agency, and K-State—and at such distance, problems would develop. One was mail limitations, getting documents from our Philippines staff to Manhattan. I find in the files my April, 1978, letter to our U.S. Ambassador, David Newsome, appealing for the use of the embassy's APO facilities by our Philippines team.[5] And, on my return from Governor Carlin's trade mission to China in 1979, I would stop off for twenty-four hours in Manila to help Wilson with some tense negotiations with Ministry officials regarding working conditions and decision-making responsibilities.

* * * * *

Winter was also a good time to visit K-State alumni groups in Arizona and southern California. On return from that trip, however, we would face the reality of a mid-February snow storm. I would be called on for a skill I had used little since my senior year in high school.

Who Can Take Off Chains?

February 13, 1978

It was about seven o'clock on a frigid Monday night at the I-70 service area near Lawrence. Shirley and I had been on a five-day swing to K-State alumni meetings in Sun City, San Diego, and Los Angeles. Due to weather, the five-day trip had become seven, and three of the six nights we had been without our luggage. Though not an easy trip, it had been rewarding; positive feedback from alums, their respect for K-State, and their eagerness for an update were gratifying.

Bad weather had prevented a connection the previous Tuesday in Denver and, from then on, our bags were generally a day behind. Then, on Sunday afternoon at Kansas City, heavy snow had cancelled our flight back into Manhattan. We had spent that night at the Airport Marriott.

With a hearing before the Kansas House Ways and Means Committee scheduled for Tuesday morning, I had counted on having Monday back in Manhattan to prepare. However, the snow had continued across eastern Kansas Monday morning, the roads were blocked, and there were no flights.

By early afternoon, some highway traffic was permitted. I called to have our campus security staff bring my legislative assistant, Barry Flinchbaugh, and my budget materials to the Airport Marriott and take us to Topeka so I would be on hand for the Tuesday morning hearing. They had wisely stopped at a Manhattan service station to have a pair of tire chains installed.

By the time we got loaded at the Marriott and headed west on I-70, highway traffic had melted the packed snow and ice. In time, a few chain cross links wore through and the loose ends were clattering and banging. We stopped at the Lawrence service area to have the chains taken off. Shirley and I stepped from the garage area into the station to wait. I knew from experience it should not take long—just release a chain clasp inside and outside of each rear wheel, drop the loosened chain on the floor and drive away.

My first job in education, at age sixteen and at the start of my senior high school year, had been driving a school bus. Wiota Consolidated was a small school, grades 1-12, with less than twenty in each grade. The thirty-six square mile school district had been formed in the 1920s. Country schools, each serving a four-square-mile area, had been replaced by a brick building in Wiota, population about 200. Town students walked to school, five buses served the rural students.

Hiring seniors to drive the buses had started during WWII, when labor was short and adult drivers could not be found for the split work hours, early morning and late afternoon. Routes were arranged so those of us drivers who lived on farms could keep our bus overnight at home. That also saved fuel.

Our farm was in the northwest corner of the district. I had a seven-mile circuitous route that ended each night in our corn crib driveway. About 7:45, after morning chores and breakfast, I would grab my sack lunch, back the 1939 Chevy bus, capacity twenty, out of the corn crib driveway and head up the road.

Though several of my fellow drivers had a few miles of paved highway (transcontinental U.S. 6) or gravel, my route was all on dirt roads. If it should rain or snow heavily during the night, I would be putting tire chains on the rear wheels while Dad finished milking and before we went in to breakfast. If it rained during the school day we would head to the bus barn behind the school at 3:20, after physics class, to put on the chains.

For handling the tire chains, I was the lucky one. The other four buses were larger, had dual wheels on the rear. My bus was smaller and each outside rear wheel had been removed during the war when tires were scarce. I could lay a chain over a rear wheel, reach behind the wheel to connect the inside clasp, pull the outside chain tight and snap that clasp. In the dry protection of the bus barn, or our corn crib driveway, I could usually do the job without getting my shirt or jacket cuffs dirty.

My reminiscing was interrupted by Flinchbaugh, "Nobody out here knows how to take off chains!"

The University sedan, its undercarriage loaded with slush and its trunk full of luggage and budget documents, was lower to the ground than my school bus. It did not take long, but I had to roll up my sleeves to keep from soiling my shirt cuffs.

* * * * *

University programs of value do not develop overnight. They may take months or years of intensive effort, perhaps negotiation, to bring them about. That was certainly the case for the Konza Prairie. This one also had, at the end, its own element of surprise.

The Konza Prairie

March, 1977

Thanks largely to Nature Conservancy and the recognized expertise of K-State's Dr. Lloyd Hulbert, the 8,000-acre Konza Prairie became a part of K-State. The Konza borders much of the west side of U.S. 177 between Manhattan and I-70, overlooks I-70 to the south, and extends west several miles.[6,7] Nature Conservancy (NC) is a national group dedicated to preservation of native prairie and natural landscapes of all types.

The first portion, 916 acres, had been purchased by NC in 1971. In 1977, that organization purchased the rest, what I had known twenty years earlier as the Dewey Ranch. I had visited that ranch with a busload of Iowa State students on an agricultural travel course. We had been hosted by then ranch manager and K-State graduate Orville Burtis. (See also A Flint Hills Rancher's View, Page 270)

The purchases by NC were with the understanding that the land would be operated by K-State as a part of the University's teaching, research, and extension programs. Hulbert had proposed such a prairie field laboratory years earlier, to help him and others understand and teach the ecology of tall grass prairie. NC had long wanted to obtain for preservation a large tract of tall grass prairie; K-State's and NC's interests had matched.

Though the Kansas Flint Hills cover a large area, few sizeable tracts that would fit the needs of NC and K-State remained. The Dewey ranch would be ideal. The initial problem was that the owner, local radiologist Dr. David McNight, had little interest in selling—until he learned just how much NC was willing to pay. Even then, completion of the purchase had required long and tedious negotiations. There existed some contracted mineral rights, the right to explore for oil and gas and to drill if such were found. Future oil and gas wells did not fit Conservancy and University purposes. The exploration contracts had to be re-purchased and voided.

In addition, to avoid heavy tax liability for McNight, a land trade had to be arranged. In time, McNight found other land of comparable value and he and NC entered into what is now called a "1031 exchange."

After some months, NC had completed the land purchase, but more negotiations remained. The ranch equipment that the University needed to run the place—tractors, trucks, and other equipment, even the diesel fuel tanks—were McNight's personal property, not included in the land sale to NC. AES Director Floyd Smith came forward with experiment station money for those items, but arriving at agreed prices for these several thousand dollars worth of equipment seemed more difficult than for the several-million-dollar land purchase. The last item was those diesel tanks; our staff and McNight could not agree. It did not get settled until McNight and I got together one evening in my office.

There had been other complications during the process, especially an issue raised by several legislators, "Is this Step One to a Prairie Parkway?" An earlier proposal had been for the state or federal government to acquire a strip of the Flint Hills, perhaps to establish a national or state park, dubbed a Prairie Parkway. It would be somewhat akin to Mississippi's Natchez Trace Parkway or Virginia's Blue Ridge Parkway, but highlighting tall grass prairie. Proposers felt a Prairie Parkway would attract many visitors to Kansas.

Opponents to that Prairie Parkway had been vocal; government-acquired land would be removed from the tax roles. Remaining property owners—and there are not many in the Flint Hills counties—would bear the total costs of county government, including schools and roads. There had been a storm of protest from ranchers, especially in Chase and Morris Counties.

The Konza Prairie was in no way connected with the Prairie Parkway enthusiasts or concept. The idea was for preservation, yes, but not only preservation. Its connection to the University would focus on research and education. It would be one piece of land, not a traffic route. It had taken a good many conversations with legislators, editors, and Flint Hills land owners to put that concern to bed. (A Tallgrass Prairie National Park would eventually be established, in 1995, further south in the Flint Hills. However, the authorizing federal legislation mandated that the National Park Service could own no more than 180 acres of the total preserve.)[8]

When it came time to publicly announce acquisition of the Konza, I felt relief. But an unnerving surprise was yet to come. It involved an item that had bothered me from the beginning. Conservancy officials had told us that the person providing the money to buy the land, heir to the 3M fortune Katharine Ordway, wanted to remain anonymous. I understood why; a major donor can become a target for endless needy projects. However, I would have liked to at least recognize and introduce the woman at the eventual dedication ceremony.

I had just taken off from the Manhattan airport in a small chartered plane (K-State then lacked its own plane), en route to a presentation in southwestern Kansas. I glanced down at the Konza with some satisfaction. I then pulled a pile of reading from my briefcase and the new issue of the Alumni Association's *K-Stater*, March, 1977, was on top. I scanned the Table of Contents and my heart seemed to stop as I read, "P. 5. Thanks, Mrs. Ordway—A donation of $3.6 million came from an elderly eastern woman with an interest in conservation."

I was reminded of two organization principles: 1) There are no secrets. 2) Communication is never adequate. *K-Stater* staff had been given the name of the donor, but had not heard the message of desired anonymity.

* * * * *

After working on several continents, one recognizes and understands the range among countries in how people see themselves, education, the role of government, and the merits of technology. One also recognizes the multiple factors that cause governments and societal sectors or tribes to function as they do.

Especially in many of the developing countries, societal cultures are far different from the cultures with which most K-State faculty are acquainted. My K-State predecessors had wisely set out to broaden faculty perceptions and, at the same time, support the U.S. policy of helping develop universities in India in northern Nigeria. The Nigeria effort was near completion.

K-State in Nigeria

Late May, 1977

K-State's and other land grant universities' successes in India had prompted similar efforts in Africa. In early 1962 K-State's Dean of Agriculture Glenn Beck had been invited to consider a development arrangement with a newly-established university at Zaria in northern Nigeria. On October 11, 1963, President McCain had signed a formal agreement with AID to "(1) establish a College of Agriculture and a College of Veterinary Medicine as part of Ahmadu Bello University (ABU), (2) coordinate as rapidly as feasible research and extension with resident instruction, and (3) train Nigerians to assume major roles in the agricultural institution as soon as possible."[9]

During my time as associate dean I had worked with several young Nigerians who had come to our campus to enroll in our plant science, animal science, or pre-veterinary curriculums. By the time I returned as president in 1975, some of those young Nigerians I had known were faculty and department heads in Ahmadu Bello's colleges of agriculture and veterinary medicine, the latter the only such college in central Africa.

The progress at Ahmadu Bello had been extraordinary, and 1977 would see the end of AID financing and K-State's formal involvement. Shirley (at her personal expense) and I traveled to Zaria in late May to represent K-State in celebrating Ahmadu Bello's achievements. About seventy-five K-State faculty had devoted several years of their professional lives to that university's development.

In that fifteen-year period thirty-eight agricultural economics, agricultural engineering, animal science, and soils faculty and thirty-seven from veterinary medicine had served, in most cases, two or more years on the Ahmadu Bello faculty. (A few of these numbers were temporary staff from other universities.) Perhaps another three dozen K-State agriculture and veterinary faculty, from such as the K-State admissions or publications offices, had been at Ahmadu Bello for short-term consultation and help. One must consider the impact these faculty experiences have had back on campus, in their classes and conversations with students.

Dr. Stanley Dennis of our veterinary college, who had served as Ahmadu Bello's Dean of Faculty and Head of Pathology, was our last remaining K-Stater at Ahmadu Bello, and was then serving as Assistant Dean for Graduate Affairs. He and his wife would depart for Manhattan July 1.

During that celebratory visit I sat with Dr. Dennis as we watched the veterinary dean and department heads, all but one a Nigerian, leading their faculty. Eighty per cent were Nigerians; the rest were expatriates from several countries.[10] A similar pattern had been achieved months earlier in the ABU College of Agriculture.

Though the initial purpose had been to support the U.S. government's effort to help developing countries, K-State, especially its colleges of agriculture and veterinary medicine, had gained enormous benefit. Multiple faculty experiences in two countries, India and Nigeria—in such areas as soil fertility, crop genetics, animal husbandry, disease diagnosis and treatment, and insect and pest control—had brought global sensitivities and knowledge to total K-State departments. Another example benefit: India was increasingly recognized as an important source of diverse germ plasm for one of Kansas' and the Great Plains' major crops, grain sorghum.

Our trip to ABU also allowed us to visit the International Research Institute in Tropical Agriculture (IITA) at Kaduna, Nigeria. It is one of fifteen international agricultural research centers prompted by the Ford and Rockefeller foundations and which the U.S. and other countries help finance. A high proportion of the calories and protein that people in tropical and semi-tropical countries consume are from yams, cassava (tapioca), and other root crops, IITA's major focus. Linkages of Ahmadu Bello and other Central African universities with IITA were important. I wanted to see that linkage from both ends, as well as understand how IITA handled their research internships and training of young scientists from multiple countries. Those young scientists would also, in time, be unlocking some of the technical secrets of the global food system.

* * * * *

Some of my more enjoyable experiences as president were in spending part of a day with county Extension staff, such as Charlie Smith in Cowley County, Winfield, or Cliff Manry in Pawnee County, Larned. Whether it was for a Rotary luncheon, an evening meeting with a county extension council, a 4-H event, or visits to several town or farm clients, my appreciation for these important university staff located across Kansas was enhanced. In those county visits I would usually hear a few stories about some of their recent encounters. All kinds of questions come to the "county agent," and sometimes a few complaints. Long-time Ford County Director Don Wiles shared this one with me.

My Stool Won't Flush

Wiles' phone rang about 2 a.m. in his Dodge City home and when he put the phone to his ear the first words were a woman's blunt message, "My stool won't flush!" It had taken Wiles a few seconds to put that message in context, why he would be getting such a call. He then recognized the voice and knew the reason for the call.

Ford County was in the midst of expanding irrigation, more wells being drilled and more irrigation systems installed. Non-irrigators were concerned these new wells would draw so much water that their domestic wells would run dry. There had been some emotional meetings in several communities.

Kansas law required that owners of domestic wells expend "reasonable effort" to deepen their wells or extend the well casing so they could reach water during the irrigation season. Drilling a well deeper or extending the casing was costly.

Kansas also has water districts, legal entities with authority to approve and set operating parameters for new wells, to balance the water needs among users within the district. Wiles' job was to work with all parties, explain the law, advise on both irrigation systems and domestic wells, and be a resource for the water district officers. With the drilling of numerous irrigation wells underway, he was identified most with the irrigators. Several non-irrigators blamed him for their domestic well problems. He had had his ears chewed more than once.

Wiles told me he looked up the phone number of the water district chairman, gave it to the caller, and went back to bed.

* * * * *

Supporting the governor and legislature when they ask for help is another state university responsibility. Whether one is a professor or president, one tries to respond. I confess that I was thrilled to do so for two trips to China. The first was a trade mission organized by Governor John Carlin and the second, to establish a sister state relationship, by the Kansas House and Senate leadership.

China: Mopeds and Doilies

August, 1979

On this first trip, led by Governor Carlin and involving about twenty Kansas leaders in agriculture, aircraft, and manufacturing, as well as cabinet officers and agency staff, I was joined by Dr. Y. Pomeranz, Director of the USDA Grain Marketing Laboratory, who also held a professorship in K-State's Grain Science Department. Veterinary Dean Jim Coffman joined me on the second China visit.

It was clear that China, with a population approaching one billion in 1979, would become a major participant in global trade, a major user of energy, and a major political force in the world. To see China in the early days of its late 20th Century development was a rich experience. More impressions from these early visits to China are detailed elsewhere.[11,12] I offer here just a few.

We visited state ministries, farms, grain research institutes, schools, manufacturing facilities, ports, and university libraries. Though I saw many future business opportunities in China I would tell my friends upon return that I would like to have just two Chinese franchises, for doilies and for mopeds. Regardless of our meeting location, whether the office of a government minister, factory foreman, or collective farm manager, the furniture and settings were identical. In every case the setting was a facing series of overstuffed couches and chairs, doilies on the arms of each. There was little differentiation in status. Regardless of size, apparent political clout, or monetary volume of activity, uniformity prevailed. And, that uniformity always included the doilies.

The bicycle seemed the exclusive form of transportation, except for a few government cars in Beijing or other major cities. To and from work and in family travel, it was the bicycle. The first motorized personal vehicle I saw was in one of the smaller (perhaps 100,000 population) towns where we had visited a school and some mushroom production. During an early morning walk I was passed by the school track team out for a run. Following them was their coach—on a motor bike! In later days, I saw a few more. It was clear to me that, with the economic development sure to come, the China market would be hot for mopeds.

As of July, 2009, there were an estimated sixty-five million motorbikes and mopeds on China's roads, and about twenty-two million were being produced each year.[13] That would have been a great franchise! However, during a 2001 assignment in China I was in government, university, manufacturing, and farm managers' offices, and I saw not a single doily!

I also share a conversation that foretold more about China's future. In a pre-banquet Beijing reception hosted by top government officials for Governor Carlin, I fell into a conversation with a junior minister of finance. He had earned a doctorate in finance at Columbia University and had been on the Columbia faculty for several years. I asked, "Why did you return to China?"

His response was matter-of-fact, "To help my country."

I followed up with several questions regarding democracy vs. communism, and how, with a degree in finance from a capitalist country, his talents could be helpful.

His response to that was uninhibited, in essence, "Communism will adapt to best serve our country's needs."

As I would see in the 1985 visit with our legislative leaders, in the early

1990s as my USDA Foreign Agricultural Service staff and I dealt with Chinese officials on grain trade issues, and in 1996 and 2001 visits to the country — and, as we all witnessed during the Beijing-hosted 2008 Olympics, Chinese Communism has adapted!

May, 1985, with our hosts at Henan Agricultural College, Henan Province, People's Republic of China. Behind me are K-State Dean of Veterinary Medicine Jim Coffman and, to his right, Kansas' Director of Economic Development Harland Priddle. To my far right is Rex Armstrong, K-State graduate from Muscotah, Kansas, who was then teaching English to Henan College faculty and graduate students. Among our hosts in the photo were the College's chancellor and vice chancellor, the head of Armstrong's department, Basic Learning, and the deputy director of the Henan Province People's Congress.

The later trip to China, in May of 1985, was led by Kansas Senate President Robert Talkington and House Speaker Mike Hayden. Because its purpose was to establish linkages with Henan Province as a sister state, the task for Dean Coffman and me was to explore opportunities for inter-university and scientist collaboration. Among the institutions visited were Henan Agricultural University, Hunan Academy of Agricultural Sciences, the Cereal College of Zhengzhou, and the Luoyang Institute of Technology. Staff of these entities outlined their interests, we saw their facilities, and we made tentative judgments regarding the potential value of establishing formal linkages. Follow-up would depend on their degree of interest and that of our K-State colleges and departments.[14]

*****

Among the annual Kansas events I should rarely miss were the late summer Grant County Home Products dinner at Ulysses, Kansas night at Kansas City's American Royal, the legislator's dinner that agricultural groups sponsored in Topeka, and Kansas Farm Bureau's summer farm tour.

The total Grant County dinner menu—potatoes, sweet potatoes, tomatoes, corn, beans, milk, beef, pork, lamb, chicken, or other—had been produced in Grant County. The food was great, but there was another reason I should attend. The crowd would include the governor, most western Kansas legislators, and First Congressional District Congressman (the first district was about everything west of Manhattan and Wichita) Pat Roberts (or his predecessor, Keith Sebelius).

All the Kansas City legislators, as well as the governor and other key leaders would be on hand for Kansas Night at the American Royal. The reason for Shirley and me being at the legislator's dinner in Topeka is also obvious. Elsewhere I have described how I was told, at one of the dinners, that K-State would be getting the nod for two major building projects.

The Farm Bureau tour was often a two-day affair, but other commitments usually made it difficult for me to join the group for more than a day or part of a day.

From Phillipsburg I'd Prefer to Walk

This year, 1977, the Farm Bureau tour was in the Solomon River watershed, with several stops in Phillips County, the home base of Kansas Farm Bureau Vice President Doyle Rahjes. Both Rahjes and Farm Bureau President John "Junior" Armstrong, of Muscotah, had become personal friends and Farm Bureau had as much political power as any Kansas organization, more than most. I was not about to miss this year's event. I had flown out with a couple of our staff to Phillipsburg for the afternoon portion of the tour and would fly back late evening, after a steak dinner and a short program.

The afternoon visits to irrigation demonstrations and crops research plots handled by our K-State agronomists, plus discussion of Nebraska-Kansas water issues, brought me up to date. Part of Phillips County drains into a tributary of the Republican River, which flows across southern Nebraska before turning south toward Milford Lake at Junction City. Both Kansans and Nebraskans tend to think the other state takes out too much water. (At this writing, the issue is still in court.)

We then gathered in a mammoth machine shed on the Henry Tien farm just south of Prairie View for a generous steak dinner and comments by Governor Robert Bennett. A cold front was on the way, a few dark clouds had appeared in the northwest. Apprehensive about the weather, we watched the clouds as Rahjes thanked Tien, those who had organized the tour, and Bennett. He then introduced a local high school girl to close the evening with our national anthem, The Star Spangled Banner.

Though the tour had been excellent and the medium rare steak among the best, I think that all of us would later say the young woman's presentation of our national anthem, in this setting, was the evening's highlight. Her stage was in front of open machine shed doors; behind her, lightning flashed against the dark clouds. Her clear voice and the anthem's verses were themselves a fitting climax.

As she sang the clouds were moving closer, loomed larger and darker. Now the lightning flashes seemed almost in synchrony with the words, "and bombs bursting in air." The setting, the dark clouds, the lightning, the words, and the young woman's voice made it a time of inspiration.

As she closed to rousing applause, my campus colleagues and I came back to reality. We would be heading back to Manhattan in that light plane, if we could get off the ground ahead of the approaching front! I had bounced around enough in both commercial and light aircraft. I had no desire to get caught inside a moving weather front.

Phillips County Extension Director Sy (Sylvester) Nyhart, had the car ready and we headed to the airport, Armstong's Farm Bureau car racing down the road ahead of us. Armstrong's pilot had his engines warmed up and his party, including Governor Bennett, jumped aboard. Their plane headed to the end of the runway and spun around into the wind. By the time our charter pilot had his engines warmed up, I could see the Farm Bureau plane headed safely toward Topeka. Armstrong and Bennett might have bounced a bit, but they were on their way.

Our pilot was confident—and determined—that we could yet make it into the air ahead of the front. He even did his "180" before reaching the end of the runway, raced the engines, flipped a couple switches, and headed into the wind.

He had been both too slow and too optimistic. Before we were far enough off the ground and had enough air speed to turn toward Manhattan, we were square in the middle of that front! The turbulence was tossing our plane up and down and side to side, lighting flashes on all sides. We had what seemed like twenty minutes, but more likely just three or four, of the roughest, jerking experience I have ever felt. I do not think being strapped to the bare back of rodeo bronco could have been more severe. At least on a rodeo bronco, one would be within a few feet of the ground!

Though the plane did not break apart and we landed at Manhattan an hour later, my preference thirty seconds into that front, had it been possible, would have been to step out and walk the 200 miles to Manhattan.

* * * * *

A concept that I believe university students should gain from faculty who have had international experience is that every culture and every country has intelligent, ingenious, and productive people. People of some countries may be handicapped in their productivity or level of living by government structure, limited natural resources, or technology, but they should be recognized and respected for their human capacities. Our time with K-State faculty in Botswana provided us such a lesson.

Plow Twice

October, 1982

By 1982, AID had made other changes in contracting, giving preference to consortiums of universities for development work. In response, K-State and its counterparts in Nebraska, Iowa, Missouri, and Oklahoma had formed the MidAmerica International Agricultural Consortium, and submitted a proposal to help develop Botswana's agricultural research and extension system. Faculty might come from any of the universities, but K-State was the lead institution and Agricultural Economist David Norman headed to Botswana in late summer to lead the effort. He was soon followed by two other faculty, John Sjo and Jim Jorns. They would help Norman assess working conditions and write a plan of work for those K-State faculty who would come for two-year or longer assignments.

About that time, by coincidence, Nigeria's University of Benin, perhaps 300 kilometers east of Lagos, had asked for a visit from K-State administration to assess and advise on their agricultural research and education programs. I wanted an early opportunity to see the task that K-State was taking on in Botswana, and Nigeria was on the flight path, so I accepted that Benin invitation.

Shirley and I were met at the Lagos airport by a Dr. Esechie, a K-State graduate and University of Benin faculty member, and driven to Benin City for a three-day visit. As with every other visit to developing countries, the openness, graciousness, and hospitality of our University of Benin hosts seemed without limit. Though we saw needs with which universities such as K-State might help, we also saw highly able, well-trained, and dedicated faculty. The government had committed additional resources and the University had a large tract of land for research. A faculty committee had developed a strong plan for forestry, fisheries, and agriculture curriculums, with undergirding in such disciplines as biochemistry and botany. I believe the main contributions from our visit—and what they needed from K-State—were for us to listen to their plans and give them encouragement to move forward.[15]

More details of these travels are recorded elsewhere, but I share several side experiences of interest. The line through customs on our arrival at Lagos had been long and slow and we were midway in the line. We, and others, were approached and offered help through customs (for a fee), but I declined. Thirty minutes later, the line was shorter, but Shirley and I were at the end of the line!

We had encountered such examples of "private enterprise" in our earlier visit to Nigeria. A reservation would not necessarily guarantee a seat on the plane; one's name needed to be called by the boarding gate attendant. As we had prepared to depart the airport after visiting IITA, we had noted that our hostess had made a transaction with the gate attendant. She still had to remind him to "Call the Ackers!" to board.

Even accommodating the gate attendant might not get a ticket-holder on the plane. K-State Department Head Embert Coles told of having made such arrangements as he was departing the project site for Manhattan. He was engrossed in a conversation when the gate attendant called "Coles!" A native Nigerian yelled "Here!" and hopped on board. The door closed and the plane departed. Coles had to wait two days for the next flight.

The University of Benin graduate student assigned to drive us back to the Lagos airport apparently wanted to be sure we did not miss our plane. The speedometer floated from 120 to 150 Km/hour (70 to 90 mph) all the way. No amount of our protest could he hear or accept. And our nervousness was not abated by the dozens of wrecked and burned out vehicles that dotted the right-of-way.

At the Lagos airport, ready to board our departing flight, whom should we encounter but K-State Sociology Professor Wayne Nafsinger. He had just arrived to do some contract research on Nigeria's rural population and would head to the bus depot for his country travel. Though the bus might be crowded and slow, we assured Nafsinger it might be a safer way to travel than in a graduate student-chauffeured sedan.

We stopped off for a week-end in Nairobi, Kenya, and a two-day safari at Governor's Camp, about 100 miles outside Nairobi. As the twenty-passenger twin-engine plane landed at the Governor's Camp airstrip, waiting to board were K-State Agronomy Professor Ernest Mader and his wife, Betty. Mader had just completed a several-month assignment in East Africa and they had taken in the Governor's camp safari on their way back to Manhattan.

Our several days in Botswana also provided some bonuses. Not only were K-State faculty at work with the Ministry of Agriculture's research and extension staff in the capital city, Gaborone, several of our former SDSU faculty were also in Gaborone. SDSU faculty, under an AID contract, were working with the country's two-year agricultural college just down the road from the ministry's agricultural research center.

Again, details are recorded elsewhere; I will describe only a two-day trip where we joined K-State's Jim Jorns to several villages north of Gabarone. Jorns had spent the previous night in a village north of Gaborone, in a "motel" rhondoval, a separate dome-shaped room of packed earth construction.

We visited two villages, where village elders were conducting outdoor "town hall" meetings on current issues. This is where Botswana's extension staff linked with their clientele. Extension staff presented education opportunities; concurrence by village elders provided credibility for them to proceed with their work.

We also visited two farms, perhaps selected for being more progressive. In both cases, the husband was away, tending the family's small cattle herd on open range. The wife and children tended the grain sorghum crop, the family's food staple. The sorghum harvest would be stored in large crockery vessels and a small, round metal bin.

Farming tools consisted of an oxen-drawn plow and a hoe. Sorghum seed saved from a year earlier was sown by hand on the ground and plowed in. This seemed to me far too crude; seeds would be at varying depths! Here was the lesson: Our hostess explained that rainfall was both low and highly variable; this variable seed depth was drought insurance. If it rained soon after planting, those seeds in shallow soil would germinate and new plants would emerge. With little or delayed rain, those deeper seeds might germinate and, in time, provide at least sufficient crop to get the family through the year.

A few watermelon seeds were also scattered at planting time. Our hostess explained that the watermelons provided both water and nourishment while she and their children were hoeing out weeds among the sorghum plants.

The food production tasks ahead for Botswana were formidable, and it was apparent our faculty could and would play a valuable role.[16] A few years later our staff would report a marked increase in sorghum grain production as a result of research and extension efforts. They and their counterpart Botswana scientists had tried a variety of cultural practices, in comparison with traditional methods. The most significant and economic sorghum yield increases had come by plowing twice, before and after the seed was sown. The first plowing loosened the soil, which allowed, with the second plowing, better seed/soil contact. More intimately surrounded by soil, seeds continually gained both moisture and nutrients from that soil. More seeds germinated and survived.

Other technologies and extension education programs would be developed over the eight-year period of K-State's involvement, among them contour strip cultivation, establishing and maintaining water conserving terraces, and preparation of a livestock management handbook that covered about everything from building corrals and shelters to bloodless castration.[17] Beyond help to the country's food supply system, this was a vivid illustration of research and extension education *at the level of need.*

How about the impact on K-State? It would be, as with other such efforts, via the Botswana students who studied at K-State and, over a longer time period, via the K-State faculty who had gained the experiences. K-State faculty who would be in Botswana for two years or longer were, in addition to Norman (eight years), were Agronomist Art Hobbs, Animal Scientist Burl Koch, and Jorns. Others who contributed to the effort via short-term assignments included geologists Charles Bussing and Duane Nellis (the latter to be, years later, K-State provost), economists Bryan Schurle, Mark Johnson (later dean of agriculture), and Art Barnaby, animal scientist Jack Riley, and agronomist George Ham. Johnson, Riley and Ham were K-State department heads.

Would not these people's international experiences in their disciplines be reflected in the content of their K-State class lectures and program leadership judgments? I offer Burl Koch as a vivid example. He had been one of the first to accept a two-year assignment in Nigeria. After about six years back teaching at K-State he had accepted a second tour in Nigeria. There followed similar intervals, teaching six years at K-State, two years at Central Luzon State University, the Philippines, teaching six years at K-State, two years as a livestock specialist in northern Botswana, then finishing his career teaching at K-State.

In the twenty-five or so years after Koch's first Nigerian tour there was likely not a single student in his animal science classes or office or hallway conversations that was not broadened in some way to the global diversity of the food and agriculture system! For those current or future administrators, would their experiences not be reflected in their priorities and emphases in curriculum and extension program planning? Or in faculty recognition?

If only a few faculty in each of K-State's academic departments could have had comparable international experiences in their disciplines, how extensive would be the resulting global understanding of all K-State graduates!

* * * * *

As I had assessed K-State's needs soon after my arrival, one that rose to prominence was the need to build a tradition of private giving among the University's alumni and friends. K-State had been without a fund-raising entity until the mid 1940s. It was then that K-State President Milton Eisenhower had called together some local Manhattan business leaders and proposed an endowment association be formed to raise and hold funds largely for student scholarships. The next chapter provides more background and describes some of our experiences in this effort.

Chapter VIII

Building A Tradition

I recalled my first exposure to K-State's fundraising efforts. It had been in March of 1962, a visit with President McCain. I was interviewing for K-State's associate dean of agriculture position, but McCain had asked me little about my experience or ideas regarding that position. Rather, he quizzed me about Iowa State's capital campaign then underway. K-State was in a multi-year Second Century Fund campaign and it was not going well.

I offer a bit of history of university fund raising, especially in Kansas. Most state universities did not get into private fund-raising until the 1940s; they relied on state appropriations and student fees. Because the universities were state entities, any donation would likely go into the state treasury and would benefit the university only if there were a legislative appropriation of that money. The University of Kansas was an exception. In 1891, KU organized an Endowment Association, and that Association soon became the recipient of 24,000 acres of farm land.[1]

When I had arrived at K-State in June of 1962, Ken Heywood, a K-State graduate and former school superintendent, was the executive director of the Endowment Association. Retired Agriculture Dean R. I. Throckmorton was helping on a part-time (and perhaps volunteer) basis. Heywood shared an office suite in the south end of Anderson Hall with Alumni Director Dean Hess. During my four-year tenure I worked with Heywood in enticing a few additional donors to establish scholarships.

When I returned to K-State in 1975 considerable progress in fund-raising was apparent. Larry Weigel had moved from assistant basketball coach to join Heywood[2] and $1,696,236 would be raised that year. It was also apparent there was much untapped potential. Though fund-raising was not yet considered a central role of a state university president, I told Heywood and Weigel that I would commit up to two days each month for personal contacts and travel on the Endowment Association's behalf, if they would identify the people I should see and make the arrangements.

I saw both an opportunity and need for some quantum steps forward in private fund raising. We had far more alumni and friends that could and should be involved in helping advance K-State.

Two Helpers from KU

March, 1978

We were fortunate to have capable and dedicated staff members in both the Endowment and Alumni Associations, and alumni board members took time from their businesses and traveled to meetings at their own expense. The Endowment Association executive committee met monthly and was visibly supportive of needs we expressed. However, we were well aware of more aggressive fund-raising programs elsewhere.

K-State's operations in these two areas were largely staffed by K-State graduates dedicated to the University. However, both they and I lacked the experiences more common in private universities and a few public universities. Private fund-raising was not imbedded in the culture of most state universities.

Nearly all of the Endowment Association's executive committee members had been Manhattan residents; the exception being Ed King of Shawnee Mission. That was convenient for the monthly meetings, some held after the weekly Rotary luncheon (difficult for King to participate). Fred Bramlage of Junction City was added and Jack Weltsch of Leawood replaced Ed King about the time I arrived.

I felt that we needed an even broader geographic presence and involvement. I had learned early that the more different experiences that can be brought to the table, whether in teaching methods, research, or other activity, the more likely programs will be current and effective. Few university departments will hire faculty with degrees from only their university and with no experience elsewhere. We needed to make some big steps in fund raising, but we did not have the collective experience to be certain of the right steps.

Heywood and Weigel had good relationships with KU's Endowment Association Director Todd Seymour and Alumni Association Director Dick Wintermode and suggested they could give us help. They were right. Seymour and Wintermode even drove to Manhattan for a session with Heywood, Weigel, and me. They shared openly their fund raising philosophy, structure, and processes. We also talked about the value of outside consultants for determining the feasibility of a capital fund drive—or in the fund-raising, itself.

I had asked Extension Public Policy Specialist Barry Flinchbaugh to join my office for a more aggressive K-State presence with members of the Kansas legislature and the governor's office. In early 1978 he and I took a few key officers of our Endowment and Alumni Associations on a chartered plane trip to learn how alumni and private fund-raising entities at Purdue, Iowa State, and Drake Universities were organized and functioned. My recollection is that Manhattan banker Al Hostetler, abstractor Robert Wilson, and Salina rancher Jack Vanier were in the small group. We came back from that trip with several steps rather well crystallized in our minds.

My calendar shows a Saturday, March 11, 1978, joint follow-up meeting of the K-State Alumni and Endowment Association executive committees or representatives. Though I find no record of participants, I believe that Alumni leaders Linton Lull of Smith Center, Mary Hewsom of Larned, and Vanier were among those involved, along with Endowment board members Hostetler, Wilson, Manhattan attorney Richard Rogers, and perhaps Bill Stolzer or Willard Kershaw. In that meeting we achieved consensus on several steps forward, including 1) that the name of the Endowment Association should be changed to K-State Foundation, a more common name for such, 2) that the Foundation would be the aggressive fund-raiser for the University, with the Alumni Association limiting its fund-raising to that needed for operations, and 3) that there would be cross representation on the two executive committees, to insure coordination.

The name change was formalized at the annual membership meeting the following October, and Alumni Association President Linton Lull of Smith Center was formally named to the Foundation executive committee. He would be followed, in June of 1979, by Bev Bradley of Lawrence.

The issue of widening the geographic representation on the Foundation executive committee was a bit sensitive and took some time. Largely local membership made for convenience and there was justifiable pride that Manhattan business leaders had started the effort at the University's request. However, by October of 1981 executive committee membership included, in addition to Bramlage and Weltsch, Ross Freeman of Topeka, Earl Brookover of Garden City, John Koger, Sr. of Holton and Topeka, Norman Brandeberry of Russell, and Donald Buster of McCracken. Committee meetings had been shifted from monthly to bi-monthly to allow more involvement by geographically-distant members. In May of 1983 Bruce Buehler of Wichita, Gene Bonnell of Bartlesville, Oklahoma, and Ed Scribante of Omaha, Nebraska, were named to the executive committee.

* * * * *

The next pages describe some other steps that we took toward building K-State's fund-raising capacity and tradition. A list of needs for private funds was one of the steps.

The Wish List

January, 1979

When Dean Hess resigned as director of the Alumni Association, Weigel was chosen to replace him (July 1, 1978).[2] Then, with Heywood's retirement, we set out to find a new executive vice president with experience in an aggressive program. Art Loub, then with Michigan State's foundation, arrived in the fall of 1978.

Over time, with some help from university funds but primarily from increased private giving, additional staff members were brought on board. By the mid 1980s, my recollection is that we had four professional staff in the Foundation.

There was another essential component to establishing a pattern and an expectation of private giving to K-State. There had not been a capital campaign since the Second Century Fund effort in the early 1960s. There needed to be a specific project that would capture the interest of alumni and friends and help open their wallets and checkbooks. What should be that project? Another scholarship drive? Distinguished professorships? An art center? Remodeling and expansion of Ahearn?

Following the advice of our KU friends, Seymour and Wintermode, the newly-named Foundation commissioned a feasibility study by an outside consultant. With input from the colleges, we put together a list of project options and their estimated dollar needs. Consultant staff interviewed a select sample of alumni and University friends, asking which of these projects they would likely help finance and to what extent. My notes dated January 10, 1979, show the project rank order of response interest.[3] (The dollar amounts were our estimate of need, not the amount respondents said they would provide.)

1. Scholarships - $5 million
2. Field house renovation - $3 million
3. Distinguished professorships - $1 million
4. Art center - $3 million
5. Nichols reconstruction - $2.5 million
6. Fine arts program - $3 million

7. (tie for 6th) Campus improvements - $0.5 million
8. Laboratory theatre - $1 million

Further responses from potential donors, steadily increasing donations for scholarships, and the determined infeasibility of remodeling Ahearn Field House (both cost and limited potential for expanded seating), led to a judgment that a new arena, largely for basketball but also serving other purposes, was the project that would most likely bring large dollar support. A six-million-dollar campaign was undertaken for what would become Bramlage Coliseum.

* * * * *

Universities and their foundations sometimes need to turn down gifts. For example, a farm may be gifted or bequeathed with the stipulation that it be used for university research. The land may or may not be suitable for research or in the geographic area where research is needed. Most important, it takes more than the farm income to operate a research unit. A gift can quickly become a burdensome cost.

Then there are those rare cases where a gift is not really a gift, where a party seeks to use a university foundation primarily for an income tax benefit. This appeared to be one of those cases.

The Donors' Direct Descendants?

Foundation Executive Vice President Art Loub came to my office to seek my support for a judgment he had made. An elderly couple wanted to establish a scholarship fund and a son was representing them in making the arrangements. His proposal included that the scholarship recipients needed to be direct descendants of the donors.

Loub's posture was that such a donation, where scholarship beneficiaries are limited to members of the family, would not meet the IRS test as a charitable donation. However, the son had pressed and said he had a legal basis for insisting on the criterion. Because he was part of a rather prominent Kansas family with many K-State links, Loub felt it prudent to run the issue by me.

As a college freshman I had been a recipient of a scholarship whose applicants each had to be a direct descendant of a WWI veteran. The scholarship fund had been established by a couple who had lost a son in the war. That scholarship fund obviously would meet the IRS test; there would be hundreds or thousands of eligible applicants, and the odds of family relationship to the donors near zero. The proposal to Loub was far different.

It did not take long for me to agree with Loub's posture. The K-State Foundation should play no role in denying IRS or the Kansas Department of Revenue its fair share of the couple's annual income.

I assume and hope that the couple did, in the end, help finance their grandchildren's education at K-State. They had other tax benefit options. Each grandparent could make an annual cash gift to each grandchild (for college cost or other) and thereby reduce their taxable estate.

* * * * *

The campus President's Home is a valuable University resource, and not only for hosting faculty, staff, campus visitors, and townspeople. I can recall only two significant donors to the K-State Foundation (or university programs) during our time that had not been a guest in our home for a dinner or a reception, or at least for one of the President's Club barbecues in our back yard. One, Katharine Ordway, had provided Nature Conservancy the money for acquisition of the Dewey Ranch for the Konza Prairie.

The second was an elderly gentleman from southeastern Kansas and whose name I do not recall or find. He stepped into the president's office late one morning and told our receptionist that he wanted to make a gift to the University in his will. In my absence, our receptionist took him to my assistant, Jan Woodward, who listened to his story. He told Woodward he had never married, had worked in the southeastern Kansas coal mines, and had saved some money. Several nieces and nephews had attended K-State and had done well, and he wanted to help other young people get K-State degrees.

He had taken a bus to Manhattan and a taxi to the campus. He wanted to get to the right person, get arrangements made, and be back at the bus station in time to catch the bus back home.

Woodward escorted the gentleman to our Foundation office where he and a staff member discussed the details. He caught his bus home, Foundation staff followed up, and years later his estate executor would send a check for several hundred thousand dollars to the Foundation.

* * * * *

The young women and couples who lived in our home and helped Shirley and K-State Union staff deserve a lot of credit for the hosting we were able to do. June Palacio, a graduate student in Foods and Nutrition, and her husband, Moki, moved into our third-floor quarters to join our effort in the early 1980s. Of Maori descent, Moki was a showman, and he made one our Presidents' Club barbecues especially memorable.

A Maori Blessing for the Roast Pigs

September 12, 1983

One of our major efforts in building this giving tradition was to increase the membership in the Foundation President's Club, those donors who had given or pledged $10,000 or more. Ten thousand dollars may seem a small figure for an elite donor group at this writing, but it was a significant sum in the late 1970s. We increased membership from 141 in June of 1979 to 296 in June of 1980 and, by 1985, we had 693 President's Club members.[4]

To help recognize membership in the Foundation's President Club, and to foster more, we began to host a Club luncheon in our back yard prior to a football game. Though the K-State Union staff always did a fantastic job with functions in the Union, we knew that to be invited to the President's Home, even the back yard, was a bit special. Shirley tried to vary these events from year to year. This year June and Moki suggested a Hawaiian luau, with roast pig as the entre.

The Animal Science Department offered to help; the pigs would be roasted in their meat lab ovens. The Union would provide the balance of the menu and help with service. When all our guests had assembled and were ready for the meal, Moki, dressed in a "lava lava," colorful and traditional Hawaiian chieftain garb, was carried in on a large plank by several husky students. He then said a Hawaiian prayer over the pigs. Our guests were impressed.

June would share with us much later that, though Moki was of Maori descent, he had been raised in California and did not know the native Hawaiian language! He had improvised, built his "prayer" around the Hawaiian-sounding name of a Los Angeles street that he remembered!

June also reminded us of an unfortunate residue of the event. Our little black Dachshund, Tena, had spent her time under the serving table, lapping up the dripping juices from the pigs—and was ill all night.

For the late winter, 1984, President's Club event, we took opportunity to acquaint donors with a campus building that might need some private investment. We arranged for the K-State Union to cater the meal in Farrell Library. Farrell's reading room, with our dinner guests surrounded by books, proved an awesome setting. (A few alumni confessed this was the first time they been in the library's reading room.)

Farrell Library reading room with the K-State Union student serving staff ready to receive Foundation President's Club members for dinner, March, 1984. Just visible, upper left, is the alcove where the Music Department string trio would provide background music for the dinner guests.

From the overlooking alcove high on the reading room south wall, our Music Department string trio provided the dinner music. Though I do not find the record, I know Warren Walker was in the group and likely Ralph Winkler on the violin and Chappell White on the viola.

Feedback from the Farrell Library dinner was so positive that we continued the concept of hosting President's Club dinners in an academic setting. The March, 1985, event would be in newly completed Engineering II, later to be named Rathbone Hall. The March, 1986, event would be in the foyers and open halls of rebuilt Nichols.

* * * * *

It is often the private funds that allow a university to provide its students "frosting on the cake," such as exposure to nationally recognized artists or speakers. Several of the University visits described in the next chapter were so financed.

Chapter IX

University Guests

Not all of a university education and broadening of the mind occur in the classroom or laboratory. K-State continued to be blessed by an extraordinary array of guest lecturers, artists, and entertainers. The McCain Artist Series for 1985-86 included the New York Opera National Touring Company for a performance of *Faust,* the Tulsa and Houston ballets, the Hungarian State Symphony, and the Dresden Chamber orchestra. Among those of earlier years: San Francisco ballet in 1980; jazz interpreter George Shearing and the great violinist, Itzhak Perlman, in 1981; and Cellist Yo Yo Ma, the Tokyo String Quartet, and the Vienna Boys Choir in 1984.

Several lecture series, most notably the Landon Series on Public Policy, exposed students, faculty, and the public to major thinkers and leaders of the day. Ahearn Field House was filled to hear Alex Haley, author of *Roots,* as part of another lecture series.

If the reader is a current college student, you may not recognize the names of the two entertainers mentioned in the first piece. If so, ask your parents—or grandparents—who they were.

Red Skelton

September 14, 1977

On a wall just inside the side door of our farm home, the entry that Shirley and I use most, is a self portrait of Red Skelton, the clown. It is a continuing reminder of Shirley's most admired guest to our K-State campus home.

Skelton had been invited by K-State's Union Board as evening entertainment for Parents' Day. Though Parents' Day was scheduled to attract a larger crowd for a pre-season Saturday afternoon football game, it would be the two hours of Skelton's slapstick and mime that evening in Ahearn Field House that most parents and students would remember.

The headliner the year before had been Bob Hope and he had joined me at halftime on the 50-yard line to be introduced. Never before had I heard a more thunderous greeting from the stadium. That evening, his near two hours of quips and perfectly timed one-liners kept the crowd in an almost continuous bout of laughter.

Skelton would do as well, with a different kind of humor, more slapstick and mime. The audience response was the same as that afforded Hope. But two things set Skelton apart.

The first was that he showed up on campus several days early. As I recall, he drove a rented car down from an earlier Nebraska performance. He had alerted our dance and theatre staff that he would like to sit in on some of their labs. Of course, there was no way he would just sit in. It was his modest way of saying that he would enjoy sharing with K-State students and staff some of his techniques and skills.

During those several days, Skelton was available to K-State and the community. I picked him up at his motel on Wednesday afternoon to take him downtown to the local cable company studio for an interview. He had quite a time folding his long legs into the passenger seat of my small four cylinder Honda hatchback.

That evening we hosted a reception in our campus home for Skelton. We had invited perhaps fifty or sixty students, faculty, and townspeople to meet him. No introductions were necessary. Skelton stationed himself just inside our living room and greeted each person with both eye contact and personality. Our guests became so engrossed that they would delay moving on to the punch or coffee table. Or, they would return with cup in hand to listen in.

Shirley and I marveled at the process. Though Skelton was the center of the other guests' attention, he was alert to any who had just joined the group or who might be reticent. He would, by words or gesture, pull that person into the conversation. He never missed!

No one left our home that evening not having felt they had had a close interaction with Red Skelton. The next morning a student drove Skelton up to our home to bring Shirley a red Kalenchoe plant (another reason Skelton was her favorite guest).

We had never seen a person work as hard as Skelton did on Saturday night. At the close of the performance it was my privilege to join him on stage to express thanks and to present him with a remembrance gift. Only then did I realize just how hard he had worked. His clothes, even his shoes, were

With comedian Bob Hope after he was introduced to the Parents' Day crowd, September 11, 1976, above, and with comedian and mime artist Red Skelton after he was introduced at Parents' Day, September 14, 1977, left. (Skelton photo courtesy University Archives and Royal Purple.)

saturated with perspiration. Though already admired by millions, Skelton had put every ounce of his physical and mental being into giving this audience the fullest and best he could provide.

To stand next to this great comedian was one of my most humbling experiences.

* * * * *

Among the many features that foster respect for K-State is the Landon Lecture Series, named for former governor and 1936 Republican presidential nominee Alf Landon. The annual series had begun in 1967 and generally featured three to five nationally known personalities qualified to speak on public policy issues of the day. Thirteen of the forty-one Landon lectures during my presidency, along with nine of earlier years, are recorded in a twenty-year Landon Series book put together by two of the four faculty who chaired the series during my time, Charles Reagan and Bill Richter.[1]

We were always on the look-out for ways to attract top caliber and nationally recognized speakers. Here I describe our opportunity for acquainting Shirley Temple Black with the Landon platform.

Shirley Temple Black

April 10, 1979

Those of my generation recall the little girl with ringlets who would sing and dance her way into the hearts of movie goers in the late 1930s. By the late 1970s, Shirley Temple Black had served as U.S. representative to the United Nations and ambassador to Ghana.

There is sometimes a bonus in these Landon lectures or other events; an important colleague or member of the family comes along. Malcolm Forbes had been a Landon lecturer early in my time as president and his then relatively young son, Steve, as he said, "carried his briefcase." In this case, it was Shirley Temple's husband, Charles Black, both a political leader and entrepreneur whose businesses included a fish farm in nearby Missouri. By coincidence, Black's co-worker at that fish farm was a brother of Amos Kahrs, manager of our poultry research unit.

The story here, though, is how she became a Landon lecturer. The major reason, of course, was that she had all the qualities we sought. Her public status embraced more decades than any other invitee I might recall. And, her qualifications were without question, personal work with the United Nations and in Africa.

The second was a chance circumstance. Dr. Bill Hoover, president of the American Institute of Baking and former head of K-State's Grain Science

Escorting former President Gerald Ford from his Landon Lecture, "The War Powers Resolution," to a luncheon for Landon patrons, February 20, 1978. Manhattan Mayor Russell Reitz is in the background.

A pre-dinner visit with NBC News Anchor Tom Brokaw, who is to Shirley's right. To my left is Ed Seaton, Manhattan Mercury Publisher and chair of the Landon Lecture patrons. Brokaw would be the 40th Landon lecturer during my presidency, speaking on "The Role of Television in our Lives" March 23, 1986.

Department, was invited to speak at a national food editors' convention in Hawaii. He had a scheduling conflict and suggested me. My schedule would allow it, the Pineapple Growers Association of Hawaii was paying for the travel, and I rationalized that Shirley deserved a mid-winter break in the sun, so I accepted. Shirley Temple Black was also on the program and at an evening reception I suggested the Landon series as one that deserved her presence. Perhaps the Landon name tapped her Republicanism; she responded with evident interest and we simply followed up.

* * * * *

I might illustrate the strength of the Landon Lecture Series by relating a specific lecturer and topic to a major U.S. policy issue, both then and today. Though many of the forty-one lecturers during my time in the presidency would serve that purpose, I choose James Schlesinger, his topic, and a few quotes.

American Security and Energy Policy

April 28, 1980

I introduced Energy Department Secretary James Schlesinger April 28, 1980, for his lecture, "American Security and Energy Policy." He had been director of the Central Intelligence Agency and Secretary of Defense. Schlesinger was, and is today, perhaps the most knowledgeable and credible person in the country to speak on that policy issue.

In 2004 I would join about ten other U.S. agricultural leaders to bring focus to both the responsibility and opportunity for U.S. land owners and operators to contribute to U.S. energy security via wind, solar, and geothermal energy conversion, and conversion of biomass to transportation fuels. Though I saw, in this effort, another market for our land's productivity, and that renewable energy use could limit carbon emissions, my major motive was to enhance U.S. energy security and, in turn, our economic security. Our group's vision became, in essence, that 25 per cent of the total U.S. energy consumption should come from the land by 2025. (www.25x25.org)

Since that 1980 Landon lecture I had heard Schlesinger at several major conferences and had followed some of his writings. His messages regarding energy security are both sobering and inspiring. What I had learned from Schlesinger and others was in large part the basis for my joining what became the 25x'25 effort.

Here are a few excerpts from his 1980 Landon lecture: "We remain dependent - - America and the Free World … upon the resources of the Persian Gulf. … It has been a common illusion in American life that somehow or other, through the waving of some wand, we could alter this condition of dependency quickly and easily. We cannot. The OPEC nations collectively possess 82 per cent of the world's proven reserves of oil. … Down through the Straits of Hormuz each day move some 20 million barrels of oil … 60 per cent of all the oil flowing in international commerce; 40 per cent of all the oil consumed in the free world. And that flow of oil has become increasingly vulnerable for a variety of reasons. … From that condition comes a political vulnerability."

At this writing, 2010, one would make little change in the words of that last paragraph.

* * * * *

Why would one identify a K-State lecture as a "Non-Landon lecture?" We certainly had other lecture designations. For example, a speaker could have been invited to be part of our campus Convocation Series. There were reasons for this designation, however. Here is the story.

The Non-Landon Lecture[2]

October 31, 1980

For the second night in a row we sat in our living room, the President's Home, 100 Wilson Court, discussing and negotiating. Who were "we" and what were we negotiating?

"We" included faculty senate and student body officers, Provost Owen Koeppe, Vice President for Student Affairs Chet Peters, identified leaders of black students and faculty, Vice President for Facilities Gene Cross, Barry Flinchbaugh, my assistant who handled invitations to potential Landon lecturers, and me.

The topic? Ian Smith, former president of apartheid Rhodesia. A few days earlier it had been announced that Smith would be coming to the K-State campus as part of the 1980-81 Landon Lecture Series.

Apartheid had been discredited in the global court of public opinion, and members of the white minority in Smith's country were no longer in leadership roles. Rhodesia had been replaced in the lexicon of countries by the name, Zimbabwe, and apartheid was also well on the way out in South Africa. However, Smith's perceptions of what had been, what was, and what would be in the country he had led should be of interest, especially on a university campus. Inquiry and understanding should guide most of what a university is about.

After I had approved extending the invitation to Smith, there had been some difficulties in communication and meshing available dates. And, once

Smith accepted and a date established, time was short for getting invitations mailed to Landon patrons (a long list of alumni and others who paid $300 per year to help finance the series and a post-lecture luncheon).

Those issues and Flinchbaugh's other responsibilities had given him too little time to alert key persons among black faculty and students. They were caught unaware when Smith's planned lecture was announced. A number expressed outrage, others at least shock, that a former leader of an apartheid state had been invited to the K-State campus. A few demanded that the invitation to Smith be cancelled.

The feelings behind the protests were understandable, and it seemed to me it would be best to get some key people together to talk it out. I was convinced that a healthy discussion by respected campus leadership would bring everyone back to a basic premise of a university, that diverse ideas, experiences, and perspectives should be available. Students and faculty should have the opportunity to listen, debate, think, and make their own judgments.

Koeppe, Peters, Flinchbaugh, and I made a list of nearly twenty-five people and invited them to our home that evening to talk and, especially, for all to listen to concerns.

To the assembled group I clarified our purpose, to let everyone speak their piece, express their concerns and thoughts, and then to reach a consensus on a course of action. I asked Flinchbaugh to spell out the details of the invitation to Smith. In the process of doing that he apologized to the group for failure to make contact with black faculty and student leaders before proceeding with the invitation or, at least, to alert them to Smith's acceptance before they read about it in the media.

I then turned to the group, "Let's hear your thoughts."

Apartheid was the initial focus. There was anger that apartheid had existed, that whites had perpetuated it and resisted its demise. Then the focus was Smith. One expressed outrage that Smith had been invited and said the invitation should be withdrawn. Another, "Why should K-State provide an audience for a defender, a one-time leader of apartheid?" This was echoed in several forms, from both black and white participants.

Others countered, "But apartheid is a reality of history. Do we not study or listen to other history components now discredited, other elements of history we may today despise?" "Should we not try to learn about the transition?" "Should we not hear the perceptions of a key participant, one who has been there?"

Those latter statements seemed to sink in. In time, there was general consensus, or at least acceptance, that the invitation should stand.

It seemed to me that at least half the problem was that the black faculty and student leadership had felt blind-sided. Not involved in the invitation process nor alerted to the invitation, they had had no ready rationale when Smith's lecture date had been announced and others had protested to them.

The focus of the discussion then shifted, "Isn't K-State honoring Smith by bestowing the designation of Landon Lecturer?" Debate on that issue continued for some time, and occupied most of the balance of the evening. Those most concerned persisted with the idea that for Smith to be introduced by the K-State president as a Landon Lecturer was bestowing an honor on a champion and perpetuator of apartheid.

About 11 p.m., I suggested adjournment, to meet again the next evening. We had made progress. Each should come the next evening with specific suggestions on addressing that issue of "an honor." We would also hammer out the logistic details, addressing the concerns of those present and other risks related to Smith's appearance. Landon lectures were always open to the public; certain people might try to disrupt the lecture or even Smith's movements on campus.

The next evening was also a long one; there was much to be nailed down. However, by the time we adjourned there was full consensus that:

1. The invitation to Smith would not be rescinded.
2. Flinchbaugh would contact Smith, explain the circumstances, describe our discussion, and seek his concurrence to come as a university lecturer, without the Landon designation.
3. I would not appear publicly with Smith, but would receive him in my office for a brief visit prior to the lecture.
4. Demonstrations would be permitted outside the auditorium in a prescribed area. Every effort would be made by security and facilities staff to avoid or control confrontations. Attendees to the lecture would not be screened.
5. Smith would be introduced at the lecture by the faculty senate chair, Physics Department Head Charles Hathaway. That would underline that Smith's appearance was within the spirit of academic investigation of ideas and issues. The normal Landon lecture platform party, including me, would sit in the audience.
6. The traditional post-lecture luncheon for Landon patrons would not be held in the K-State Union. Rather, it would be at the Elks Club in downtown Manhattan, and I would not attend.

As Smith rose to speak in McCain Auditorium following Hathaway's introduction, there were scattered and loud hecklers. Security staff had to eject a few from the auditorium. With patience and persistence on the part of Hathaway and the endurance of Smith, the complete lecture was delivered.

Smith gave the audience much to think about. He challenged their naïveté and their lack of acquaintance with the history, economic development, and status of Africa. He presented evidence of the capacity of Zimbabwe's minority whites to supply economic leadership and he gave rationale for his widely known philosophy.

Follow-up seminar sessions at campus locations, with speakers of opposing views, had been arranged and were well attended. I believe that most observers would agree that Smith's campus presence, his lecture, and the debate and discussion that followed were a true intellectual experience for many of the K-State family, for all who chose to participate.

For me there was a feeling of tremendous pride and satisfaction. Our faculty and student leadership, especially black and other minorities, had helped insure that an invited speaker, though controversial, could speak. His right to be heard had not been infringed upon; his experiences, his perceptions, and his thoughts had been exposed to those who wanted to hear.

In recent years I have learned of at least a dozen instances where a university-invited speaker was either disinvited or prevented from speaking. In some cases the invitation was cancelled because of campus or external objections. In others, an unruly audience drowned out the speaker or forced him or her off the stage. In most cases, the invited speaker or the topic was recognized as controversial. However, in one case; the spouse of a U.S. president was so treated.

In my opinion, such responses or behaviors just do not belong on a university campus. If a university can not provide an environment where a controversial or politically different speaker will be heard, where should it be provided?

Though it had taken two long evenings in our living room, ways had been found to accommodate the concerns Smith's invitation had engendered. We had let free speech happen!

* * * * *

K-State's role as a place for free expression would be tested again. In this case, we encountered a far greater problem than we had anticipated.

Jeers and Howls![1]

March 28, 1983

The first words by Saudi Oil Minister Sheik Ahmed Zaki Yamani, to thank me for his introduction, were drowned out by jeers and howls bellowed from scattered sections of McCain Auditorium.

Yamani had been invited as the third speaker in K-State's 1982-83 Landon Lecture series, to give his perspective on the global oil supply and market. Near East oil had long fueled most of U.S. transportation. As Saudi Oil Minister and key member of the OPEC decision-makers, Yamani was at the center of that global supply and market. He could provide a perspective of high interest to our faculty, students, and Landon patrons.

We had feared heckling of Yamani by some of the few Saudi or other Arabic students at K-State, or from nearby campuses. Many Saudis were not sympathetic to the Saudi royal family (and are not at this writing). We had security staff on hand in case they might be needed. However, the extent and magnitude of the jeers and howls were far more than we had expected.

We turned up the volume; perhaps Yamani's voice could overcome. He started again. But the jeers and howls were even louder, and continued without let-up. Finally he turned to me, "They won't give up. Their feelings are so intense! It is no use."

Fortunately, we had planned for an overflow crowd, so had provided TV viewing areas in the K-State Union. Yamani and the balance of the stage party remained seated while I huddled with Facilities Vice President Gene Cross about our options. It was evident to us that there was only one option, and it was not to cancel the lecture!

I stepped to the microphone and announced, "You came to hear Sheik Yamani and for that to happen, we will first clear the auditorium and the building. K-State students, faculty, and Landon patrons will be individually readmitted on the basis of their I.D. Any persons not readmitted may view Mr. Yamani's lecture via TV in the K-State Union." I asked deans, vice presidents, and a few others to assist our security staff at each of the re-entry doors.

We learned, in due time, that most of the jeers and howls had come from university-age men and women not among K-State's student body. They had come from campuses as far away as Colorado. Their demonstration and protest had been well-planned. They had arrived early enough to place themselves at scattered spots in the auditorium. That had amplified and made most effective their disruption. It had also precluded easy removal.

The process of clearing everyone out of the auditorium and readmitting took nearly an hour, but when Yamani was re-introduced he could be heard by all.

What about Yamani's message? It was, in a nutshell, that OPEC's existence is good for everyone. He cited first the risks, to both users and sources of oil, of fluctuating oil prices and that "price volatility tends to obscure the real value of oil." From one who had control of a major share of the world's known oil reserves, it was a logical argument. However, it was not a message that a free-market economist would endorse.

He did give some credit to the market, with "The existence of a controlling body (OPEC) is also necessary for setting out the right price *as signaled by the market*." (Italicizing is mine.) I would have enjoyed hearing the discussion in campus business or economics classes the next day.

Though I could not accept Yamani's basic thesis, I was thrilled he had accepted K-State's invitation. He had helped move the Landon series to a more global perspective, and his perspective could not but challenge the audience to think more seriously about the country's energy future. We also got a taste of the intense emotions that prevail in the Near East, in this case relative to Saudi Arabia's controlling royal family. Also, Shirley and I would say that Yamani was among the most gracious of campus guests that we had the privilege of hosting.

There were two bonuses from the auditorium disruption. For the chair of the Landon patrons, *Manhattan Mercury* Publisher Ed Seaton, it was nearly an hour interview and visit with Yamani in a backstage room while people left the building and were being re-admitted. For K-State, the bonus was national media exposure, and not just as a setting for comments by a key OPEC leader. Network coverage emphasized that, though there had been expected disruptions, at Kansas State University the invited speaker spoke and was heard!

* * * * *

I drafted this next recollection in the first hours of a fourteen-hour flight from Los Angeles to Hong Kong, October, 2008. Shirley and I were looking forward to eighteen days experiencing current Vietnam and Cambodia. However, my thoughts returned nearly a quarter century to a Landon lecture at Kansas State by Los Angeles Mayor Tom Bradley, whose name is affixed to the terminal we had just raced through.

No Impossible Dreams

April 16, 1984

The Tom Bradley International Terminal is a bit like Tom Bradley. It is large (we nearly missed our flight because of the distance from our arrival gate); Bradley was tall, had a big frame. A terminal building is unassuming; Bradley was unassuming. His manner suggested he was simply available for whatever good purpose life would bring.

Bradley's name on the terminal reflects his stature and success as mayor, especially his forward focus. Thousands who traverse the Pacific each day leave from or arrive at that terminal. Bradley's forward focus helped make the L.A. airport ready for today's traffic volume.

How and why did we attract Bradley, who had gained national exposure and stature with his city's successful hosting of the 1984 Summer Olympics?

First, the why: Bradley was one of the most highly respected—in my opinion, the most consistently respected—of several black mayors of major cities during the 1970s and early 1980s. Though a number of blacks had attained national stature, a criterion for Landon invitees, there had been only one black among more than sixty Landon lecturers. That had been U.S. Information Agency Director Carl Rowan, during my second year in the presidency.

Most important, because of Los Angeles' history of racial problems, especially the 1965 Watts riots, I felt that Bradley's perceptions would be carefully listened to. His perspective would be respected by an audience that, though mostly white and certainly Midwestern, were highly sensitive to social change.

There was also a personal reason. Shirley and I knew Bradley. We knew something of his beginnings and his path before he became mayor and rose to national stature. In the fall of 1967 we had spent ten days with Bradley and about a dozen other Americans as guests of the West German government, to help commemorate the twentieth anniversary of the post WWII Marshall Plan. How Shirley and I came to be included in that group is another story. The important matter here is that we learned to know Bradley.

Bradley was then a member of the Los Angeles city council. We learned his early career had been on the L.A. police force. He had attended college at night and earned a degree so he could do better. In time, he had built a political following and was elected to the city council. Two years later, in 1969, Bradley ran for mayor. Our respect, and that of others of our Marshall Plan group, had prompted both moral and dollar support for his campaign. He did not win, but we sent him the message, "Your time will come; plan now for the next election." He was elected in 1973 and would serve five terms, an unprecedented twenty years!

I felt Bradley's very life, as well as his stature and his perceptions, should inspire and broaden the perspective of the Landon audience.

We had maintained intermittent contact. I called Bradley, told him about the Landon series, our criteria for invitees, and mentioned several recent speakers. I also told him why I wanted him, his life, and his perspective on the Landon platform, for our students, faculty, and patrons. I also suggested that a day in the relative tranquility of a university campus in the Kansas

Flint Hills might be a welcome respite from his mayoral schedule—and that Shirley and I would be honored to host him.

I did not need to mention the fact that his name had surfaced a few times as a potential Democratic candidate for president or vice president. The value of being a Landon lecturer on the campus of a well-known Midwestern university, and to spend time with a popular second-term Democratic Governor, John Carlin, would not be lost on Bradley or his advisers.

Bradley arrived late afternoon on Sunday, spent the evening and overnight with Shirley and me. We reminisced, talked about the continuing power and consequences of the Marshall plan. West Germany's great economic growth, evident to us on its twentieth anniversary, had been thought an impossible dream. There had been almost complete devastation of Germany's industry at the end of WW II. Secretary of State George Marshall, President Harry Truman, and a willing Congress had believed, though, that with prudent financial help, full reconstruction of both Germany's infrastructure and economy was possible.

Bradley's lecture, "No Impossible Dreams for Possibility Thinkers," was fitting.

* * * * *

Especially in the leadership of universities and government agencies, where one deals both internally and in the external political arena, one gets well exposed to how and why people act and react the way they do and, consequently, how things get done. Here is such a story, shared by a Landon lecturer and speaker of the U.S. House of Representatives.

Tip O'Neill and the Chrysler Bailout
April 22, 1985

This Landon lecturer, Speaker of the House Thomas P. "Tip" O'Neill, loved to tell stories. He also liked to hear good stories and he remembered them. During Ronald Reagan's presidency, though strong opponents during the day (Republican vs. Democrat and the Executive Branch vs. Congress), the two Irishmen would often get together after hours for a drink and to tell each other stories.

I had met O'Neill before and when I greeted him at the Manhattan airport he recalled the event. It had been in South Dakota, where he had come to help our first term South Dakota congressman, Frank Denholm, in his re-election effort. Now, this is a different Frank Denholm than the long-time Manhattan resident of the same name. (The two Frank Denholms had met once, when the Manhattan Denholm was in South Dakota on Farm Bureau insurance business.)

It is common for senior members of Congress, those whose seats are safe from challenge, to spend part of the campaign season helping their newer colleagues get re-elected. It sends a message to the latter's constituents that their less-senior representative or senator is close to those Congressional leaders that have clout.

O'Neill also remembered the story I had told when I introduced him at a Brookings, South Dakota, luncheon. O'Neill, a native of Boston and having represented that city in Congress for decades, had told me during the meal that, except for Los Angeles and San Francisco, he had never been on the ground west of Chicago. He had flown over the Great Plains many times, but had never been on the ground. He also said he had voted a number of times for rural and agricultural programs, including USDA's Watershed Program (small dam construction to control floods and prevent soil from entering major streams). However, in regard to watersheds, he had "never seen one!"

The story he recalled? In introducing him to the audience of Denholm supporters I mentioned that O'Neill was from Boston and had spent virtually all of his life breathing the industrial and vehicle fumes of Boston and Washington, D.C. Denholm and I had met his plane at Sioux Falls, we had walked through the terminal, and, when we got outside and O'Neill took some deep breaths of the clear and clean South Dakota air, he had collapsed! We had to drag him over to the curb and put his head under a bus exhaust to revive him!

O'Neill had obviously enjoyed the story.

At the time of O'Neill's visit to K-State, the Congressional bail-out of the Chrysler Corporation had just happened and O'Neill, as speaker, had been a key actor. I raised the topic and he was quick to follow up with his story.

In the early 1980s the Chrysler Corporation was in financial difficulty and dragging far behind General Motors and Ford in sales. Lee Iacocca, the man behind the Mustang early in his Ford career, later Ford CEO, and then fired by Henry Ford II, had been hired by the Chrysler board to salvage their company. Chrysler needed an emergency loan from the government. No bank or set of banks had the risk capacity or willingness to loan what Chrysler needed. And, though by law the Federal Reserve is the "lender of last resort," it was not then willing to taking on such a risk.

According to O'Neill, Iacocca had hired several Washington lobby groups to press Congress to approve the massive loan that Chrysler needed. However, the lobbyists were not having much success. O'Neill met Iaccoca at some event, and Iacocca confided that he was worried.

With typical Irish humor, O'Neill shared with me what he had told

Iacocca, in essence, "Young man, you've got this all wrong. You don't need to hire those high-priced lobbyists to pester my colleagues and me. The person I want to talk to is you, the CEO! Why don't you just fly into Washington and come see me. We'll go into my office, have a good visit, and maybe we can work something out." As we all know, that loan was approved by Congress.

As I listened to O'Neill's Landon lecture, "Half a Century of American Achievement," later that morning I could not but wonder how many of those "American Achievements" got their impetus from legislation that was "worked out" during some key person's visit in the office of the Speaker of the House or the Majority Leader of the Senate.

* * * * *

Attracting top government leaders to K-State's Landon platform also meant that those leaders' jobs came with them. At no time were they separated from their major responsibilities or the need for their timely judgments. Here may be an example.

The Decision to Bomb Libya
April 14, 1986

President Ronald Reagan's decision to unleash a joint air force, navy, and marine corps airstrike against Libya the next day, in retaliation for apparent support of international terrorism by Libyan President Muammar al-Gaddafi, may have been made or at least confirmed during a noon-time phone call Secretary of State George Schultz made from Director Walt Smith's office in the K-State Union after Schultz had delivered a Landon Lecture. I can not document that, but circumstantial evidence is convincing.

Libyan involvement had been implicated in a series of terrorist actions, including Rome and Vienna airport attacks in late December, 1985, and, on April 5, 1986, an explosion at a West Berlin disco frequented by U.S. servicemen. Two of our servicemen had been killed and a number wounded in that event. U. S. diplomatic talks with several European countries regarding potential sanctions toward Libya had not been productive. It was clear in media reports that Reagan's patience was wearing thin.

As I escorted Secretary of State George Schultz from his lecture in McCain Auditorium to the patron's luncheon in the Union's ballroom, he told me he first needed to make a phone call. His aide had handed him a note as we had left the McCain stage, and there had seemed an element of urgency in the aide's manner. I was not surprised, considering events of recent days.

At the Union, Smith gave Schultz and his aide the privacy of his office, and I proceeded to begin the luncheon. Schultz joined the head table just as serving began, no outward sign of concern apparent. Shultz was experienced—cool and unflappable.

Following the meal, I introduced Shultz again and he gave Landon patrons "their money's worth," fifteen minutes of informal comments about some of the issues that face a secretary of state. Neither Libya nor Gaddafi was mentioned. However, his lecture earlier in the day, "Moral Principles and Strategic Interests," had sent a clear signal. In the body of the lecture he devoted some time to terrorists, "No tactic is too gruesome in their destructive manipulations" and to a necessary response, "the sternest test for all free nations . . . is to summon the will to eradicate this terrible plague. Because terrorism is a war against ordinary citizens, each and every one of us must show a soldier's courage."

We would learn later that Reagan had arranged to alert key Congressional leadership to likely action, but his secretary of state, normally a key person for both the final decision and that briefing, was in Manhattan, Kansas, giving a lecture.

After bidding Schultz goodbye at the Manhattan airport, I flew to Wichita for a 3:30 meeting, and that evening to Washington, D.C. The next day, just outside of the House International Relations Committee room in the Rayburn House Building, whom should I encounter? It was Secretary Schultz, obviously heading in to brief the total committee.

That evening I learned that Gaddafi's compound just outside Tripoli had been hit. Fourteen F-111 strike aircraft, flying from Royal Air Force Lakenheath base, plus twenty-seven attack aircraft from U.S. carriers in the Gulf of Sidra had struck five targets during a ten-minute attack in and near Tripoli. Gadaffi had been alerted by a telephone call from Malta's prime minister, so escaped injury, but two sons were injured and an infant adopted daughter was killed.

In October of 2008, Libya paid $1.5 billion into a fund to compensate relatives of those killed in the 1986 Berlin bombing, in the destruction of Pan Am Flight 103 over Lockerbie in 1988, and in other terrorist events in which Libya had been implicated.

* * * * *

Though Shirley and I became well acquainted with many students, their time with us was short. It was the faculty and staff with whom we would have continued interactions and where we would develop and retain a good many life-long friendships and feelings of mutual respect. As with students, there were many faculty and staff successes and actions that brought me satisfactions and a few that brought disappointments. The next chapter includes both.

Chapter X

Faculty and Staff

When I accepted the presidency I vowed that I would devote more time and effort encouraging, commending, and recognizing excellent faculty and staff work than might be required in addressing problems. As I look back on my eleven years in the presidency, I fear that I failed to fulfill my vow. Many courses became popular or retained popularity; faculty led student teams to wins in national competition. Many Extension faculty saw increased and continued large attendance at their educational meetings. Many researchers published highly important papers, or developed and released valuable technologies and genetic lines. There was much creativity among music, art, writing, theatre, and design faculty, earning acclaim locally and nationally.

Though I would express commendation when I learned of outstanding work or, by my presence, show support at department events or off-campus field days, too often there were time conflicts. Monthly board meetings, legislative hearings, or selling the University at service clubs or state conventions demanded my time. Also time was required to handle issues a vice president or dean may bring, or about any issue that might reach the regents, legislators, or the governor.

Such is the circumstance of the presidency in a large university. Outstanding faculty and staff performance do not demand being conveyed to the president's office, but serious problem cases do.

* * * * *

In the third week of August fall semester gets underway. My 1976 pocket calendar shows the key events of a typical opening week. We had a faculty/staff convocation in McCain Auditorium on Tuesday at 4, where I introduced new department heads and other administrators and provided a brief "State of the University." On Wednesday I welcomed new students in the Union Ballroom at 9:45, spoke to parents in the Little Theatre at 10:15, and Shirley and I had a coffee for parents at our home that afternoon. Thursday afternoon, while registration for most students was underway in the Field House, Chet Peters and I were at a student senate retreat at the little red schoolhouse north of Council Grove. Student registration continued on Friday.

Words I chose for each event were important. Though most faculty at meetings in which they were involved were old hands and had heard it before, new faculty would likely listen well, especially at a smaller event for them just after the semester began.

Specific to New Faculty

September 2, 1976

The faculty senate welcomed new faculty in a late afternoon reception in the K-State Union. This was my only opportunity to speak to these twenty to fifty each year as a special group. For many, this would be their first job on a university faculty. I recalled my first days as a new instructor at both Oklahoma State and Iowa State, how I had "soaked in" what the dean or president had to say. Following are major points I would make to these new colleagues.[1]

1. Be a part of the University community. Acquaint yourself with the campus, the major buildings, and their histories. Partake of such as student/faculty concerts, track meets, the dairy bar, theatre, the recreation complex, and horticulture field days. Make use of, appreciate, and enjoy the resources of the total university.
2. Develop your educational philosophy, especially a philosophy of helping students achieve the standards for which K-State is known.
3. Each new faculty member is a highly capable person, with talents and skills that K-State needs. We will do our best to reward effective and productive employment of those talents and skills.
4. Take home every evening and every semester some satisfactions. Do those things that will help insure you have a career that brings satisfactions. I would emphasize, "The salary you are paid will disappear—on living expenses, investment in a home, or a retirement account. But, the satisfactions will endure; they will last a lifetime."

* * * * *

With the total Manhattan population less than two times that of the campus, there was much interaction between the University and local business and professional people and elected officials. We were together at church, in service clubs, and at the many public events on campus, including music, theatre productions, and sports. Shirley worked with many townspeople, as well as with faculty and their spouses, on a number of community boards and committees. The town and University were, in essence, a seamless continuum. There were many personal friendships which Shirley and I yet cherish.

A Party for Town and Gown

August 19, 1977

An early effort to enhance the town/gown relationships almost got us in trouble with our state senator, Donn Everett. Long-time friends, music professor Paul Shull and his wife, Joan, joined Shirley and me in planning a Flaming Forties party, built on the theme of 1940s dress and music. We each made a list of couples to invite, from various segments of the campus and community. Some would be well acquainted with each other, some not.

To make it more interactive and suspenseful, we sent unsigned invitations for only the date and time, August 19, 7:30 p.m., and the theme. The invitation did not include the location (our campus home) or the names of the hosts. RSVP was to a Post Office Box.

Virtually all of the thirty-eight invited couples accepted (we learned later that one couple thought it a hoax and discarded the invitation). We then sent details. Certain invitees, designated drivers, were sent a clue as to the two couples they were to pick up. We also included for each a phone number (an unlisted number for our home) for any baby sitter or emergency purposes.

One couple to be picked up had a clue for the first stop on what would be a treasure hunt to find the party. Each group (we hoped) would eventually find and follow four successive clues. The final clue, to the party's location, was the same for all groups. It read, "The Library is named for the man who lived here when the '40s began."

(This was before the recent addition to and renaming of the University library; the structure was then Farrell Library. Frances David Farrell was K-State president from 1925 to 1943.)

I confess Shirley and I had our fingers crossed the night of the event. Would the invitees figure out the clues? And when they got to that last clue would they believe it was the University President's Home? We would stand at our door, watch cars go slowly up Lovers Lane, the street between our home and Justin Hall. We could imagine the car occupants re-reading that last clue. Several cars entered the Farrell Library parking lot and stopped. Eventually, they would leave the lot, come slowly down the hill, and enter our drive. Someone, more likely a non-faculty person, would ring our doorbell, "Is there, by chance, a party here?"

It was soon apparent the party would be a success. Several cars arrived before eight o'clock; people shared the fun of figuring out the clues and the questioning of that last clue. Merriment and conversation were well underway.

We then counted noses; had everyone found their way? Oh, oh! It was well after 8:30 and one car was missing! Whose car? It did not take long to identify, State Senator Donn Everett's.

We wondered, "Where did they get stuck on the clues?" Could there have been a mix-up when we sent out the clues? Could one of the planted clues have blown away? Had a clue led them to a dead end?

This was well before cell phones, so there was only one place to check. I called Everett's home—and the senator answered. I could hear lively conversation in the background. They were likely re-reading the clues and trying to decide if they should call that emergency phone number.

"Donn, we're at a party and we miss you."

"Where the hell is it?" his response reflecting some frustration.

The Everetts and their riders, the Marc Ollingtons (director of McCain Auditorium) and the Bill Richards (manager of the Ramada Inn) were soon at the party.

We did have a couple more parties, not necessarily of the treasure hunt type, but fun. And, for his remaining time in the state senate, Everett continued as a robust supporter of K-State.

* * * * *

In a faculty of a thousand, there are annual losses, including retirements, a professional move up on another campus and, for a few, a new and different occupation. The most unfortunate are the premature deaths of valued faculty. In this case, we felt the decedent deserved recognition and honor before some of her appreciative students. And, it might remind all graduates that their teachers are mortal, each with finite lives.

A Eulogy in a Proper Setting
May, 1978

Following the death of one of our outstanding teachers, the 1978 Spring commencement gave what we felt was the proper setting for inclusion of a eulogy. Not only were a number of her students among the graduates, but what should be said of her would be an inspiration for all. For my commencement address' theme, persistence and determination, Professor Helen Williams' time at Kansas State was a fitting illustration. The address[2] excerpt:

> *"In 1974, one of our new English professors, Helen Williams, revived our literary magazine, Touchstone. Professor Williams was a resolute and persistent woman. She believed students could learn about good literature and that they could create excellent poetry and prose. Touchstone was to be the students' showplace.*
>
> *In 1975 Touchstone was selected by the Coordinating Council of Literary Magazines as the best college literary magazine published in this country. That same year, Helen Williams learned she had cancer.*
>
> *In 1976, she taught two sections of freshman honors English, and two classes she had created herself. At the end of the academic year, she was cited for the all-University award for excellence in undergraduate teaching. At that time, she said, 'Teaching is a love—a love of material, a love created within the group that allows both student and teacher to do their best work. I teach by believing in my students, believing that they can do their best work when I expect it of them.'*
>
> *In addition to being a dedicated teacher, Helen Williams was a prolific poet, and her work appeared frequently in elite literary magazines.*
>
> *Professor Williams, her cancer in remission, taught full time both spring and summer terms of 1977. This last fall she began the semester teaching one composition class on campus. That was the limit to her endurance. However, she offered two poetry classes in her home. Of course, those classes were filled almost immediately. On October 1, she had to give up her classes. October 17, at age 37, Helen Williams died.*
>
> *Her students and colleagues remember her as a warm human being and as a teacher who persistently believed in the intellectual and creative abilities of students. She lived the tradition of a true educator."*

A fitting eulogy in a proper setting.

* * * * *

Most faculty get plenty of recognition for their work. I felt that our classified staff also deserved recognition. Early in my time as president I had asked our personnel office to develop a recognition program for both years of service and outstanding performance. When the program had been designed, I asked the Foundation for modest funds to finance it.

Deserved Recognition

March 19, 1979

An early January 1979 issue of the *Manhattan Mercury*[3], under the heading, "Eighteen Still in Running for Employee Recognition," described a K-State staff recognition program then in its third year. The article said, in part:

"Eighteen Kansas State University employees with an average of 12.6 years of service to the University remain in the running for the honor of being KSU's 'Classified Employee of the Year.' The semifinalists were selected by the Classified Affairs Committee from among the 77 individuals nominated this year. There are approximately 1,800 classified employees at the University. The Classified Affairs Committee will reduce the number in the running for the 1980 honor to six finalists on January 16."

For both the classified staff and for me, this would be the third year for a new event in the goings on of K-State. Public focus is usually on administrators and faculty; they get most of the exposure and recognition. Faculty not only perform before their student, scientific society, or extension clientele audience, they are shown as publication authors, team coaches, and directors of music or theatre productions. Administrators get media coverage when appointed or promoted, for initiating new department or college programs. or for appearance before legislative committees.

However, neither administrators nor faculty would get much done, nor would they get it done with efficiency and comfort, were it not for staff that heat the buildings, clean the classrooms, reproduce the class outlines and exams, wash the laboratory glassware, feed the research animals, or keep track of the finances.

In asking our personnel office to design this recognition program I had emphasized it should be University-wide, including county extension offices and state-wide research locations. The first classified employee of the year, in March of 1977, was an equipment operator in our campus facilities division; the second year it was a secretary in our Cowley County Extension office at Winfield.

Few events in a given year would yield more pride and satisfaction for those involved, including me, than that ceremony.

* * * * *

Though a university presidency brings with it many formal and expected roles, once in a while the opportunity comes along for what I call personal privilege. In this case, I could spend an evening with a long-time acquaintance at an event we might both enjoy.

My Special Guest

March 22, 1980

This night was the annual K-State Faculty Social Club dinner dance in the K-State Union. I should be there, but Shirley could not; she was in China with Extension Home Economist Eleanor Anderson and a People-to-People group.

To go alone did not appeal and it had struck me that here was an opportunity to invite as my guest someone who might not otherwise go. My mind had gone immediately to retired and recently widowed Professor David "Davie" Mackintosh. I called Mackintosh at home and he accepted.

Most senior and retired faculty knew Mackintosh, either personally or through his campus reputation. He was a long-time professor of meats in the Department of Animal Science, a gregarious person who had retained a good bit of his ancestral Scottish accent. Having taught courses in both the agriculture and home economics curriculums, Mackintosh had had several current faculty as students. Also, he was one of several professors that, at alumni meetings across Kansas or across the country, I would be asked about. "How is Professor Mackintosh? I suppose he is retired by now. If you see him, tell him 'Hello' for me."

Several things had brought Mackintosh to mind. First, though he enjoyed faculty colleagues, he might pass up the event. Widows and widowers often have difficulty, especially the first few years, feeling comfortable going alone.

Second was a personal reason. Mackintosh had been the first K-State faculty member that I had met, in late January of 1951. I was a junior at Iowa State and member of the meat judging team. En route back from our intercollegiate contest in Ft. Worth, where we had competed against his K-State team, we had stopped in Manhattan so he could show us through K-State's new meat lab, in what is now known as Weber Hall.

My meat team coach, Ed Kline, had been one of Mackintosh's students and had entertained us with stories about him. Kline claimed Mackintosh used a meat cleaver to get students' attention. If a student's mind or conversation was off point in a meat-cutting lab, he might slam a cleaver, flat side down, within inches of the student's hand.

There was another personal reason. In December of 1961, just a few days after I had received a letter from Dean Glenn Beck inviting me to visit K-State to discuss the associate dean position, I had received a letter from Mackintosh. He asked if I would consider a faculty position in meats, working alongside him.

Though the Beck letter and associate dean position were more in line with my interests and aspirations, I was as complimented by Mackintosh's letter as by Beck's. He knew me, while Beck did not. We had heard each other's presentations at meat research conferences and his interest spoke to his appraisal of my scientific and teaching skills.

An important feature of a small population state and a land grant university's statewide relationships is that one can become well acquainted across the state. A couple I had come to know early in my presidency had been Liz and John Oswald of Hutchinson. When I learned that she was Mackintosh's daughter, it cemented our relationship. Coincidentally, Liz would later become president of the K-State Alumni Association.

Though I missed having Shirley at my side for the Social Club dinner dance, I could not have had a more appropriate substitute, partner, and guest than Davie Mackintosh.

* * * * *

When tenure for teachers comes up in general public conversations, it tends to be discussed in a negative way, "I suppose they can't get him (or her) to retire and, with tenure, they can't get rid of him (or her)." Perhaps tenure is too often leaned on as an excuse by administrators unwilling to face their responsibilities. I will leave public school tenure for others to defend. In universities, however, I consider academic tenure's existence essential and here is why.

Academic Freedom and Tenure
Spring, 1981

Some readers may recall Adrian Daane, head of K-State's Department of Chemistry in the 1960s. He came from an academic family. Daane's father had been head of the Agronomy department at Oklahoma A&M, now Oklahoma State, and had been fired as part of a political purge in 1928. The undocumented but often-told story is that the root of the purging was Governor William H. "Alfalfa Bill" Murray's displeasure that the Agronomy department was doing research on inorganic fertilizer and presenting the research at farmer meetings.

At both Iowa State and in my earlier time at K-State, I had seen irate farm leaders march into my department head's or dean's office urging that "Professor X" be fired, or at least reassigned to some other topic, because his research or his presentations at extension meetings revealed data or included statements not in those farm leaders' interests. One had reported comparatively low productivity of a sheep breed; flock owners would lose ram sales. Another had estimated the societal cost/benefit of alternative real estate and property tax policies; land and cattle owners worried the legislature would use the data to their disadvantage.

During the 1981 Kansas legislative session, academic tenure in the universities had come under attack. Several Board members then picked up the issue and raised concerns. I knew that the general public, exposed to some tenure problems in public schools, might need a bit of reinforcement on the whole issue of tenure and academic freedom in universities.

That had prompted me to devote both my spring 1981 commencement address[4] and service club presentations[5] across the state to the issue of academic freedom and tenure. I felt it critical that key people in the state understand why academic tenure exists in universities, what it protects, what it does not, and why. People needed to be reminded that freedom of inquiry is essential to a university's continued credibility. I include an excerpt from those presentations:

> *"Throughout the centuries, there has been pressure to limit the freedom of expression or the freedom of research in universities. Sometimes it has been accepted with calm and at other times resisted with vigor.*
>
> *Historically, within the United States, the climate often has seemed inhospitable to unorthodox thought. The religion vs. science controversy, characterized by the famous Scopes trial in 1925, a generally hostile attitude toward radical political thought, and the resistance to a third political party are examples. These may suggest an atmosphere in which the academic freedom of a professor is uncertain.*
>
> *But let me quickly say that it is in the United States that the battle for academic freedom has been fought most vigorously. And, the battle has been fought by the citizenry, as well as by professors. I'll list several examples.*
>
> *In 1903, the trustees of the Board of Trinity College, now Duke University in North Carolina, defended the academic freedom of Professor John S. Bassett. He had written an article in the South Atlantic Quarterly in which he criticized racial inequality and predicted a future state of equality for the American Black. He was at once attacked by newspapers and organizations which called for his expulsion. Professor Bassett submitted his resignation. However, the Board met, refused to accept his resignation, and issued a declaration of principle supporting his right and responsibility to speak out.*
>
> *In 1894, Richard T. Ely, a distinguished economist at the University of Wisconsin, was accused of believing in collective bargaining. He was tried by a committee of regents and the expectation, given the tenor of the day, was that he would be dismissed.*

Instead, the trial resulted not only in Ely's exoneration but in a declaration that some now refer to as the "Wisconsin Magna Carta." It says: 'As regents of a university with over a hundred instructors supported by two millions of people who hold a vast diversity of views, we could not for a moment think of recommending the dismissal or even the criticism of a teacher even if some of his opinions should, in some quarters, be regarded as visionary. Such a course would be equivalent to saying that no professor should teach anything which is not accepted by everyone as true. This would cut our curriculum down to very small proportions. We cannot for a moment believe that knowledge has reached its final goal or that the present condition of society is perfect. We must therefore welcome from our teachers such discussions as shall suggest the means and prepare the way by which knowledge may be extended, present evils be removed and others prevented. We feel we would be unworthy of the positions we hold if we did not believe in progress in all departments of knowledge. In all lines of academic investigation it is of utmost importance that the investigator should be absolutely free to follow the indications of truth wherever they may lead.'

In 1943, at another land grant university, Iowa State University (then Iowa State College), faculty economists were assigned the task of preparing a pamphlet on the efficient use of various foodstuffs in a national emergency, World War II. In the publication, eventually known as Pamphlet Number Five, the economists suggested that oleomargarine was as nutritious and appetizing as dairy butter. The state's dairy industry was furious and put great pressure on the president of the college to act. He named a committee to review the publication; the committee asked for revisions in the publication. While no resignations were sought, two of the economists, the head of the Department and the lead author of the pamphlet, resigned, feeling they could not work in an atmosphere which they believed encroached upon their freedom to express ideas that were counter to prevailing opinion.

In October of 1979, while visiting that same university for a seminar, one of those economists, Dr. Ted Schultz, learned that he had been awarded the Nobel Prize for excellence in economics. (The reader may note the irony.)

Academic freedom is the freedom to seek and to teach the truth, as one knows it, in his or her discipline. For university faculty, the bulwark of academic freedom is tenure. Tenure, given after a probationary period, usually six to seven years, permits the faculty member who can continue to demonstrate competence to hold his or her professional post continuously until the age of retirement. The only reason for tenure is to protect academic freedom."

I should add that academic freedom is not the same as freedom of speech. A discussion of the difference is provided in other writings.[6]

* * * * *

If I wanted to preserve tenure, I had to be sure that my university was using it appropriately, to protect academic freedom. Unfortunately, at K-State, tenure was also being used for another purpose.

Where Tenure Doesn't Belong

May 28, 1982

Soon after my return to K-State as president I became aware that many administrative service personnel, in such areas as finance, facilities, student affairs, and physical plant, carried what was called administrative tenure, described in the faculty handbook as providing "continuous appointment of unclassified staff."

Use of the tenure term for those with no research or teaching duties, either in the classroom or in Extension education, seemed to me both illogical (no academic freedom to protect) and unnecessary. State and federal policies, as well as societal expectations, provided all kinds of employment protection. The practice seemed well imbedded in the University, however, and I had no personal desire to molest it.

However, the 1981 Kansas Legislature's attack on tenure and related discussions by members of the Board told me there could be a movement to limit or constrain academic tenure within the state's universities. It was incumbent upon me to defend tenure for the one purpose for which it existed, to protect academic freedom.

How could I credibly defend tenure when my own university was abusing its use? Our personnel office identified eighty-five valuable staff that held administrative tenure, or were scheduled to be given the designation after specified years of satisfactory work. The eighty-five included two in my office!

As we discussed the issue in Anderson Hall, one of my colleagues suggested that if we removed administrative tenure, those staff would think of themselves as second-class citizens. I had not seen that on other campuses. People are respected for their jobs and their professionalism. To suggest that inappropriate employment protection adds dignity or respect is bogus. Yet, it was obvious that the designation carried some feeling of intangible value.

How could we make the shift, yet retain these valuable staffs' undiminished feeling of being appreciated?

I named a committee of administrative service staff, headed by Acting Student Affairs Vice President Earl Nolting, to draft a policy that would honor existing institutional commitments. Work with that committee, a faculty senate administrative caucus, and legal counsel resulted in a conclusion (and a letter this date to the eighty five affected staff) that administrative tenure would no longer be used for newly hired or those then on a "tenure track." The latter, after five years of service, could be dismissed only in the case of financial exigency.[7]

There were no legal grounds to remove administrative tenure from those to whom it had been granted. Remnants would remain until the last of the persons holding it retired.

One of my colleagues criticized me for spending time on this issue, "in the weeds," he said. However, I had learned in my youth that, if unchecked, weeds can damage a crop. In this case and at this time, the crop was academic tenure, under some attack. One of the weeds was tenure's inappropriate use.

* * * * *

An outstanding faculty, such as at K-State, yields successive celebrations and reasons for pride. Then, reality strikes; there appears a human frailty that may cause pain to the University or to a faculty family. Here is an example.

Distant Temptations

I knew this visit would not be easy, but it was necessary. The dean had alerted me to the rumor, a professor on a several-week assignment more than a thousand miles away and perhaps involved there in a liaison with a co-worker. The wife had called my office to ask for an appointment. He was a well-respected scientist and they were a well-regarded couple in the community.

She laid out the problem rather directly. She knew her husband had special skills, was valuable to the University's programs, and that he enjoyed working with students and faculty in collaborative research efforts with other universities. She also knew his weaknesses; apparently he had had earlier liaisons in such situations.

Though his current assignment had been scheduled for just a few weeks, she had just learned that he was extending his time there. She was certain the young co-worker was a part of the reason.

She had no desire for legal action or divorce, and certainly no public exposure of the situation. But, could not the University just bring him home? And, could not the University find someone to replace him, at least for future collaborative efforts?

We both acknowledged that the University had limited ability and no legal standing to control the relationships of a staff member, whether in Manhattan or elsewhere, but it was a reasoned and reasonable request.

His current assignment would be his last to that location.

* * * * *

Among more than two thousand faculty and staff, including units allied with the University, more than one may succumb to temptations.

Local Temptations

Few of us may be as cautious in our behavior as the depiction of Harry Truman, pulling a postage stamp from his billfold for a personal letter he had written at his Oval Office desk. We may use the office copy machine to make a file copy of some personal item or the office phone to make an urgent personal long-distance call. In my years of university and government work, I recall only one case of the latter that was clearly abusive and it happened to occur during my presidency.

In that era we had WATS phone lines, flat-rate and low-net-cost lines to which we could connect for 24-hour long distance calling on university business. Our central finance office billed University departments for WATS line use. Bills showed the time, call origin, number called, and length of call. (For personal long-distance calls, most of us carried a telephone charge card; we would use a regular line and give the operator or dial in our charge card number.)

One unit had received an unduly large WATS line bill from our finance office. The unit head had just resigned and moved on, and the acting head questioned the bill. Call details on the bill, plus other information, eventually told the story. For months before his departure, the former head had been making daily calls to his distant girl friend.

Finance Vice President Dan Beatty took on the personal task of getting reimbursement for the University, and I know he had repeated contact with the departed head. However, I do not recall that he collected a dime.

A few years later that offender's replacement was also involved in a problem, though of a different type. He allegedly used the same revolving account that had been used to pay those WATS line bills to buy a computer for his home and family use. It was not lost on our auditor that many staff, at that time, had no idea how to use a computer. However, their children did.

There was another case. We had a food purchasing cooperative that served most of the fraternities and sororities. It was supposed to save money for member groups, but was not doing well and some of the participating groups' leaders started asking questions. After a bit of checking by our auditor, the junior staff member serving as custodian of the cooperative's account quietly resigned and moved two states away.

Then there was the case of the staff member who, when traveling on behalf of the University, was reported to gather restaurant receipts from his fellow traveler, after each had paid for their own meal. Now, why would one do that?

He was in a unit allied to the University, the unit's income and expenditures handled through one of those revolving accounts. Because his duties included arranging meetings and, in the process, sometimes hosting others for lunch, claiming reimbursement for one or two additional meals would raise no red flag.

It is coincidental that I write these cases at a time, 2009, after four or more nominees for cabinet level or other high federal governmental office have been publicly exposed as having fudged on their taxes. The U.S. public is disappointed. It is even more disappointing that all but one were confirmed to their high office by the U.S. Senate and that no fewer than a dozen members of Congress are under a cloud for financial improprieties!

If there is any place in society that must, by example, demonstrate integrity it is the University, in the classroom and research lab, in athletics, and in financial operations. (That statement should also apply to the Congress and the U.S. Executive Branch.)

Though there may be a touch of humor in some of the cases I have cited, each is a tragedy of some proportion, especially for the involved individual. I take no joy in relating these cases. However, to avoid sharing them would deprive the reader of some of the reality with which a university president deals.

* * * * *

Every year we fought for faculty and staff salary increases, to move K-State salaries more in line with those at peer universities, or to at least equal or exceed inflation. Most years my Kansas system presidential colleagues and I were successful; one several-year sequence I would call the Golden Years.

The Faculty's Golden Years?

January, 1983

As I listened to Governor John Carlin's annual budget message to the state legislature and watched members of that legislature struggle with balancing state needs with revenue expectations, I wondered if our university faculty's series of golden years, in terms of salary increases, would be interrupted. In recent years, the Kansas Regent universities had had good treatment by Carlin and the legislature. The following table, for K-State, shows how good.[8]

Average Nine-month Salaries at K-State[8]

Rank	1978-79	1982-83	Dollar increase	Per cent increase
Professor	$25,992	$34,166	$8,174	31.4
Associate Professor	20,446	25,882	5,436	26.6
Assistant Professor	16,549	21,146	4,597	27.8
Instructor	13,712	18,501	4,789	34.9
Average of averages	$19,175	$24,924	$5,749	30.0

In a four-year period, the average salaries for the four faculty ranks, instructor through professor, had increased a calculated 30 per cent. As applied to individual faculty persons, the average salary increase was likely more than 30 per cent. The reason is that a number of faculty had been promoted in rank during that four year period—and had moved to the next rank and salary strata. It should be emphasized that the bottom line figures in the table are not necessarily the average K-State faculty salaries for the respective years; there were different numbers of people in the several ranks.

Why the significant increases? I give major credit to Governor Carlin, a K-State graduate, and legislative leaders for their dedication to higher education. They clearly wanted to help state universities hold our good faculty and attract more. I should also mention the effective work of legislative contact people from K-State, Barry Flinchbaugh and Mike Johnson, and their colleagues at other universities in the Kansas Regent system. With rare exception, they and their respective university presidents, especially after 1980, worked on behalf of the total system's faculty.

The willingness of new KU chancellor Gene Budig, who arrived July 1 of 1981, to join me in presentations to service clubs and other groups across Kansas was, I believe, a factor. When I learned from a regent that Budig, then at the University of West Virginia, was to be named KU chancellor, I called him to suggest he join me in a series of service club presentations I was planning for that fall. It was clear to me that legislators and the public wanted a united voice from the state universities. As heads of the two major universities, we were the logical persons to provide that united voice. (I did have another motive, KU had an airplane!) Beginning in September of that year, the two of us made nearly thirty joint presentations, from Coffeyville to Goodland and from Liberal to Leavenworth.

A reader may ask, "How about the twelve-month faculty, a high proportion of those in research (financed in part by the agricultural and engineering experiment stations and grants or contracts) and in Extension? The table shows only nine-month faculty salaries." My pocket notebooks show twelve-month faculty salaries for only F'83, so I have no record of their increases over the four-year time span. Though we had smaller percentage increases in federal formula funds for the AES and the CES, and most twelve-month faculty were partially paid by those funds, every effort was made to provide them the same percentage salary increases as for those who were financed exclusively by state money. To do that sometimes required cutting a lower priority program or leaving a couple positions open to free the needed money.

By 1983, the early 1980's farm crisis was negatively impacting businesses across the state and, consequently, state tax revenues. We were in for a couple difficult years with limited salary increases. Were the golden years over? Not forever. In more recent decades there have been some more golden years for faculty salaries, sometimes outpacing the Consumer Price Index. At the time of this writing, 2010, however, university faculty in some states are experiencing salary reductions or partial furloughs because of sharply decreased state revenues.

* * * * *

Personnel issues have brought me to faculty grievance committees (or the court room) on several occasions. Faculty handbooks outline a grievance procedure for use if a person feels improperly treated, such as on salary level or, as in the following case, employment termination. It is incumbent on administrators to adequately defend their action.

Are Notes Worth $100,000?
July 12, 1984

To avoid challenges to an employee termination, or to win when challenges occur, there are three basic rules: 1) Have written personnel policies and procedures. 2) Follow them. 3) Keep a written record of performance reviews and, where there is termination risk, dated notes of every related conversation. When a university loses a case, the cause is usually failure on Rule 2 or 3.

For more than five years, department heads and deans in two K-State colleges had dealt with internal and cross-college battles involving this tenured professor. It seemed that no change in the professor's teaching assignment, course and curriculum structure, or staff organization would lower the stress.

Rather, it intensified. Eventually his department head and dean recommended his termination and the provost approved. Though not directly involved, I had learned so much from so many quarters that I was not surprised.

The professor filed an appeal, as provided in university policy, with a faculty senate panel of tenured professors. Following nine days of testimony the panel unanimously recommended to me that the professor not be terminated.

What went wrong with the University case? I concluded the case was lost the day I learned that two of the involved administrators had based their testimony to the panel solely on their memories. They had no notes, from conversations back as far as five years, to back up their testimony. They had been so sincere and optimistic in their solution-search efforts that preparing for a potential termination and legal challenge was apparently not considered.

For the University to pursue the case in court could not be justified. Odds of winning were low. Our attorney negotiated a settlement, more than $100,000 payment to the professor in return for his resignation and no further litigation.[9]

The reader might ask two questions: 1) Considering that ethics panels in Congress and professional societies find it so difficult to discipline members for egregious behavior, can a panel of tenured university faculty ever concur in terminating a colleague? Yes, such a panel can and will, if the case is solid and the involved administrators have followed those three rules. More than once, before an internal appeal panel or in court, dated and initialed conversation notes pulled from the files have given my administrative colleagues and me credibility, comfort, and a win. 2) Could there have been an early error, in granting tenure to this professor? I do not know enough about the professor's early functioning to make a judgment. Based on other cases I have encountered, I always advise, in regard to granting tenure, "If in doubt, don't!"

* * * * *

The next entry, on grades given by K-State faculty, is an interesting inside story. I recall no external publicity; such would not have been helpful to K-State. In fact, I had forgotten about it until I was reviewing data in one of those pocket notebooks I had carried during my presidency.

Inflation in the Grade Book

Fall, 1984

I had noted early in my presidency, as I reviewed historic academic data, that there had been a steady rise in average grades given to K-State students. This was especially surprising to me in that the average ACT (American College

Testing program) scores of K-State's entering freshmen had declined over a several-year period.

Though average ACT scores of K-State's new students had dropped from 22.4 in the fall of 1970 to 20.9 in the fall of 1975, the average grades reported for K-State freshmen had risen, from 2.33 (4.0=A) in the 1969-70 academic year to 2.63 in 1974-75. For all undergraduates, the grade average had risen from 2.54 to 2.80 in that time span.[10] The magnitude of change, 0.3 of a grade point for freshmen and more than 0.25 for all undergraduates was remarkable! It would have been remarkable even if the ACT scores of entering students had remained level!

Students know which are the "pud" courses, sources of an easy "A" and a boost to one's grade average. However, no department or university wants to be known as a "pud place."

I needed to find out and understand what was going on! Was this grading pattern just a K-State phenomenon? Was there some internal cause for the higher grading trend at K-State? Or, was the trend evident at other universities across the country? Could it simply be a reflection of the societal trend then evident, the increasingly prevalent attitude that no one should fail, that a low grade might forever ruin one's self-image.

Regardless, should the grade inflation trend be allowed to continue? If the trend should be reversed, how does one go about making that happen? Grading is a faculty prerogative!

At no time during my classroom years had I been told how to grade students, what grade average or range I should try to meet. There had been no university grading policy of which I had been aware. In my first semesters as an instructor at Oklahoma State, however, I had checked my grading range and average with colleagues who were teaching the same courses. I wanted to be in tune with the grading standards of my colleagues.

As an associate dean or dean, I had encountered a few cases of what seemed unduly harsh grading by some instructors, most often in a freshman or sophomore service course. When I would follow up with the department head, either outside or in my college, it was often a case of the instructor being a fresh Ph.D. wanting to impress both students and his colleagues with his or her "high standards." The Department head would generally remind the instructor that student achievement is a function of both student ability and the instructor's effectiveness, and that too many low grades, especially among able students, raises a question of teaching skill.

I had never been aware of any steady or unexplained rise (or lowering) in average grades in a total university, or even in a college or department.

I started asking questions, especially of Academic Vice President John Chalmers and several deans. Most expressed surprise at what the data showed and no one could provide a specific rationale. They emphasized to me that there had been no overt encouragement for instructors to lighten up their grading. I had also asked several individual faculty and department heads. They, too, were surprised. Some were not only surprised, they were downright concerned!

That concern gave me some comfort. No one at K-State wanted their university, college, or department to get the reputation of being a "pud" place! It suggested to me that the mere sharing of the data with faculty, department heads, and deans would trigger some self-correction in the grading trend. Over time, K-State's grade inflation would likely slow, stop, and perhaps reverse.

My comfort level was also enhanced when I learned that K-State was not alone in grade inflation. Pieces on the issue began to appear in the *Chronicle of Higher Education* and elsewhere; it was apparently a nation-wide trend. This gave credence to the thought that the easier grading behavior may be largely a reflection of a societal attitude that no one should fail. I became increasingly confident that exposing our data internally, plus the *Chronicle's* and other pieces that our faculty would be reading, would bring some self-correction at K-State.

K-State's average grades soon leveled off and modestly declined.[11] By the 1977-78 academic year, the average freshman grade had dropped 0.12, to 2.51. By 1982-83 it had lowered another 0.15 to 2.36, very near the 1969-70 level. For all undergraduates the decrease had been less; it was still 0.2 higher than for the 1969-70 level. Though there would be variation from year to year, grades appeared to have stabilized at about these levels.

Another important point: The decreases in K-State grade averages were more significant in that by the early 1980s the average ACT of entering freshmen *had moved back up*, from 20.9 in the fall of 1974 to 21.4 in the fall of 1984![12]

Presidents sometimes like to say they took bold and aggressive action to address an issue. I can not claim that in this case. In fact, to have invaded the grading prerogative of a thousand faculty would not have been especially prudent! Simply exposing the data—and faculty seeing the issue discussed in national media—did the job.

This self-correction in grading by our faculty also reinforced my long-held belief that when university faculty have the appropriate information, they will make good judgments. It also reinforced the value of an institutional research office and staff, the source of these data. I give credit to Institutional Research Director Don Hoyt and his colleagues for gathering and tabulating the data.

* * * * *

Space does not allow mentioning all the individual faculty whose extra efforts deserve recognition—chairs of the faculty senate, advisers to department and interest clubs or publications, team coaches, and, especially, the music, theatre, and dance faculty. Those latter faculty were always ready to perform, or prepare and lead student groups to perform, for campus events and visiting groups. All of these people were dedicated to their students, their respective roles, and doing their best for K-State. These people deserve much of the credit for the successes cited in the next chapter.

Chapter XI

Students and Surprises

My first thirteen years in university work, from instructor at Oklahoma State through associate dean at K-State, had focused largely on teaching and advising. In the intervening years, with responsibility for research and extension programs as well as for instruction, plus work with industry groups and legislators, I had had less opportunity to work with students. One practice had continued through those years, Shirley seeing to it that our home was available for student recognition events and often receptions for graduating seniors.

At K-State Shirley would have many interactions with students visiting our home as a class project. The Restaurant Management students once asked Shirley if there might be an event at our home where they could practice preparing and serving a meal, getting ready for national competition in their to-be profession. She was planning such a dinner for deans and spouses, so their need fit perfectly. Shirley and the home were also resources for visits by Interior and Landscape Architecture, Horticulture, and even Journalism students.

Shirley and I would enjoy many dinners at college or department student events, or with residence groups (residence halls, fraternities, or sororities). I would work directly with elected student leaders and sometimes join a table of students in the K-State Union or a residence hall dining room. We would have many chance encounters with students on campus (or at our front door). Otherwise, my attention would be *about* students, with deans, student affairs staff, faculty, or parents.

Shirley and me on our front steps being serenaded by the men of Pi Kappa Alpha Fraternity on our 34th wedding anniversary, March 23, 1986.

I offer here an example of the good judgment of K-State students—and the wisdom of Student Affairs Vice President Chet Peters in letting them make judgments.

It had been a total surprise when, at a regents meeting, one regent moved that the student union at one of our sister universities be allowed to sell beer. To my knowledge the issue had never been openly discussed. Within seconds, the motion was amended to include all campuses and approved. I called Peters to alert him. His response, "We should let the Student Union Board decide if they want to sell beer."

Beer was flowing in student unions on two other campuses by noon the next day, but our Union Board held back and decided to seek broad student input. In time the Union Board decided against selling beer. One member observed, "We may like beer, but Aggieville is the better place for beer sales."

K-State students were high energy, inquisitive, responsive, and, sometimes, challenging. So often, their skills and good judgment, individually or as a group, brought credit to the University! It was the unexpected, though, that often provided humor and spiced our life during our eleven years in the presidency.

* * * * *

Those who have taught high school students tell me that to stay ahead of both students' good and questionable behaviors, one has to make full use of both inductive and deductive reasoning, and consider all possibilities. A university dean of students or vice president for student affairs is well served by doing the same. Vice President Peters shared this case with me.

Early Morning Calls

A history professor came to Peters with a problem. Periodically he would get early morning calls, about 4 a.m. He would rouse from sleep, answer the phone, but get only a dial tone.

The calls persisted and the professor contacted Peters again. "This time," Peters told me, "A light came on." As a student, Peters had worked at the dairy barn, had to be up early for the morning milking. "Could it be?" he wondered.

He asked the professor to bring him lists of students from recent semesters. He then called Dairy Department Head Charlie Norton, and asked for a list of students who helped with the morning milking.

Bingo! A match!

Peters called in the student, asked him about his work at the dairy barn and what time he reported for the morning milking. He then went on to mention that Professor X had been receiving calls about 4 a.m. and that it was really rather bothersome. "Now, I don't know who would be making such calls to Professor X," Peters said, "but if they don't stop, I know a young man who has a problem."

The calls stopped.

* * * * *

It seemed that in my first year in the presidency I had spent a majority of my time introducing myself to student groups, alumni, and athletic booster clubs, letting them see and assess this new guy who had replaced the only K-State president many had known. I had had too little time to listen to these University clientele about things beyond athletics. I wanted to hear what they had to say about K-State's teaching, research, and extension education programs. One message I would hear was loud and clear.

Teaching in Their Second Language

Spring, 1977

Early in my second year in the presidency, I asked our Alumni Association to arrange some citizen forums across Kansas, where alumni, parents, and others interested in K-State could express to me any concerns they had and what they expected from the University. From the latter part of 1976 through November of 1977 I was in all corners of the state, Liberal, Garden City, McPherson, Pratt, Dodge City, Pratt, Hays, Kansas City, Wichita, and elsewhere, for two-hour sessions. Issues raised by participants ranged from extension and research programs to athletics, but the most common concern pertained to the difficulty their sons and daughters had in understanding some of the graduate teaching assistants (GTAs) from other countries.

I was not surprised the topic was raised. Universities with large research programs attract many foreign graduate students, students for whom English is not the first language. Most of these universities also have large enrollment and not enough senior faculty to handle the many sections of freshman and sophomore courses. I was surprised, though, at the intensity and consistency of the concern in the early forums.

Back on campus after my first series of forums, Academic Vice President John Chalmers, long pressed for teaching positions and having accepted foreign-born GTAs as a necessary given, had some trouble believing and accepting this concern. For some of the next forums, I took Chalmers and a dean with me.

Soon after the next series of forums we established a policy that every teaching assistant for whom English was not their first language would audition before a three-person committee, generally composed of a student, an assistant or associate dean, and a faculty member. The committee would have the authority to approve the GTA for teaching, prescribe corrective training and a second audition, or insist on reassignment. This would be fully implemented by the beginning of the 1977 fall semester.

A few department heads objected, "What if I committed to a teaching assistantship when the student applied for graduate study?" Our response, "You took a risk. Transfer the person to a research assistantship, and move one that can be understood from a research assistantship (GRA) to the GTA."

I would emphasize to all—forum participants, deans, department heads, and students—that we live in a global society; many graduates will work in other countries, or perhaps work in the U.S. under a person from another country. We all need to be attentive to the accent and cadence of those for whom English is the second or third language, and be willing to work at understanding. But some level of communication skill in English, our language of instruction and learning, had to be insured in K-State classrooms.

Over time, certain features were added in implementation of this policy. I find a 1982 memo that reinforced the policy.[1] Every new GTA with native language other than English was scheduled for a fifteen-minute presentation of the discipline they expected to teach. For each GTA's presentation, one faculty member from the discipline department would be a part of the judgment panel.

* * * * *

When one who enjoys teaching moves to a full-time administrative position, one feels a void. Though I would usually speak to several audiences every week, from alumni to legislative committees to a convention group meeting on campus, I truly missed the challenge of explaining a new subject or concept to students, and connecting it to their previous knowledge or experiences. I also believed that by teaching a class I could underline, as president, my regard for the teaching function. This is increasingly important as a major university builds its research program. I was therefore glad for another reason to get back to the classroom.

Back to the Classroom

Fall, 1977

As my third year in the presidency approached, my publisher gave me a reason to get back in the classroom. My textbook, Animal Science and Industry, needed up-dating, sections replaced with current data, industry practices, and scientific concepts. For earlier editions, it had been the drafting of lectures, choosing illustrations, and watching student reaction as concepts and data were presented that let me put together a book that had been well accepted on many campuses. I could do a better job on that third edition if I were teaching a section of the introductory course, for which the book was designed.

It would be a busy semester. Presidential demands would not necessarily change; I would just have to be cautious in scheduling off-campus travel. As an associate dean, I had established some guidance for instructors involved in off-campus research or extension duties, that they should have a teaching substitute no more than five per cent of the time in an undergraduate course or more than ten per cent in a graduate course. I was determined to abide by my own guidelines. Secondly, I had been advised early in my career that I should block out an hour prior to each lecture, avoid interruptions, and concentrate on both the lecture outline and supporting material. As president, that was not easy to do, but my secretary was most helpful in blocking my door and holding calls.

Completed during my time at Iowa State, the first edition of the book had come off the press during my first fall as associate dean at K-State and carried a 1963 copyright. During my deanship at South Dakota State I had revised and updated the book, adding several chapters.

Now spending less time with the industry, I felt the need to ask several animal science and veterinary faculty for help with certain chapters, suggesting what should be deleted, modified, or added. Their personal compensation would be only their names in the book's acknowledgment section and whatever credit might accrue to K-State by the accuracy and currency of material (and that the author shown on the title page was professor and president of Kansas State University). They were generous with their help. Textbook royalties do not make an author rich, but of what I received from that edition, most went to K-State's Meat Industry Foundation for the Department's use

Revising a text in a dynamic industry is not easy. We added five new chapters, including Nutrition of Horses and Ponies, and Animal Behavior, but consolidation of several chapter pairs let us hold the book's length to a net increase of one chapter. We made room for new sections on goats, embryo transplanting, price protection and the futures market, and tax considerations, and we doubled the glossary. It took two years, mostly week-ends and vacation time, to get the job done.

Teaching the course also helped my university-wide responsibilities. It sharpened my alertness to classroom acoustics, light and temperature control, and the unique needs of physically-limited students. A hearing impairment necessitated one of my students using a tape recorder so he could review the lectures and discussion.

* * * * *

As president I would have but two opportunities to convey my philosophy or advice to most K-State students, a welcome when they first came to campus and, on their departure, their commencement ceremony. From the students' perspective, these were the two opportunities for most to know, in person, who their president is and that person's thoughts. I include here my charge to the Class of 1979. It not only marked the end of my first four years in the presidency, the content is not unlike other of my commencement addresses. I wanted all to leave K-State with pride in their university and, therefore, pride in themselves for having graduated from such a respected institution.

Charge to the Class of 1979

May 19, 1979

At the close of spring semester, Veterinary Medicine and Graduate School degrees were awarded at Friday afternoon ceremonies in McCain Auditorium. Bachelor and honorary degrees were formally awarded and university-wide recognitions were given in a Saturday morning ceremony in the football stadium. Following that, at various campus locations, undergraduate colleges held ceremonies where each graduate could be individually introduced and receive their diploma from the college dean.

Following is my charge to those 1979 graduates, as presented at the Saturday morning ceremony.[2] I include it here for several reasons: 1) its condensed history of the land grant university concept, 2) former K-State President Joseph Denison's quote regarding women, 3) the citing of significant accomplishments by K-State students and faculty, and 4) the prominent mention of K-State and other land grant university alumni in both the business world and government leadership.

> "To each of you, I extend my personal congratulations and those of the entire University on the degree you will receive today. From here (the podium) you do, indeed, look wise— learned, prepared, and eager for the next challenge.
>
> This is your day, and I share it with you for a special reason. Four years ago, many of you and I entered Kansas State University together. I became president July 1, 1975, and near the end of August, many of you entered as freshmen. To all of you, we have come through all or part of the last four years together.
>
> Why is it we have both emerged wiser and more learned, but only I appear older and grayer?
>
> When you and I came to this university, we became part of an institution marked by a tradition of excellence and by a special caring for individuals. Kansas State University is a member of a most important family. It is a land grant institution, by definition dedicated to providing quality education, equally, to all.
>
> The land-grant institutions were born of the idealism of Lincoln's America, and it appeared to be an untimely birth. The nation was at war. There was no guarantee this revolutionary educational idea would work, and there was serious doubt that it would pay off economically. The Land-Grant Act of 1862 was an act of faith—in the future of the nation and in the future of its young people.
>
> President Lincoln signed a bill that would profoundly influence the lives of millions. The action represented an affirmative revolution. It called for a university supported by society, open to all regardless of economic status.
>
> From the beginning, the land-grant movement took leadership in broadening the scope of American higher education. These land-grant schools were co-educational. K-State President Joseph Denison was approached by a few persons within this state who objected to the admission of women, but he quickly pointed out, "By what right

would they be excluded? The federal endowment was not given to a particular portion of our citizens."

Frederick Jackson Turner, author of the brilliant analysis, "The Significance of the Frontier in American History," said the rise of the land-grant university replaced the disappearing frontier as the path to opportunity, as guarantor against a closed hierarchical society based on inherited wealth and social position.

Today, the land-grant universities are among this nation's most revered institutions of higher learning. And, the sons and daughters of the working classes, those for whom the legislation was designed, have marked this nation with their brilliance and their intellectual and pragmatic productivity.

In this winter's edition of Encounter, Harvard sociologist David Riesman surmised "that in the Fortune Magazine list of 500 major American corporations, there are more top executives who are graduates of Purdue or Texas A&M and other land-grant universities than there are of Ivy League institutions."

Prompted by his statement, the National Association of State Universities and Land-Grant Colleges decided to see if he was right. Indeed he was. The president of Standard Oil is a graduate of Texas A&M. The President of Bethlehem Steel was graduated from Cornell University. The chairman and president of Monsanto is an alumnus of Penn State. The chairman of the Board of Boeing was graduated from Iowa State University, the president of Minnesota Mining and Manufacturing from the University of Nebraska, the chairman of the Board of Knight-Ridder Newspapers from the University of Missouri and the president of Wells Fargo and Company from Rutgers. All these executive officers were graduated from land-grant universities. The survey showed that more than half of the presidents and chairmen of the Boards of these top five hundred corporations were graduated from land-grant universities.

Twenty current state governors attended land-grant universities. Thirty per cent of the representatives in Congress and 40 per cent of the U.S. senators attended land-grant universities.

This year thirty-two Rhodes scholarships were awarded to America's outstanding students. On the list were students from K-State, Iowa State University, the University of Arizona and Cornell—all land-grant schools.

When the John Simon Guggenheim Memorial Foundation announced the awarding of its prestigious fellowships this year, 129 scholars, scientists, artists from this country's state and land-grant universities were named as recipients. The list was headed by land-grant schools. The University of California had nine awards and Cornell University had eight.

Yes, Kansas State University is a member of a most important family. And we are a member in good standing. A member of this class, Ann Jorns, is a Rhodes Scholar. K-Staters are regular winners of Fulbright scholarships. Two of our students are now in Europe studying under this program. A member of this class is a Phi Kappa Phi fellow, one of only thirty-two college graduates in the U.S. to be selected this year for this honor. This is the fourth year in a row a K-Stater has received a Phi Kappa Phi fellowship.

During this past year, alone, K-State faculty have won dozens of important national awards. An Alexander von Humboldt Foundation fellowship, one of the most prestigious awards available to young scientists was awarded to one of our professors in the Chemistry Department. A KSU assistant professor in physics was awarded an Alfred P. Sloan Fellowship on the basis of his potential to make creative contributions to scientific knowledge. He is the third K-State faculty member to receive this fellowship since its introduction in 1955. The list of special awards and recognition to our faculty members is long.

Today you will graduate from this fine university. Its students, its faculty, its alumni, and its programs are among the best in the nation. You should have great pride in the degree you are about to receive and know that today you will join a prestigious group of K-State alumni.

K-Staters now serve as the director of the National Zoological Park in Washington, D.C., minority leader in the U.S. House of Representatives, Senior Vice President of Phillips Petroleum, and president of Occidental of California, both of these companies among the Fortune Magazine top 500. One Alumnus with us today, Mr. M.D. "Pete" McVay is president of Cargill, the world's largest wheat exporter. K-Staters are governor of this state, speaker of the Kansas House of Representatives, president of the Kansas Senate, and chief justice of the Kansas Supreme Court.

Today, you will take from Kansas State University the mark of excellence. But, it is also my belief that during the past four years, we—you and I—have given to the stature of this institution. I have listed for you a few of the honors of your classmates. But I cannot list all of your achievements or all the ways you have strengthened this university as student leaders, as student spokespersons on University committees, or as student journalists who consistently monitored this university's progress. I think today we deserve an opportunity to talk about our contributions.

During these four years, many new programs have been initiated, including an M.F.A. in art, which represents a significant step forward for the University in program breadth. During these four years, K-State became part of the National Merit Scholarship Program.

During these four years, a student and alumni legislative network helped achieve increased appropriations. Three new campus buildings are under construction—a classroom-office building for the College of Education and the Department of Psychology, a Plant Science building and a recreation complex. The latter is student-financed, and students voted a fee increase to help finance a new sports arena.

During these four years, the excellence of the KSU faculty has shown brightly. The level of federal, foundation, and private grants received doubled from $8.8 million in fiscal 1975 to $17 million in fiscal 1979. These grants go to the productive scholars and respected universities, and these years were a time of financial constraint in most granting agencies. About 9,000 acres of range land for ecological research (the Konza Prairie) was made available to the University by a private foundation.

During these four years, intercollegiate athletics was strengthened. Net worth became positive, management controls were implemented, and the audit this spring indicated proper recruiting and scholarship awarding procedures were being followed. Win-loss records in major sports sharply improved. This year, we did not have to wait until commencement to see K-Staters in the end zone.

During these four years, the confidence of the private investor in Kansas State University has increased. Gifts received by the Foundation increased from $1.7 million in 1975, when we entered KSU, to $3.4 million in 1978. During these four years we have worked together to improve the campus appearance. We have done well.

As we now prepare to part, I have for you a charge and a promise. My charge to you is that you exhibit your pride in this institution. Kansas State University is an important member of what has become this nation's most productive and prestigious family of universities—the land-grant universities.

It is my observation that persons who come to land-grant schools are by nature cautious and deliberate. They are not careless in their enthusiasm or flamboyant. They make their judgments based on facts. Today I have given you the facts.

No institution in any state has greater impact on that state—its economy or the quality of life of its citizens—than the land-grant university. In Kansas, that is Kansas State University. By every measure K-State is a number one institution. Let's not keep that a secret!

Land-grant people tend to be modest. As K-Staters we have been far too modest. As you now begin your contributions to this state, this nation and/or society, I urge you to be proud of your accomplishments, the accomplishments of this university and your affiliation with Kansas State University. I charge you to spread widely the name of your alma mater. Say it loudly and speak out boldly on its behalf.

I charge you to let everyone around you know about K-State, its excellence, its accomplishments, and its promising future. I charge you to continue your support in will and in spirit. From this graduation day forward, let me hear the proud voice of the class of 1979 in support of its alma mater.

In response, I promise you I will continue diligent work to advance this institution's excellence. We will keep a strong faculty. We will strengthen academic advising to assure full utilization of our quality education, and we will further improve the physical environment of this campus so when you come back, this university's excellence will be fully reflected by clean, green lawn, well landscaped grounds, and well-kept buildings.

Please return to Kansas State University. Return bearing the scars of your battles and the banners of your victories. Your alma mater will be proud of both. Turn always to Kansas State University for encouragement and refreshment. How happy your alma mater will be to pour them out in abundance upon you."

* * * * *

The postal carrier to our campus home most of our early years was Melvin Dale, a mid-1960s neighbor with whom we had worked to prevent a 7-11 type retail shop in our residential neighborhood, at the corner of Browning and Kimball. Following Melvin was Jim Lundberg, whose wife, Lynne, I would bring from the Arts and Sciences dean's office to be my secretary in 1982. Both Melvin and Jim brought us some surprises.

What the Mailman Brings

"Did you order some sauce pans?" Shirley asked as I stepped in the door for an unusual lunch at home. A set had arrived C.O.D. and, knowing that I would not even know what sauce pans were for, she had refused to sign. The supplier had been duped, no doubt, by some K-State student.

More than once I received enlistment materials from the U.S. Marine Corps or the U.S. Army. I also refused to sign! And, we received three-month trial subscriptions to Esquire and Playboy.

* * * * *

Beyond the mailbox, Shirley and I were daily reminded of student creativity and enthusiasm. She would greet and be greeted by students as she walked Tena, our small black Dachshund, or crossed the campus to and from her thrice weekly lap swims at the Natatorium. In the fall she would hear the marching band on their practice field, just east of our home, and would often step down to watch. Other than at student events and meetings, most of my encounters were in the halls of Anderson, this one when I stepped out for a drink at the water cooler.

At the Water Cooler

The best place to find out what is really going on in an organization is usually at the water cooler or in the coffee room. While leaning over the water cooler down the hall from my office I caught fragments of a conversation between two young women seated on an adjacent bench. They were oblivious to my presence, but seemed distressed.

Perhaps there was a problem I should know about. In a large university, some problems do not get communicated to the right person, and so are not addressed. I listened, remaining bent over the fountain.

I had not caught the topic, but it appeared their complaints had not brought change and they were frustrated. Soon, one blurted out in bravado, "I think I'll just go down and see Duane about that!"

By then I recognized the voice, that of a young woman I knew—and I had met her parents. I could not resist! I raised my head and turned toward the two, "Is there something I can take care of for you?"

After the I-wish-there-were-a-hole-in-the-floor expression, the three of us had a good visit. The issue was not a big one, just a minor problem that impatience and idealism of youth thought should not exist.

Several months later this young woman stopped me in the K-State Union. She had had a good story to tell her parents and she shared with me her dad's response, "I told you that mouth of yours would get you in trouble!"

* * * * *

Now to a serious and high-priority topic, academic advising. The following is lifted from my presentation to deans, vice presidents, and presidents at a National Conference on Higher Education, Washington, D.C. I include it here because it summarizes a philosophy I carried into the presidency and which I would share at every opportunity with K-State deans, department heads, and faculty.

Academic Advising: Nine Steps[3]

March 6, 1980

"When a university admits a student, it assumes the responsibility to permit the student to succeed, within the standards of that university. Academic success cannot be guaranteed, but the mechanics of the University, the effectiveness of instruction, and the advice and counsel given the student should help cause the student, when he or she leaves the University, with or without a degree, to feel the experience has been successful.

Effective academic advising requires that the institution give attention to several steps:

1. Summarize the relative academic success of current students. For example, calculate the percentage of your students whose grades warrant academic honors, who may be on probation, or who may be dismissed at the end of the term. Compare percentages with comparable universities or units within your university, or with the situation five years ago. Perhaps more important, classify each student according to the chances for success you would have assessed at the student's entry. Compare that assessment with his or her current status.
2. Set goals for academic success—persistence and graduation—of your students. Base these goals on the requirements for graduation and the measured academic talent (test scores or high school grade average) of entering students. Recognizing that some may transfer to other curriculums, perhaps the goals should be stated as pertaining to those who stay in the curriculum.
3. Establish the academic advisers' responsibilities. I suggest a brainstorming session within each college, involving advisers, department heads, and perhaps personnel from the dean's office. Here is a list of advisers' responsibilities that emerged from such a session at Kansas State:

   a. Know the advisee—high school courses, grades, ACT or SAT scores; career objectives, interests, motivation, and fears; some non-academic background knowledge, such as family support, hobbies, university residence.
   b. Let the advisee know the adviser—as an adviser, professional faculty member and one interested in the advisee.
   c. Know the University rules, procedures and policies which affect the academic program.
   d. Be familiar with courses normally taken by advisees, some of those courses' instructors and their relative effectiveness.
   e. Find the key that motivates the advisee.
   f. Exercise real judgment in guiding the student, based on knowledge of that student and previous advising successes and experiences.
   g. Be available, at scheduled times, by pre-arranged appointment, and/or by phone.

4. Establish the (college or department) administration's responsibilities. The brainstorming session mentioned above brought out these:
   a. Choose the right people as advisers, those who can be effective.
   b. Provide time and workload credit for the advising responsibility.
   c. Provide information to advisers—each advisee's academic and other information available anywhere in the University, plus university rules, policies and procedures.
   d. Provide clerical help for appointments, filing, etc.
   e. Help develop advising philosophies and provide assistance with problem cases.
   f. Keep roadblocks to good advising out of the way, such as unnecessary limits on credit load, proliferation of course prerequisites, or rules that prevent a student transferring to another adviser or curriculum.
   g. Commend and reward good advising.
   h. Insure that incoming students understand the role and responsibilities of their adviser.
5. Budget time and dollars for the academic advising (item 4b above). This is perhaps the most critical step; it sets the stage for all others. For the function to be well performed, all administrators

and faculty, especially the advisers, need to fully understand that the University considers academic advising to be important enough to be identified as a budget item.

6. Train the adviser. An adviser needs to know a bit about psychology and motivation, what ACT or SAT score mean and how to interpret a high school transcript—and how they relate to course selection, especially the first semesters.
7. Monitor the effectiveness of advising. Because the Department head makes initial recommendations for salary increases or promotions, he or she has the first responsibility, but might be aided in that by a college assistant or associate dean who monitors students' credit loads, grades, persistence, etc.
8. Transfer the complete student file when a student transfers to a different adviser, department or college. The new adviser needs the total story.
9. Recognize and reward good advising. Though mentioned above as Item 4g, it is critical that this be college and university policy, expected, and supported by the University administration.

Effective advising is a key to academic success of students and can also help maintain higher enrollment and lower cost per student. Academic advising is an important university function, to be budgeted for, trained for, monitored, and rewarded."

The reader may ask, "Did K-State do all these things during your time in the presidency?" I believe we came close, but I cannot claim all colleges did all these things. When I became president, each college had its own way of assigning and supporting staff for the advising function. Most students in the College of Agriculture chose a major on entry and were assigned an adviser in that major department. Advisers were all of faculty status, instructor or above, and their tenths of time for advising showed in the printed budget. It was a rather formal system, led by Dean Carroll Hess, Frank Carpenter, and David Mugler.

The Colleges of Business and Arts and Sciences had one or more staff in the dean's office that served as adviser to many of their students, especially those who had not yet chosen a major within the College. Some advisers were full time in that function; others taught courses in their discipline. For those who had chosen a major, departments varied in their system of advising.

I did not insist that there be a single system imposed on all colleges. I chose simply to emphasize the value of advising, that I expected it to be effective, and spoke to the points above at any appropriate opportunity. I believe the bully pulpit has some value and impact within a university. I also believe that, with perhaps extremely rare exception, we had high dedication to student success in every college. I also believe that such dedication—and the time individual faculty spend encouraging, advising, and challenging the individual student—is more important than the specific system.

* * * * *

It seems appropriate that the first recorded anecdote of an academic year would involve the football team. However, in this case it was late night and far from the gridiron.

The Football Team is Stealing our Rock

Fall, 1980

It was after 11:30 on a Saturday night when the sharp ring roused me from that deepest of early sleep. The caller sounded almost in panic, "Mr. President, the football team is trying to steal our rock!"

"What?" I was hardly awake and the words did not make sense.

The caller explained. He was president of the SAE (Sigma Alpha Epsilon) fraternity. A stone, perhaps three feet across and near the street, marked their driveway. I now understood; I remembered the stone.

"They came by last night and tried to steal it and we drove them off. Tonight they are trying again!"

"How do you know it is the football team?"

"I recognize some of the players," and he named a couple.

"Why didn't you call Coach Dickey?"

"I couldn't find his phone number."

I was now fully awake and knew exactly what to do. I gave him Head Coach Jim Dickey's phone number and went back to bed.

* * * * *

Our K-State faculty were well supported by professionals in our student counseling center, student health center, and international student advisers, but we sometimes encountered student problems that we just could not solve. Following is one of those problems.

No Homeland

May, 1982

A few days after Shirley had been at a reception for spouses of international students, she received a call from one of the young women with whom she had visited. She thanked Shirley for her interest during their visit, said she had a problem, and wondered if Shirley would have time to talk. She mentioned she and her husband lived in Jardine Terrace, married student housing. Always empathetic, especially to young student wives distant from their home countries, Shirley told the young woman she would be taking our dog to the veterinary clinic that afternoon and would just stop by her apartment.

After the call, Shirley had second thoughts, "What could be the problem; should I get involved?" She called Gwyn Johnson, wife of my assistant, who had been with Shirley at the reception. Gwyn might have a clue to the woman's problem. Gwyn's response, "No, but Mike had mentioned this woman's husband had a problem and just might be irrational."

Shirley then called my office for Mike (I was out of town) and he was quick to advise, "Don't go to Jardine. In fact, be cautious en route to the veterinary clinic and when you get home, lock the doors." My secretary would call the young woman and tell her Shirley had encountered a conflict.

The young man's problem? He and his wife had come from the Near East to K-State for him to earn a doctorate in microbiology and then return home. But, he had become a perpetual student. Perpetual students are not unknown in universities; a few young people just do not want to leave the comfort of academe and face the world of work. But this was a special case.

He had started Ph.D. programs at K-State in three successive disciplines! In each case, as he was about to complete his thesis research, his data would somehow get destroyed or lost. Or, he would lose confidence in the research and claim it was invalid. I had learned of the problem only when he was well along in his third effort, in Veterinary Physiology under Dr. Stanley Dennis.

The student was able and a good research worker. Considerable money had been invested in his research assistantship (half-time salary) plus research supplies. Dennis felt the research was valid, could be incorporated into a quality thesis, as well as papers for refereed journals, and the degree wrapped up. However, the young man had refused to write up his research data. Dennis had become exasperated.

In time, the apparent root of his problem had come out. He said he could not return to his homeland, the Gaza Strip. Ethnic conflict had made return there far too dangerous for him and his wife.

Dennis, having served several years at Ahmadu Bello University in Nigeria, had obvious empathy for the student's plight. He had consulted for solutions with Associate Graduate Dean John Noonan, international student advisers, and others, but the eventual conclusion, in the fall of 1981, was that Dennis had to terminate the assistantship and drop the student from the graduate program. The student would then lose the privilege of residing in Jardine, lose his student visa, and need to depart the U.S.

The young man subsequently applied for readmission to the graduate program. That application was considered and denied, but this month, May of 1982, he made repeated visits to Dr. Dennis' office pressing for readmission. In time, he became irrational and threatened violence to Dennis and two of Dennis' Pathology Department colleagues. To Dennis, "I will destroy you before leaving the University. I will destroy Dr. (Horst) Leipold and I will destroy Dr. (Sam) Krukenberg." To Dr. Leipold directly, on more than one occasion, "I am going to get you."[4]

The campus police had been called, the Riley County attorney investigated and chose not to prosecute, but an assistant Attorney General charged the young man with "communicating a terrorist threat." He was convicted, and that conviction, on appeal, was upheld by the Kansas Supreme Court.

I have always held that for every problem there is a solution, and Dr. Dennis and others did all they could to solve this one. However, in dealing with students of many political and ethnic circumstances, there are times that the University has to leave the solution to others. This was such a case. In response to a credible threat of physical violence, it had to be the legal system. And, after the conviction, without a passport and his student visa expired, the young man and his wife would face deportation.

* * * * *

One of Murphy's Laws as applied to state universities is that a student who runs afoul of a university policy or deadline is likely the son or daughter of a legislator, regent, or highly influential alum. Here is one of several such cases.

Murphy's Laws

August, 1981

Our K-State residence halls were exceedingly well managed, under the leadership of Director Tom Frith. Staff were well trained and motivated, facilities were high quality, food was good, and management kept the System's finances in the black.

Each spring most hall residents would sign contracts for the following year and there was a firm August 15 cancellation deadline. If a student cancelled before that date there was no penalty. If after that date and there was a waiting list of students who could use the room, the penalty was $100.

This year eighteen upper class women who held residence hall contracts went out for fall sorority rush; all received invitation bids and chose to pledge, intending to move into their sorority houses. Sixteen had cancelled their residence hall contracts before August 15; two had not. Of whom were these two the daughters? They were a member of our alumni board and next door neighbor of our regent chair.

For a day or so, the two girls were in panic, worried about lack of a waiting list, and our office received a couple calls. Fortunately, there was a waiting list and the families could handle the $100.

* * * * *

Another law, not the Murphy type, is that every year there emerge some outstanding students who can and do compete with the best. Also, there are always one or more faculty who take on the task of encouraging and preparing such students for that competition. Among universities, in Rhodes Scholar competition, K-State competes with the best.

Kansas State, Harvard, and Yale

K-State's first selected Rhodes scholars were well before my time, one each in the 1920s and 1930s. In a five-year period, 1974-79, K-State had three Rhodes scholars, Roger Sorrell of Garden City, Elaine Hefty of Valley Falls, and Ann Jorns of Manhattan. Only thirty-two were chosen each year and for those years, K-State's record matched those of Harvard and Yale.[5] Another K-Stater, Virgil Wiebe, also of Garden City, was chosen in 1986. Credit goes not only to those selected students but, especially, to Arts and Sciences student adviser Nancy Twiss, who prepared them well for their interviews. I also credit her dean, Bill Stamey, his predecessor, John Chalmers, and other faculty who encouraged and helped prepare our applicants. I took much pleasure in mentioning that Harvard and Yale comparison fact to alumni audiences.

K-State students did well in competition for other prestigious and high-dollar scholarships awarded in national competition. In 1984, a K-State student, Dan Robinson of Winfield, was one of 30 Marshall Scholars; he received financing for two or three years of study in Great Britain. There was also the Truman scholarship program, established in the late 1970s and covering four years of education (about sixty scholars named each year), and the Phi Kappa Phi graduate fellowships (also about sixty each year). The reader may know some of these recipients, named during my time at K-State.

Truman Scholars	Phi Kappa Phi Fellows
Kent Bradley, Lawrence	David Niemann, Newton
Lori Shellenberger, Ransom	Gregory Case, Salina
Patty Hipsher, Wichita	Marc Brack, Hoisington

Cindy Leighton, Overland Park	Janette Roth, Wamego
Brad Russell, Topeka	William Buck, Jr., Maryville
Tracy Turner, Great Bend	Cheryl Sales, Valley Falls
David Carlin, Smolan	Dwight Jury, Clifton
Mike Gibson, Portsmouth,NH	Hussein Khalil, Manhattan
Peggy Grosh, Manhattan	Patrick McFadden, Laramie, WY
	Mark Spurrier, Topeka

These winning students came to their competition from diverse K-State curriculums. No college of the University had a corner on academic excellence. And, these students had come to K-State from high schools large and small. At this writing, the lists of K-State national scholarship recipients continue to lengthen, and I applaud that fact.

Another way to assess the academic ability of K-State students, in this case academic competitiveness, is how those who take their pre-professional work at K-State do in seeking admission to certain professional schools, in comparison to national averages. In the 1984-85 academic year 95 per cent of K-State applicants to law schools were admitted vs. a national average below 80 percent. For medical schools, it was 74 per cent vs. a national average of 46 per cent. It is of interest that not all of K-State's medical school applicants had majored in pre-med. Two earned degrees in music and one each in anthropology and modern language.

Every 1985 K-State Veterinary graduate passed the federal accreditation exam. That was the case for only one other of the approximately 20 U.S. veterinary colleges—and the K-State students had the highest average scores. That year K-State was the only university in the country that had two accounting students among the top 100 in the national CPA examination.

Each year the National Geographic Society selected six to eight students from across America to serve an internship. For three consecutive years, 1983, 1984, and 1985, a K-State student was chosen. Over a fifteen-year period ending in 1985, our students had won ten of thirty-two scholarship recognition awards given by the international geography honorary, Gamma Theta Upsilon.

The American Society of Engineering Education, which sponsors Washington internships, chose a K-Stater to be one of fourteen in 1985. Of six students recognized by the American Society of Landscape Architects for their achievements that year, three were from our campus.

Had there been an upward trend in scholastic stature or achievement at K-State during our time in the presidency? That would be difficult to document but, if so, most of the credit should go to those who made faculty hiring and promotion decisions in earlier years. We do know that there was some upward trend in average ACT scores of admitted students. We also know that, with our joining the National Merit Scholarship program and the Foundation raising funds for such, the numbers of National Merit semifinalists at K-State had increased from seven in 1977 to fifty-two by the fall of 1985.[6] We would expect some of these to be among Rhodes, Marshall, or Truman scholarship recipients in future years.

* * * * *

Though my friends who have spent a broiling summer in basic training at Ft. Riley might disagree, Shirley and I would say that, among the states where we have lived, Kansas' climate was the best. One reason is that heavy snow is rare. This date we had that rare event, and a creative student took advantage.

Classes Cancelled?

Tuesday, February 1, 1983

A heavy snow had continued all day through central and eastern Kansas. It had begun long before daybreak. On such days it was not uncommon to receive a call at home about 7 a.m., "Will there be classes today?" The answer from Shirley or me was always "Yes," and that might bring a second question, "Have you been outside to see how much snow there is—or how cold it is?"

On snow days I would try to be in my office well before 7:30 classes began. If my office was dark when students trudged through Anderson Hall at 7:20, a note might be left under my door, "Dear Mr. President: If we have to be out on a day like this, you should be, too!" and signed, "A lowly student."

This morning I was at my desk at 7:15, the office lights on. A call came from the head resident at one of our residence halls, "We just received a call from someone claiming to be in the President's office and who said classes are cancelled for the day. I just thought I'd check." I assured her it was not true and commended her for checking.

I quickly called the local radio station, KMAN, assuming they had also received a hoax call—or soon would. Manager Lowell Jack knew such information would come from our director of information, but I did not want to risk a reporter on early duty being duped.

By 11o'clock the storm had intensified. I became concerned that roads to outlying communities, where many of our faculty and students lived, would be treacherous, even blocked in some cases, and called a meeting of key staff to assess the situation. We quickly made three decisions, 1) continue classes through the day, 2) cancel night classes, those beginning at or after 5:30, both on campus and at off-campus locations in north central Kansas, and 3) authorize department and unit heads to release staff early, where warranted, so they could get home before roads were blocked.

Communications Director Charlie Hein would put out a release to KMAN, KSAC (the University station, which shared a frequency with WIBW, Topeka, and would come on the air at 12:30) and KSDB, the 50-watt student operated station, as well as other outlets. The release would include that Wednesday classes would be in session. Weather reports had indicated the storm would subside by evening. Roads and campus walks would be cleared by morning.

With night events cancelled, Shirley and I would have a free evening. However, she had some business to discuss with a fellow hospital board member, Accountant Roger Sink, so we arranged to meet Roger and his wife, Connie, for dinner at the Ramada Inn, just across the street from the campus.

The storm was over by the time we had finished dinner and the walk home was one to remember. A bright moon outlined the barren trees and shimmered on the fresh snow.

We opened our front door about eight, hoping to catch the last half of K-State men's basketball game at Oklahoma State. Our phone was ringing.

"I just heard that classes are closed for tomorrow. Is that true?

"No," I said, "Classes will be in session." Click

The phone rang again. "I just heard on the radio that K-State classes will be closed tomorrow. Is that true?"

"No, classes will be held." The phone clicked before I could ask what radio station he was listening to. We had not even gotten to our radio to tune in the game!

Another call, "Are there classes tomorrow?" This time I inserted a question, "Why do you ask?"

"I was listening to the ballgame," she said, "and the announcer interrupted to say they had just been informed classes would be closed, the K-State Union and the library would be closed, and there would be no food service in the residence halls."

"What station?" I demanded.

"I don't know," she said.

I dropped the receiver and grabbed the phone book. There were two chances, KMAN and KSDB, and I guessed KSDB, the student station. KSAC went off the air at 5:30. By contract, WIBW originated the play-by-play for all stations; a local announcer came on during time-outs with commercials and announcements.

Before I could complete dialing the seven-digit KSDB number, I had to handle several more incoming calls. When I finally got KSDB on the line I identified myself and asked for the announcer. "This is President Acker. Did you recently announce on KSDB that classes will be closed tomorrow?"

A reticent, "Yes."

"What was your source of information?" My voice no doubt conveyed some irritation.

"Oh, no! Did I get duped?" He followed up, "A fellow named David called and said he was calling for the K-State Union, that classes were cancelled for tomorrow, the library would be closed, and there would be no food service in the residence halls."

"Yes, you've been duped! Any announcement of that type would come only from me through our director of communications!" I may well have added "You should know that!" My next words were more command than a question, "Would you get back on the air and inform your listeners?"

A very embarrassed apology followed and while I was dialing KMAN—just to be sure they were not also a victim—Shirley, listening to KSDB, heard the young announcer say, "Your announcer has made a very dumb, sophomoric mistake and I've just gotten the word from a very unhappy president. There will be classes tomorrow, the K-State Union and library will be open …"

I was able to catch only the last few minutes of an agonizing defeat by the Oklahoma State Cowboys.

P.S. Eight years later, as administrator of USDA's Foreign Agricultural Service, I attended a Washington dinner hosted by a visiting Kansas Farm Bureau group and also attended by most of Kansas' Congressional delegation. An aide to then Congressman Pat Roberts asked me if I recalled the evening that a KSDB announcer had erroneously told listeners that classes would be closed the next day. He had been that student announcer.

* * * * *

Any faculty member is complimented when a couple students ask if they can take your photo. But from these K-State coeds I would learn there was another reason.

Out of Film

I answered the doorbell on a Saturday afternoon to two young women students with a camera. "Would you be willing to have your picture taken?" one asked.

"I would be honored," I said, and led them through to the back of the house for a good setting—green grass and flowering shrubs, with the white deck railing against the limestone house as background. I posed with one and then the other as their partner snapped the photo.

Just then Moki Palacio who, with his wife, June, was helping Shirley get ready for a group scheduled for our back yard, came around the corner of the house. I suggested to the young woman holding the camera that she hand it to Moki; he could take a picture of the three of us.

"Oh, no," she said, "We're out of film." Then she added one of those uninhibited truths that might come from a K-State coed, "That is why we came by. We've been taking photos of the campus and had just two shots left. We needed to finish the film so we could get it developed yet this afternoon."

* * * * *

Student groups representing K-State are generally on their best behavior and build respect for the University. However, from time to time there are mishaps. I would never learn if this problem was caused by K-State students, or if it was just that the K-State President's home was closer than those of my counterparts at Wichita State and KU. Regardless, my visitor unloaded his frustration.

Residue from the Canoe Race
September 24, 1984

Our doorbell rang just before nine this beautiful Sunday morning and I opened the door to greet a man, perhaps in his late thirties, with controlled but seething anger and carrying a large paper sack. He introduced himself, completely—name, rural route and box number, Maple Hill.[7]

Not about to invite him in but also not worried about physical harm from one who had so completely identified himself, I stepped out to hear whatever it was he had to say. Listening usually helps.

My visitor handed me a county map, his land adjacent to the Kansas River marked, and told me, through rather clenched teeth, that the University canoe race teams (KSU-WSU-KU) use his picnic area as a change point. "They were welcome to use it this year and they will be next, but," as he thrust out the sack, "I don't want any residue left!"

Before I could respond or react, he dumped the contents—banana peels, beer and pop cans, and even a pair of shorts—on the porch floor, folded the bag, got in his pick-up, and drove away.

I thought of my former SDSU president, Hilton Briggs, who was asked in a state fair barn (Briggs had several show horses at the fair), how a university president feels having to fork up horse manure. He responded, "At least out here in the barn I can call some of the stuff I'm obliged to handle by its real name."

I picked up the garbage and carried it to the cans behind our garage.

* * * * *

At this writing, 2010, few professions discourage entry by either sex. Not so in the 1950s and 1960s. It was during my years in university administration that much of this change occurred. Enrollment changes in Engineering and other sex-identified disciplines at K-State illustrate what was going on across the country.

Freedom to Choose

Fall, 1984

Much change had occurred in engineering enrollment since I had spoken in April of 1978 to the K-State student chapter of the American Society of Women Engineers. My pocket calendar for that year supplemented my memory. After a 6:15 dinner with another group, I had walked over to Room 254K of Seaton Hall to meet with our to-be women engineers.

The national organization had been founded in 1950, but student chapters on major university campuses had only recently been established. I considered this organization and the K-State chapter to be evidence of society's progress toward what I might call true freedom, the freedom of young men and women to choose their profession without regard or, at least, less regard to any stifling tradition.

The yearbook for my graduation year, 1952, at a comparable university, Iowa State, shows but one woman among the 322 Engineering graduates. Among the 310 Agriculture graduates pictured there were four women; there were no women among the 63 who had received the Doctor of Veterinary Medicine degree.

How about men among Home Economics graduates? Among the 238 photos, there was not a single male.

I consider it fortunate to have been involved during the time that traditional gender bonds were being broken in such professions as engineering, veterinary medicine, chemistry, restaurant management, architecture, fashion merchandising, and accounting. The data below illustrate both the change and the relative speed of change, more rapid by women than by men.

Undergraduates, by gender, in selected K-State colleges.[8]

College	Fall, 1975		Fall, 1984	
	Men	Women	Men	Women
Architecture & Design	919	146	621	173
Engineering	1,377	103	2,332	301
Veterinary Medicine	336	51	268	146
Human Ecology	48	1,388	68	924

While total enrollment in the College of Engineering had increased about 78 per cent, from 1,480 to 2,633, in the nine-year time span, the number of women enrollees had almost tripled. And, while the enrollment limit in Veterinary Medicine had been increased seven per cent (from 387 to 414), the number of women in that program had also nearly tripled!

Data for some individual curriculums would tell a more vivid and revealing story of the changes underway. In the fall of 1963 at K-State, my second year as associate dean of agriculture, only 2.5 per cent of the undergraduates in that college were women. I do not have curriculum data for those years, but my recollection is that those few were largely in Horticulture and Animal Science. Ornamentals and horses seemed to have attracted the young women. By the late 1970s, there were women enrollees in almost every agriculture curriculum.

A component phenomenon was pointed out to me by Engineering Dean Don Rathbone. In the mid 1970s virtually all the freshmen women in his college were in the top 10 per cent (above the 90th percentile) of their high school graduating classes. Each had scored especially high in mathematics and the physical sciences. By the early 1980s, however, the high school grade point average and SAT mathematics profile of women enrollees in Engineering were more comparable to those of the freshmen men. More were from the 80th and 70th percentiles. Young women from a wider spectrum were choosing engineering.

Another phenomenon became evident as I watched scholarship recognition and student leadership at the 1982, 1983, and 1984 Engineering banquets, always a Saturday night in March. Relative to the enrollment ratio, more women than men were among the top ranks!

What motivates a young man or young woman to choose a career and curriculum different from tradition? Increasingly since the 1970s, motivations have been the same for men and women, a mix of their awareness, exposure, encouragement, and skills.

While seated beside a young man at the head table, the annual Restaurant Management club banquet (College of Human Ecology, formerly Home Economics), Shirley asked what had prompted him to choose that major.

His response was a story of early exposure, "We happened to live right next to the American Legion Club, a popular eating place in Larned. From the time I was about ten, I hung around the back door and told the chef I wanted a job. He told me I wasn't big enough. I kept pestering and he kept telling me I wasn't big enough. One night I asked how big I needed to be."

He shot back, "When you are big enough to reach the sink!"

"I got a box, pushed it up to the sink, and started washing dishes." He had chosen his career— and college curriculum.

One might ask if there were many models among the faculty, women faculty in engineering, agriculture, or veterinary medicine, or men faculty in home economics. I do not have the numbers, but I do have faculty percentages for the fall of 1982: 1.78 per cent women faculty in Agriculture, 8.57 per cent in Veterinary Medicine, and 3.02 per cent in Engineering. In Home Economics (Human Ecology) 25 per cent of the faculty were men.[9]

In more recent years, as I read publications from land grant universities with which I have been associated, I note with interest and pleasure the continuation of these trends. In fact, among the University animal science and veterinary medicine programs with which I have recently worked, women students outnumber men.

For most curriculums and professions, there is freedom to choose.

* * * * *

In the case of athletics, conference and NCAA tournament championship banners may hang in the coliseum or are listed in event programs and seen by many. For competitive excellence in judging, debate, music, theatre, or other student team activities, recognition is less public, perhaps limited to department hallways or bulletin boards. I want to highlight some of these latter K-State team winnings.

Teams and Trophies in Academics

Perhaps best known in the academic arena are judging and debate teams, but others also bring credit to K-State. I urge the reader to take a breath after each illustration, and consider the hours and energy in each case that a coach or adviser, as well as the students, invested in preparing for their team performance.

I had long been acquainted with K-State's winning livestock and meat judging teams. I was therefore not surprised, during my first year in the presidency, to see the junior livestock team place first at the National Western Show in Denver.[10] More first places had followed: 1977 – meat judging at Chicago's International Show, 1982 – wool judging at Houston, and both 1981 and 1982 – livestock judging at both Ft. Worth and Kansas City's American Royal.[11]

In 1985 an interdisciplinary team from the Colleges of Engineering and Human Ecology won national competition to design a new glove for use on the space shuttle. And a team of interior architecture students won three of five international design awards, including "Best in Show," at the International Student Furniture Design competition.

In six of eight years prior to 1985 Agricultural Engineering senior teams won the national design competition sponsored by the American Society of Agricultural Engineering. The K-State Research Foundation filed for a patent on their 1984 design, a device for straight-line baling of windrowed forage.

An eight-person Engineering team had entered an energy-efficient vehicle in the national Student Competition on Relevant Engineering in 1979, hoping to repeat the grand prize won in 1977 by a K-State team.[12] That 1977 team entry, an engine powered by ethanol produced from Kansas grain sorghum and a Savonius wind machine, won over fifty-six other collegiate entries.[13]

K-State's Dance Troupe won the American Dance Festival Association's Midwest Regional Competition in 1985.[14]

In the case of university music competition, it is more a case of which universities get invited to certain prestigious settings than it is direct competition. K-State's Jazz ensemble was invited to perform at Switzerland's Montreux Jazz Festival and our glee club was one of eight invited to participate in the International Music Council's annual seminar at Harvard University in 1986.

In 1976 Speech Department Head Norma Bunton had initiated a forensics program and two faculty, Harold Nichols and Lynne Ross, quickly developed it into a powerful force. They helped form the American Forensics Association National Individual Events Tournament and hosted that national tournament in 1984. Our undergraduate forensics team placed third in the nation in 1979 and second in 1984. It had individual national champions in the late 1970s or early 1980s in five events, Informative, Impromptu, Extemporaneous, Persuasion, and Dramatic Interpretation.[15] As of 1985, forensics teams had placed among the top five in the country five of the previous eight years.[14] In the process of developing winners in forensics, the program also yielded a number of Master of Arts graduates and what has been called a coaching family tree, with graduates leading college forensics programs in at least six states.[15]

There are other team efforts outside the classroom—leadership and activities of student department clubs, publications, residence units, or other student interest groups. And, there is competition among universities in many of these sectors, with success in the competition giving more assurance of K-State's relative stature.

As of the fall of 1985, K-State's Panhellenic Council (the organized council of K-State's sororities) had been ranked among the top five in the nation continually for a decade, and had been honored in 1981 as the nation's top. The previous year, three of K-State's twenty-eight fraternity chapters were chosen top chapters by their respective national organizations. Much credit in this arena goes to Greek Adviser Barb Robel.

The *Kansas State Engineer*, edited by a team of students, won four national awards in the 1984-85 year, bringing to twenty-one the number of such awards earned over an eight-year period. Though I have no measure of the degree to which other colleges of engineering advanced and encouraged minority students, I was proud that our faculty and students had formed K-State chapters of the National Society of Black Engineers, the Society of Hispanic Professional Engineers, and the American Indian Science and Engineering Society. The sensitivity of our College of Engineering had come through.

The reader may recall that part of the federal land grant charter, "not to exclude military science." K-State has continued to interpret that as "to *include* military science." The Reserve Officers' Training Corps (ROTC) was considered an integral part of university academics and student development. During a four-year period in the early 1980s, the K-State chapter of the Arnold Air Society, Air ROTC honorary, had received each year "The Most Outstanding Squadron" award of the U.S. Air Force.

There was a four-year parallel in K-State's Construction Science Department. For the fourth year in a row, our student chapter of the Associated General Contractors (AGC) was named the top chapter in the country. (Concurrently, Associate Professor Merrill Blackman was named the first recipient of AGC's Outstanding Educator Award.) For ten years in a row, the K-State chapter of the Institute of Industrial Engineers earned the national organization's "Award of Excellence."

History, too, has its national honor society. It is Phi Alpha Theta, and its national association named the K-State chapter the best university club for 1983-84 and 1984-85.

In 1984, for the first time in history, both the yearbook and student daily newspaper of one university were rated "Pacemaker" by the Associated Collegiate Press, K-State's *Royal Purple* and the *K-State Collegian*!

Elsewhere I mentioned that an important day in the life of a university is the day that faculty hiring or promotion and tenure decisions are made.

Another is the day when a faculty member is chosen to be a team coach or the faculty adviser to a student group or student publication. Effective coaches and advisers see their work as valuable teaching and student development opportunities, and take on the task with relish. Whether it is a judging or debate team, the student section of the Civil Engineering Society, the Rodeo Club, or the *K-State Collegian,* serving as a team coach or faculty adviser is an important and respected responsibility. Their work is appreciated.

* * * * *

Murphy's law still functioned. This time it was a case of allergy to early morning classes.

No 7:30 Class!

August, 1985

A young woman student was on the phone to my legislative assistant, Mike Johnson. The 12:30 section of a Business Management course she wanted was already full; could he help her get added to the class?[16]

Most of our seventeen to eighteen thousand students enrolled in five or six courses, and if a preferred course section was full, they would search out a second. They would solve their own problem. This case, though, was another application of Murphy's law. The caller said she called Johnson at her father's suggestion and her father happened to be president of the Kansas Senate and a K-State graduate.

The senator had been a strong supporter of some K-State items before the legislature, but he seemed to run hot and cold in his support. In the case of the separate budget for Veterinary Medicine achieved several years earlier, another senator (a University of Michigan graduate) had picked up our cause and led the effort, without his support.

Universities can also be political punching bags, for money spent on out-of-state travel, teaching loads, or foreign teaching assistants who have difficulty with English. Though we had instituted a screening process to minimize that latter problem, the senator had joined several other legislators in blasting all the state universities for using "those foreign teaching assistants."

Johnson's first step after the call was to check with the young woman's adviser. Yes, he was familiar with the problem, and had suggested she simply enroll in one of the other sections. Johnson also checked on the 12:30 section, and found that it was not only full, it had a long waiting list. However, there was room in two other sections, at 2:30 and 7:30.

Johnson called back the young woman. "How about the 2:30 section?"

"I can't do that," she responded, "I have a part-time job that conflicts."

"How about the 7:30 section? It is still open?"

"Oh, that is impossible. My two roommates and I all use the same bathroom, and we just wouldn't be able to get to class in time!"

Johnson finally told the young woman he just couldn't be of much help, and suggested she just enroll in the 7:30 class and set her alarm a bit earlier.

Of interest: The instructor for the 12:30 section that she "just had to have" was taught by a foreign-born graduate assistant!

* * * * *

Though most of the surprises came *from* students, there was one occasion where I did the surprising. Late on a Sunday afternoon, Shirley and I had rushed our Dachshund, Tena, to the veterinary clinic on the north edge of the campus. Tena had apparently swallowed a needle and the three students on emergency were at work trying to find it. Shirley and I were watching.

That afternoon had been my first racquetball game after recovery from a brief bout of flu. I always carried a quart of Gatorade with me so that after a series of games I could, over the next hour or so, replenish the water, potassium, and other salts lost from heavy perspiration. However, Tena had apparently swallowed that needle just before I had walked in the back door at home. I had dropped my gym bag and Gatorade and we had headed to the veterinary clinic.

The students had just begun their work with Tena when I felt the need to sit down on a nearby stool. A few seconds later I toppled onto the floor. I was out only momentarily and recovered quickly but, at least for a few moments, those junior and senior veterinary students thought they had two problems on their hands.

Chapter XII

Apprehensions and Satisfactions

Our eleventh year in the presidency would be one more than we had planned. Early in my presidency, noting that the average tenure of state university presidents was then less than four years, I would tell my friends that my goal was to "survive for six years and stay no more than ten." In this eleventh year, in addition to handling routine presidential duties, we would be considering "What next?" For that, we would have some apprehensions. We would also feel some pride and satisfactions from the University's progress and our efforts.

What Experiences Next?

Early Spring, 1986

In January of 1986 Senator Bob Dole publicly suggested that I should be considered for the Number Two spot, Deputy Secretary, in USDA. Both Secretary Jack Block and his deputy had resigned. Dick Lyng of California, who had served as deputy secretary early in the Reagan administration, had been nominated for the secretary position but not yet confirmed by the Senate. The deputy spot would also be a presidential appointment with Senate confirmation.

I was also contacted by Peter McPherson, Administrator of the Agency for International Development, about a role in that agency. I knew McPherson, having served since the early 1980s on AID's Board for International Food and Agricultural Development, a group advisory to the administrator. Several posts in that agency, then open or soon to be, would be both challenging and rewarding. Some of these were also presidential appointments.

As a university president, I had tried to remain apolitical; I needed to work with members of both political parties. Though I was a registered Republican, I did not work on campaigns and my financial donations had been modest. That would likely be a limiting factor in being considered for a presidential appointment.

In most executive branch departments and independent agencies, such as AID, the top three position levels, secretary, deputy secretary, and under or assistant secretary (and their counterparts in the independent agencies) are political appointments. The appropriate senate committee first considers each nomination. Committee staff gather information and then meet with the nominee to delve into any issues of concern. The next step is a committee hearing on the nomination and a committee vote on recommending the nominee to the full Senate. These processes can take months or longer, and inter-party games can easily de-rail a nomination.

In a late February trip to Washington I had interviews with two staff in the White House personnel office, one responsible for AID positions and the other for USDA. Their job was to size up people who had been suggested for posts in an agency (including evidence of financial or time contributions to political campaigns), learn if their philosophies mesh with those of the president, and probe for any affiliations or past statements that might later be embarrassing to the administration. If the person passed muster, their name would be passed on to the head of the White House personnel office and the agency head.

I also visited briefly that day with Lyng, who, awaiting confirmation by the Senate, was using an office in the Old Executive Office building. As majority leader of the Senate and a senior member of the Senate Agriculture Committee, Dole had played a leading role in Lyng being nominated by the President.

It was a generous and helpful visit. First, I was impressed with Lyng and his manner. He was low key, sincere, and obviously well acquainted with the Department and the political issues. I told him of my interest in both USDA and AID. He described the role he expected the deputy secretary to play, including coordinating many internal matters of the Department, but travel at least a day a week. He did not downplay the cost of living in Washington—said one would be lucky to break even financially. Nor did he downplay the time and risks for any nominee in achieving Senate confirmation.

I was also aware that there were non-political appointment options in either agency, especially AID. The most attractive arrangement, in many respects, would be an Interagency Personnel Agreement (IPA), where I could stay on the K-State payroll, with uninterrupted health insurance and retirement benefits. I could assume either an administrative or staff position in the Agency; the University would be fully reimbursed for all costs plus a modest overhead fee. Such an appointment could be consummated in short order, with approval only by the Agency head and our Board of Regents.

Most who leave a university presidency and return to faculty status are given a six-month or one-year sabbatical at full pay before returning to the classroom or research work. An IPA, even if I returned later to the campus, would avoid that cost to K-State's budget.

The Senate confirmed Lyng in early March and I called his office to offer congratulations. He returned my call within the hour. He had just returned from a session on the Hill with several senators, said he had found his "popularity had peaked two or three days ago." I told him I was even more interested in the deputy position than before I met with him, but that I also knew others were being considered and that he should have his personal choice as his deputy.

Word from several friends in D.C. indicated that USDA's assistant secretary for conservation, Peter Myers of Missouri (with whom Lyng had worked during his time as deputy secretary), was likely Lyng's preference. I also learned that North Carolina Senator Jesse Helms was pushing one of his constituents for the deputy position. Lyng did not need a battle with or between two influential Republican senators, Dole and Helms, and I was not about to be a part of such. I called Senator Dole to express thanks for his interest and support and that I would next call Secretary Lyng to withdraw my interest. I would plan to go to AID.

I had kept in contact with Kansas' junior Senator Nancy Kassebaum along the way. As a member of the Senate Foreign Relations Committee, she was close to the needs of AID and had high respect for its administrator, McPherson. Though she emphasized the Agency had great internal management and leadership needs where I could be of help, she cautioned me about its many bureaucratic traditions. I had encountered both in K-State's AID relationships and my BIFAD work. That did not deter me, however. I was enthused about the national value of our foreign assistance work in agriculture and related areas—and every large organization (even a university) has bureaucratic problems that need to be solved.

An IPA was soon worked out with Administrator McPherson for me to head AID's food and agriculture programs.

* * * * *

The previous section describes options for our next professional step and the process of deciding the matter. In the following I share Shirley's and my perspectives toward such a change, and how our perspectives may differ from those of others. Yes, we had apprehensions, but our long-term goals and our life perspectives overrode.

I Wish I Could do That!

The following is from a piece that served as a base for my comments to several audiences during our last months in the presidency.[1]

"On June 30 of this year, my wife and I will leave the presidency of Kansas State University. I emphasize the presidency is a joint effort, with me handling the administrative responsibilities, both of us representing the University, and my wife providing support to me and symbolizing the humaneness and family character of university leadership. She, to a greater extent than I am able, expresses and demonstrates empathy for faculty and their spouses and families, and for a good many students. And, she initiates and leads the extensive entertainment function of the presidency, both in the President's Home and at other sites on campus or in the community.

We leave the presidency at this time and stage in life because it is what we intended to do. When we returned to Kansas State as president in 1975, we set a target of six to ten years, manifesting the conviction that one makes the greater leadership contributions to an institution the first five to six years, in most instances, and based on the belief that we owed ourselves a succession of experiences in our finite lives. We would not be satisfied with a limited number of professional settings or experiences that tend to repeat themselves year after year.

We prepare to leave the University with many good feelings of satisfaction—elevated excellence in the student body as measured by ACT scores, number of national merit semifinalists enrolled, and number of national scholastic recognitions; major construction projects completed and several more funded; a significantly improved and inspiring campus appearance; a major fund-raising endeavor completed and a pattern established for future endeavors; sharply increased research funding; some restructuring of central university administration; outstanding faculty; and a very high level of leadership in the colleges.

There are a few items we sought that were not achieved, but if that were not the case, our aspirations would probably have been too low.

One major question as we approached this change was, 'What now?'

Early in our time back at Kansas State we outlined some personal goals for the next ten to fifteen years. These included a good relationship with our daughters, good physical and emotional health, an additional professional experience, perhaps in government or in the private sector, more exposure to other cultures via international travel, and the initial steps to identify a potential retirement location. After announcing (late June, 1985) our planned departure, we turned our attention to the additional professional experience, of course, and suggested publicly that we would be interested in either the public or private sector.

Beyond that, my wife and I recorded a list of about twenty-five major communities or geographic areas in which we would be willing to live, and the kinds of experiences we would like to have.

Soon after our announcement we were amazed at the number of others who said, privately, 'Gee, I wish I could do that!' They were saying, in essence, 'I wish I could leave my business, my profession, where I've lived for twenty years, or whatever, and move to a totally new and different experience.' An expression of anticipated excitement or yearning would appear, and then it would often be followed with both the words and the facial expression, 'But, I can't.'

These came from fellow university presidents, a physician, attorneys, farmers, a retailer, and faculty.

I could only guess what was behind the 'But, I can't.' For some it may have been the fear of financial risk; for some, lack of confidence in who might take over their business; for others, unwillingness to face a new geographic location or worry that the spouse or family could not accept such a move. For most, I think it was that they had not significantly changed their location or occupation before, and they were simply reticent about the total process.

Shirley and I are fortunate in having worked at five universities, twice at two of those universities; we have lived in nine different homes in those five communities. Our daughters have each attended college at two out-of-state institutions, as well as having been enrolled in three public school systems.

Each of our moves has been successful, though there are always some stresses and apprehension. We have learned that we make new friends and still retain the old each time we move, and that we can be successful in these new relationships.

So many others could be; they just have not learned that they would be.

We have settled on a position, effective July 1, as Director of Food and Agriculture for the Agency for International Development, which functions as a unit of the State Department. We have never lived east of the Mississippi nor in a city larger than Lincoln, Nebraska. We have never lived in an apartment, except for our first eighteen months of marriage, in a two-bedroom unit in married student housing, and three months here in Manhattan while awaiting redecoration of the President's Home. Both the work and the living experience will be new.

As I review our thoughts that led to these plans, they illustrate our philosophy that life is a long journey over a maze of roadways. This maze provides options for many turns, many hills and valleys, and many vistas. There are many flowers and a few thorn bushes along thc road, and many people line the road. Each of these provides opportunity for acquaintance, interaction, pleasure, challenge, and satisfaction.

We choose not to travel the same segment of road endlessly, going back and forth past the same people, the same hills and valleys, the same flowers and thorn bushes, and the same vistas. We prefer and are determined to visit the new. We intend to experience, in interacting with them, the apprehension of the untried, joy of discovery, exhilaration of success, or pain of disappointment. And we intend to experience the satisfaction of seeing new tasks achieved.

In short, we are determined that we will give ourselves significant new and rewarding experiences and that, in the process, we will make some new and different contribution to an entity, a program, a person, a sector of society, or a portion of the globe that we would not otherwise have encountered."

One of my friends recently asked, "Did you ever consider abandoning that intended ten-year limit on the presidency?" Yes, we did. After having worked through a number of major issues, establishing the provost position, and having more of my own team in place—and even K-State making it to a football bowl game—we reconsidered for a time. A university presidency is a prestigious position and it provides a good income and a stimulating environment; perhaps we should enjoy it a few more years. However, more and more of the daily issues we were handling were "repeat performances." I told my friend that we soon decided that "enjoy it a few more years" was just a euphemism for "staying too long."

* * * * *

If there would be a swan song for one leaving a university presidency, what better time and place for delivery than at the last spring commencement? However it was not easy to structure. I had to keep in mind that the major purpose of a commencement address is to encourage, charge, give promise, and convey some useful philosophy. I hope that this filled the bill.

The Halls of Ivy

May 16, 17, 1986

Following is my last commencement address to Kansas State graduates, refined here from the text and notes used for the two ceremonies, for Veterinary Medicine and the Graduate School on May 16, and for undergraduates on May 17, 1986.[2]

"This spring both you and I are graduating from Kansas State University. Most of you have devoted four years—some two or three and, I know, some five or more—at K-State. I have invested eleven years as president, plus four in an earlier role. You look forward to a new experience. I look forward to a new experience.

You have dreamed in earlier days about what this college experience would be and you likely dream today about what can lie ahead. Some of those dreams may well come true. I tell you that what you dream today is not outside the realm of possibility!

During my college years I dreamed about what my life and work might be. I often listened to a radio series (later a TV sitcom) called Halls of Ivy. It was about a university president and was a series of vignettes, usually involving a troubled student or disturbed professor who would call on the president at his home during the evening. Did I dream that someday I would live some of those vignettes?

Later, while a doctoral student and instructor at Oklahoma State University, my wife and I were privileged to know and even play cards with the president and his wife, Dr. and Mrs. Oliver Willham. Alumni members of the fraternity to which President Willham and I belonged gathered at the chapter house one Friday night each month for cards. The Willhams and Ackers did not play bridge, so we often paired up for hearts. During those evenings we learned about the University presidency and the wonderful couple who served it.

These experiences and others during my early academic years suggested that being a university president was not outside the realm of possibility and that it would be extraordinarily interesting and stimulating.

I tell you that what you dream today is not outside the realm of possibility!

During my eleven years as president of K-State there have been many experiences similar to those portrayed on Halls of Ivy. I have been reinforced by thoughts of how Oliver Willham, or other presidents with whom I have worked, would have handled the people and the situations with which I have been confronted.

As you encounter problems and opportunities in your future work, perhaps as a graduate student, a teacher, or manager of people, you will be reinforced by thoughts of how Professor X, or others with whom you have studied here, would have handled the people or the situation.

The presidency of a respected university is, to me, the greatest experience in the world. We leave it only because we intended to, after a finite time, to further enrich our lives with new and different experiences.

Attending this respected university is a great experience. You leave here because you intended to, to further enrich your lives with new and different experiences!

I share with you a few observations and thoughts that may apply to your future life and work experiences.

Timing. Some say "timing is everything." Timing can have immense impact on both success and perception of success.

In 1970, I was invited to become a university president, but my wife and I decided the timing was not right. There was much campus unrest and our two daughters were yet in high school. We waited for a different time.

So we came to K-State as president in 1975, just in time to encounter the half million dollar negative net worth in athletics and football probation. And we knew that our planned time here, six to ten years, would see an enrollment peak followed by enrollment decrease. And, some problems in the organization and leadership structure within agriculture and between agriculture and the balance of the University were to reach a climax and call out for resolution.

But, we were also lucky on some matters of timing. When we needed good action in the Kansas legislature, the right people seemed to be in the right positions—Ways and Means or Building Committee—to make the right decisions for K-State. And, we had the right faculty leadership when there were some critical internal issues.

Now you look to new experiences and may wonder about timing. Is there now a strong demand for accountants? Did I graduate in Nuclear Engineering at the wrong time? Is this the time to begin farming? Will the calls for accountability affect my teaching career? If a new Ph.D., will universities be hiring new faculty? Will the federal research budget be adequate to provide more jobs in research?

I will be moving to the U.S. State Department, to work with the U.S. Agency for International Development as Director of Food and Agriculture, on loan from the University. In this position I will have some responsibility for a series of international agricultural research centers and contracts with several dozen universities. But a key Congressional committee chair is now threatening to cut the AID development budget by 45 to 50 per cent! Is this the right time for that job?

There are always challenges and risks in any position, especially in an important profession or a position of major responsibility. And, the luck of timing is ever-present.

When you are lucky, you just give thanks. When you are not, you just swallow hard, analyze the situation with a clear eye and clear mind. You do not blame others; you just move ahead with the task at hand and do your job in a professional manner.

If you are in management, you are forcing and facing issues, making decisions, and supporting others to make theirs. And, you do these things with a positive attitude.

This may be the right time be an accountant or to start farming, better than three or five years ago. There are opportunities in nuclear medicine. And the well-equipped teachers will meet and surpass the standards of accountability. They will pass the tests that society will impose. If you are a new Ph.D., this may be the exact time that the right teaching or research job will open up for you.

Memories. You will have memories of your time at K-State. These memories will be important. Our memories of the K-State presidency are important to us, and I want to share a few.

I remember, after several years as president, being bitten by a large Dalmatian, and noting that my skin had toughened so the dog's teeth did not even penetrate.

I remember the recent campus visit by Vice President George Bush and the challenging talk he gave and which many of you heard.

I remember the K-State visit and concert by the famed violinist, Itzhak Perlman.

I remember a visit here this past winter with actor Don Ameche, whom I had watched as a child and who this spring received an Oscar for his supporting role in Cocoon. Ameche is a student of horses and the training of horses, and had come to K-State for discussions on muscle physiology and training regimes with Dean Jim Coffman and Dr. Jerry Gillespie of our Veterinary faculty and Dr. Don Good of Animal Science.

I remember a 10:30 p.m. run to Swanny's with two students. (This was Swanson's Bakery, on the south side of Poyntz between Second and Third Streets. After normal business hours, the ovens were put to work on other than dinner rolls and angel food cakes and the back door was opened to a different clientele. When we arrived, the line of K-State students extended well out into the alley.) Those students thought I should know the tasty goodness of Swanny's yum-yums.

And, I remember ten other spring commencements, with men and women in academic garb, relieved that their papers are all in, tests done, classes over, and with a sense of excitement about what was to come.

You have similar and vivid memories, all important to you.

For you, it has been a thrill to live in this rich academic community, as a student in an exciting department and college.

It has been my great thrill to live and work in this rich academic community as president.

As you move on to a new assignment and experience, with our congratulations, I invite you to keep the University in your thoughts and to call upon the University and faculty.

In my new assignment with the State Department and AID, in Washington, I will also be calling upon K-State.

Turn always to Kansas State University for encouragement and for refreshment. How happy your alma mater—the faculty you know and respect—will be to pour them in abundance upon you."

* * * * *

Though one of the Chapter title's key words is Satisfactions, most of the *credit* for those satisfactions should go to others. I also have *pride* in many university achievements. In the following piece I differentiate among the terms.

Satisfactions, Pride, and Credit

In greeting newly arrived faculty each fall, I would urge that each find some satisfactions to take home from their work each day, each week, or each semester. I would suggest that each of us is well paid for what we do, but the money gets quickly spent or invested. What will endure in our conscious memories and sustain our self-worth will be the satisfactions from what we do.

For Shirley and me, as we moved from the President's Home in early June of 1986, most of the salary received had paid our daughters' college expenses, remodeled our week-end and vacation retreat, or gone into a supplemental retirement fund or investment. The money had come and gone. But we each held personal satisfactions that we would carry for our lifetime.

We had gained so many friends, including faculty, students, townspeople, alumni, and University supporters across Kansas and beyond. Shirley, especially, had the satisfaction of having hosted, in the most open, hospitable, and comforting way, according to our guest books and other records, thousands of people in our campus home.

I recently asked Shirley to list some specific satisfactions she carried from our time in the K-State presidency. She highlighted these:

1. Making the President's Home a welcoming place for so many members of the K-State family, especially students and faculty, the latter both campus and statewide; supportive townspeople, alumni groups, and commencement parties; and many campus guests.
2. The feeling of being appreciated by the likes of Red Skelton, who delivered a kalenchoe plant the morning after our home had been the setting for his gracious interaction with a number of faculty, students, and townspeople.
3. Hosting a Faculty Social Club-sponsored international style show, with international students and spouses modeling their native attire. Though Shirley held the title of Honorary Chair of the Club, she was cautious in deferring to elected leaders regarding the Club's activities. But when the idea of this international style show came up, she quickly volunteered to host the event in our home.
4. The opportunity to serve as a board member of St. Mary Hospital, First United Presbyterian Church, and Home Health, plus considerable work with United Way, the Senior Citizens' Center, and the Manhattan Civic Theatre. She recalled our moving our piano, the piano on which our daughters had practiced in earlier years, to our back deck for a brief performance teaser, part of a Theatre fund-raising event we hosted.
5. The rich working relationship with those undergraduate and graduate students (and spouses, in two cases) that lived on our second or third floor and helped with house care and entertainment in return for their room. She recalled the unexpected wedding of a graduate student helper, where she served as witness and quickly organized a reception for the couple's friends.

She has far more good memories, some shared elsewhere in student, faculty and staff, or other sections.

For me, it seems appropriate to differentiate among the words, satisfactions, pride, and credit. Though I may have pride in all of the K-State achievements during my tenure, personal satisfaction varies in accord with my personal involvement and the circumstance. There is no way that a president should be given or assume credit for all the good things that happen to a university during his or her tenure.

The two-volume dictionary on my book shelf offers these definitions:[3]

- Satisfaction (noun) – gratification … occasioned by some fact, circumstance.
- Pride (noun) – pleasure … in something conceived or reflecting credit.
- Credit (transitive verb) – to give reputation or honor, to ascribe to a person.

I carried and continue to carry immense pride in the work of our campus faculty, deans, department heads, coaches, and classified staff, and their counterparts at branch research stations and in area and county extension offices, as well as in greater Kansas City. I also have considerable satisfaction in having helped hire some of these people, gain funds for their work, and encourage their endeavors. However, it is those people who earned and would carry for their lifetimes the most enduring and vivid satisfactions. They did the work; they created, taught, and led. I credit them for making good things happen.

Pride. It seems appropriate that I first list those K-State accomplishments that gave me pride and some satisfactions *because* of the leadership of these people. For these listed items I cannot claim a major role. Financial commitments for some projects were achieved largely by my predecessor, James McCain; others were initiated and led by deans, department heads, or individual faculty. As K-State president at the time of each I have much pride and, of course, helped move these along. However, major *credit* belongs to others.

1. **Durland Hall and Engineering II, later named Rathbone Hall**, the first and second of the three-building Engineering complex on the central campus' west side. Durland was near completion when I arrived. We obtained the money for Engineering II (Rathbone), beginning with the 1978 legislature.[4] That was not difficult, due in significant part to K-State's well-

understood land grant role in "agriculture and mechanic arts," its relative engineering strength within the state, and that legislators had long understood that Durland was only part of a planned three-building complex. I should also give some credit to good friend Jim Olsen, then president of the University of Missouri. He called to tell me he planned to offer Engineering Dean Don Rathbone the chancellorship of their Rolla campus.[5] I shared that with members of the Board of Regents, got quick endorsement for seeking appropriations for Engineering II, and the legislature did its part.

Dedication of Phase II of the new Engineering complex on the campus' west side, September 30, 1983. Billed then as an addition to Durland Hall, which had been completed in the early 1970s, this Phase II would be named for Dean Don Rathbone at his retirement. (Photo courtesy University Archives and Royal Purple.)

2. Completion of the three-building **Veterinary Complex**. The third building, the diagnostic facility and hospital, was designed and construction had begun when I arrived, and credit goes to my predecessor and the Veterinary College faculty and leadership. Still, officiating at the 1978 dedication gave me pride.
3. **King International Center**. As I visited with retiring President McCain a few months before assuming the presidency, he told me that Mr. Ed King, a K-State graduate and founder of Olathe's King Radio Corporation, wanted to provide funds for such a building. It seems that at some point, perhaps a Foundation trustee's meeting, McCain had outlined the need for such a

center and King had come forward to say he would like to provide the funds. I followed up with an early call on King, he made a formal commitment, and planning proceeded. I was proud that this would be the first of a number of ground-breakings during my presidency.

4. Construction of the **dairy research and teaching center** north of the campus in 1976-78. Though the final appropriation came and construction occurred during my time, credit for it being high on the University priority list for legislative consideration goes to a Lawrence area legislator before I arrived.
5. The **Peters Recreation Complex**, dedicated in 1981. The initiative for this came from the students; they passed by a three-to-one margin a resolution calling for a $15 per semester fee increase to accommodate both bond retirement and a major part of the facility's operation.[6] The complex became not only a fantastic facility for students and faculty, it was fitting recognition for Student Affairs Vice President Chet Peters, beloved by students and his staff and an enthusiast for intense physical activity.
6. The **first post-season football bowl game** in K-State's 85-year history, the Independence Bowl, December of 1982. Any university president would be proud of such a ground-breaking event. (In 1982 there were only about eighteen bowl games, in contrast to the thirty-six in 2009-2010.) Credit goes, however, to Head Coach Jim Dickey and Athletic Director Dick Towers. Dickey's strategy had been to red-shirt a number of players for the falls of 1980 and 1981, to stack up some strength and maturity for seasons ahead. It had worked; 1982 was a winning season and the team was eligible for bowl consideration. It was Towers, though, who so impressed the Independence Bowl committee, that clinched the invitation. My role was simply that I had told Dickey in the fall of 1980 that I would back him all the way in the red-shirting strategy.
7. AID funding for major **agricultural development projects** in the Philippines (1976) and Botswana (1977). Credit goes largely to International Programs Director Vern Larson and Vice President for Agriculture Roger Mitchell. K-State had the successful history of AID-financed work in India and Nigeria, Larson had the confidence and familiarity with agency officials, and Mitchell had a long-time personal acquaintance with AID's Philippine development officer.

8. Dedication of the **Konza Prairie** in 1980, after purchase of the tract for K-State research and education by Nature Conservancy. Primary credit goes to Botany Professor Lloyd Hulbert, who held a national reputation in the ecology of tall grass prairie. Hulbert had proposed such a facility and worked closely with Nature Conservancy in the Konza acquisition.
9. Re-location of the **American Institute of Baking** (AIB) from Chicago to Manhattan. Grain Science Department Head Bill Hoover (who would, in time, be named president of AIB) had worked closely with AIB's leadership in analyzing the advantages of proximity to K-State's flour milling and baking research and education program. The K-State Foundation made nearby land available and Vice President Peters helped work out arrangements for use of campus recreation facilities by AIB students. My role was to endorse and encourage.
10. Formation of the **Kansas-Nebraska College of Veterinary Medicine**, a formal agreement involving commitments by both state legislatures and both boards of regents. The arrangement, led by Veterinary Dean Jim Coffman, provided for accommodating a specific number of Nebraskans in K-State's facilities and providing all veterinary students clinical experience with dairy and swine at or near University of Nebraska facilities and the USDA Meat Animal Research Center at Clay Center, Nebraska.
11. Relocation of the **Conservatory** from the designated Bluemont Hall site to a site on Denison, in front of the old Dairy Barn, now Glenn Beck Hall. The conservatory was, to me and others, an important and highly appreciated feature of the campus. The new site was advanced by Vice Presidents Cross and Mitchell and endorsed by our campus planning committee.
12. The **Ruth Hoeflin Child Development Center**. There was obvious need to expand the Stone House child care training facility on the northeast edge of the campus, which accommodated largely children of faculty and staff. There was also desire to give deserved recognition to retiring Dean Ruth Hoeflin, well known in the child development discipline. A Foundation fund drive provided the money.
13. **Quinlan Gardens**. This grew out of the recommendation by Landscape Architecture Department Head Robert Ealy to recognize long-time Professor Leon Quinlan by enhancing what had been the rose garden across the street from Weber and

naming it for Quinlan. My regard for both Ealy and Quinlan made this an easy approval.

14. **The Fire Training Center** on K-State land at the corner of Claflin and Browning. The City of Manhattan needed a station to serve the growing northwest residential area and a training facility for its personnel. I asked Facilities Vice President Cross to work out the location with city officials and Animal Science staff. I supported the arrangement because it would give more fire protection to our campus. Beyond that, about my only direct involvement was to insist that the design mesh with campus limestone structures. The red stripe lets all know it is part of the fire protection system.
15. Two new centers in the College of Engineering, established in 1977. **The Energy Center** was prompted by federal legislation that would provide funds largely for extension education type programs in energy conservation. Credit goes to Dean Don Rathbone and his staff who came forward with proposals for both it and the **Center for Occupational Safety and Health.**
16. A $6.2 million expansion of the **Macdonald Collision Facility** in the Physics Department in 1985. Credit goes to that department faculty and the reputation it had earned, and to Arts and Sciences Dean Bill Stamey for his steady support.
17. A new undergraduate major in **Dance** and a new interdepartmental masters degree program in **Recreation**, both brought about by outstanding faculty performance and student interest.
18. Removal of the last of the **temporary academic buildings**, which had been necessitated by the post WWII enrollment surge and retained for use after two major fires in the 1960s. Completion of Bluemont, Durland, and the first section of Throckmorton allowed those temporary buildings to be razed.
19. The **K-State Research Park** west of Manhattan. Our expanded contract and grant research, as well as engineering and agricultural experiment station funding, was yielding some break-through and patentable technologies. We needed a facility for some joint private-University ventures. Engineering and Agriculture Deans Don Rathbone and John Dunbar and several Manhattan business people, along with the K-State Foundation, carried the ball for this effort.
20. The **Kansas City semester** for students in the College of Architecture and Design. Development of this center, to provide urban experiences for our students and to increase K-State's

presence in the metropolitan area, had been a charge to then new College Dean Mark Lapping. He and his staff worked with Kansas City leaders to bring it about.

21. Establishing a **Parsons headquarters** for the University's agricultural research in southeastern Kansas. Vice President Roger Mitchell was helped in this effort by a $450,000 legislative appropriation to remodel a Parsons State Hospital building for that headquarters.

Satisfactions. Of K-State's achievements and steps of progress during my presidency there are several where it was my role to force or face the issue, make decisions, and perhaps aggressively support others to make their decisions. Of these, which gave me major *satisfactions*? The following are yet vivid as I write these words a quarter century or more later. For some, fascinating and sometimes surprising details are provided elsewhere. Most would have long-term positive impact on the University

1. Establishing **the provost position**, July 1, 1980. Early retirement of a vice president for academic affairs provided the opportunity for establishing a university-wide position to assist the president in supporting and guiding teaching, research, and extension programs for the total university.
2. Gaining funds for a new **chemistry/biochemistry building** and an addition to and renovation of **Weber Hall**, both at one time, in the mid 1980s. For several years I had been pressured by the politically strong livestock industry to move the Weber project ahead of chemistry/biochemistry and, at the same time, pestered unnecessarily by a couple of my Anderson Hall colleagues who feared I would cave in to that pressure. Both projects were approved in one legislative building committee meeting. Planning money was provided in that legislative session and construction money for both came in later sessions.
3. Reconstruction of the burned-out shell of **Nichols Gym to become Nichols Hall**. The Nichols shell had stood for eight years when I became president and I pledged I would resolve its future. It took longer than I expected, and there were many twists and turns, but Nichols did get reconstructed and dedicated during my time.
4. Putting K-State **Athletics on paths of financial integrity and**, especially in football, **abidance with NCAA and Conference rules**, and significant steps toward **equality in women's sports.**

For the former it took several years and personnel changes before some generous supporters would believe and accept my posture that a *pattern* of violations would bring termination of a coach and a *repeated pattern* would bring termination of the athletic director. A critical step to eventually bring equality for women's sports was to have a single department. We were the first in the then Big 8 Conference to make that move, effective July 1, 1976.

5. Construction of **Bluemont Hall** and the first section of **Throckmorton Hall**, as a pair, in the late 1970s. It had been the same issue here as later with chemistry/biochemistry and Weber, a matter of competitive priority. The difference was that regents' staff had switched Throckmorton from second to first priority on an apparent whim. An impromptu visit with the governor, including a convincing commitment, let me get them back in order and obtain appropriations for both at one time.
6. **Bramlage Coliseum**. Though the structure was not completed until after I had left for other duties, this facility had my involvement during most years of my presidency. I saw Bramlage as far more than a coliseum; it was a vehicle for getting the entire K-State family involved and familiar with the idea of major giving to their university.
7. Sharply increasing the membership in the **Foundation's President's Club** (donors of $10,000 or more). Part of the process was adding staff, changing the organization's name from Endowment Association to Foundation, charting a course for aggressive fund-raising efforts, and hosting spring and fall galas for Club members.
8. Regent approval in 1978 of the **Master of Fine Arts degree in Art**. What made this satisfying for me was that it had been turned down at least twice before my arrival. The key was the degree's definition, in essence, the practitioner's degree. That made clear that the degree was appropriate for the state's land grant university.
9. Demonstrating that **freedom of speech at K-State** includes insuring that an invited speaker will be heard. It took clearing the auditorium and readmission on one occasion, and two nights of negotiation with faculty and student leaders on another but, in contrast to some other campuses, all of our invited speakers were heard.

10. Re-establishing **a single leader for agricultural programs** in 1980. Stress among the key officers had gotten in the way of coordinated leadership for teaching, research, and extension.
11. Appropriations for establishing the **International Trade Institute** in the College of Business, plus the **International Grains Program** and the **International Livestock Program** in the College of Agriculture. The Colleges of Agriculture and Veterinary Medicine had long held a global posture, but these three programs made it increasingly clear the State of Kansas expected K-State to think and function globally.
12. Joining the **National Merit Scholarship Program** in 1977. I had been surprised, on my return to K-State, that the University was not a participant. Though 140 to 200 National Merit semifinalists graduated from Kansas high schools each year, only nine were enrolled at K-State in the fall of 1977. On joining the program, we set a long-term goal of attracting half of Kansas' semifinalists each year. The number at K-State had reached fifty-two in the fall of 1985.
13. Commitments that would lead to the **Dole Regents Educational Telecommunications Center.** Though this facility was built and the program established after my time as president, and much credit goes, therefore, to others, we had placed it top on the University priority list and had obtained endorsement by the Board of Regents to seek state funds. We had also obtained the support of Senator Dole for line-item provision of federal funds.
14. Naming the **first minority to a vice presidency** in the history of K-State. Though Dr. Bill Sutton was chosen for the student affairs vice presidency because of the skills and experiences—both urban Chicago and rural Mississippi—that he brought, the naming helped to symbolize the importance of minorities in the University. By the early 1980s the proportion of minorities at K-State had reached near half the proportion of these groups in the Kansas population.
15. A separate **line item budget for K-State's College of Veterinary Medicine,** provided by the Kansas legislature effective July 1, 1978. My effort began with a letter to the Board of Regents in the spring of 1976.[7] A separate budget released this high-cost program from a system-wide funding formula based solely on full-time-equivalent student numbers. The resulting appropriation also provided several new positions and increased operating funds.

16. Dedication of **Edwards Hall** in the fall of 1978. Ownership of this former athletic dormitory, in disrepair and heavily mortgaged, had been transferred from the Foundation to the University and residence hall funds had financed renovation. Athletes were henceforth housed along with other students.
17. **A staff recognition program**, with pins and certificates for years of service and identification of some top "employees of the year." This program included both campus staff and staff in all statewide K-State offices.
18. Increasing the proportion of the University's "education and general" budget allocated to **the University Library**. Though the percentage unit change was not large, the dollar differential would put the traditionally underfunded library on a path toward **its millionth volume,** celebrated April 3, 1986, and our goal of membership in the Association of Research Libraries by 1988.[8] I include here creating and funding the University **Archivist position** in 1982.[9] (Little did I know that a quarter century later the archivist we chose, Anthony Crawford, and his colleagues would be of such important help in this book effort.)
19. A series of **land acquisitions, trades and sales** in 1976 and 1977 for university expansion, buffering, and related development. Tract names would have little meaning to the reader, but University ownership of Edwards Hall, university-related developments adjacent to College and Claflin, land for agronomy research, and a large acreage of grazing land to buffer then new livestock facilities from residential development were among the beneficial consequences.
20. Combining the separate vice presidencies for finance and facilities into **a single vice president for finance and facilities**, effective July 1, 1984.

Some of these developments involved considerable time, effort, and emotional energy. For a few, there was some political risk. That is why each gives satisfaction. At the same time, I emphasize there were other important actors for most. For those involving legislative action, considerable credit goes to Max Milbourn, Barry Flinchbaugh, and Mike Johnson, who served, sequentially, as assistant to the president.

In terms of my time and effort, the first and the last stand in contrast to the rest. These changes required little effort; they were simply decisions on my part after two retirements and one resignation made them possible. (These changes and the title change in agriculture resulted in our moving, during my presidency, from five vice presidents to one provost and two vice presidents.)

I also carry satisfaction for one proposed change that was prevented! I refer to an effort to remove K-State from the joint use of the AM 580 radio frequency (and the state-wide and beyond exposure it gave K-State). Low numbers on the AM dial are valuable because of their large signal radius. By long-term contract, K-State shared the frequency with WIBW, Topeka, and provided the afternoon programming, 12:30 to 5:30. It took some help from several regents, but we managed to resist considerable pressure to trade that time on 580 for a higher frequency with a much smaller signal radius. (KSAC became KKSU during my time, but that was only to achieve consistency with K-State's earlier re-naming, from "College" to "University." Though I am aware of later changes, KKSU then stayed at 580.)

* * * * *

Though we tried in several ways to express our thanks to the many who had given help and support to our presidency, there was no way to express personal thanks to all. There was one group of people, though, to which Shirley wanted to convey her personal appreciation.

Cookies from Big Mama

June, 1976

Redecoration of the President's Home was not yet finished when we had arrived in the summer of 1975, so we had spent several months in sub-leased apartments. Shirley was at the President's Home most days, reacting or making decisions on such items as paint colors or cabinetry details. Eager to get out of an apartment, settled, and ready for entertaining, she had donned jeans and spent several days sanding, painting, and varnishing alongside the crew. When it was all finished, including some exterior plantings, she had insisted that our first open house would be for those workers and their families.

For what seemed a steady flow of events at our home, physical plant staff always had the shrubs trimmed or the drives and walks cleared of snow. And, they were quick to respond if there occurred a problem with the heating system or otherwise.

On several occasions she told one of the workers that their little service vehicle looked like fun; she would like to ride in it sometime. But, she had not had the chance.

In reference to Shirley's size, 4' 11" and barely 100 pounds, the word at the staff shop, when workers were heading to 100 Wilson Court, apparently had become, "We'll get that done for 'Big Mama'." She was not supposed to know about her assigned nickname, but found out through a student helper and appreciated the endearing humor.

Our last week in the presidency, she still had not ridden in that service vehicle. She called the physical plant shop to ask if one of the staff would drive it down to the house. She had made some cookies for them and she wanted a ride up to the shop to join them for coffee. It was all she could do to resist putting a note on the cookie tray, "With appreciation, from Big Mama."

* * * * *

Having worked in four Great Plains states, I had learned that Plains people are more candid than most. What they like, they will tell you, and what they do not like, they will tell you. I appreciate that. It saves time and avoids misunderstanding. Among the Plains people, ranchers tend to say the most with the fewest words.

A Rancher's View

It was in late May, a few weeks before our scheduled departure from K-State. My secretary, Lynne Lundberg, interrupted a meeting I was having with a dean, "Can you take a call from a Mr. Burtis? He is calling from a retirement home in Council Grove."

"Certainly!"

This was the Orville Burtis who, in the summer of 1957, had driven my thirty Iowa State Agricultural Travel Course students and me over what was by now the Konza Prairie. He was manager of the Dewey Ranch, and he was showing us how he managed Flint Hills grass and the cattle that flourished on that grass. An early K-State graduate, Burtis had been a county extension agent, but ranching had been his goal.

Burtis and I had become reacquainted in the early 1960s while I was associate dean, at a dinner honoring Vice President A.D. Weber on the naming of Weber Hall. By then Burtis had acquired a ranch of his own. We had had little contact since my return as president, but I knew that he and his wife had moved to a Council Grove retirement facility

Burtis' voice came through loud and clear, "Doc, I just wanted to call and thank you for the job you've done at K-State. You've done a good job!" I thanked him for the call and for his comments.

Burtis then continued, with words that reflected his experience handling horses, especially riding a newly broke mare, "Running a university is kind of like riding a ticklish bitch!"

I had to agree, "It was a challenge to stay on, and the ride was fun, but it will also feel kind of good to get off."

Many others expressed appreciation during those late spring days. Shirley and I were feted at a faculty and townspeople reception at the rather new Manhattan Holidome, both arranged and, I believe, financed by local businessman and appreciated friend, Jack Goldstein, and others.

A few days later, several hundred gathered—from as far away as Kansas City, Wichita, and Colby—for a farewell dinner and a bit of toasting and roasting. There were also a couple gifts. For Shirley, it was an item for which she had longed, a hand-made stand-alone Amana pendulum clock. For me it was a hand-made desk and file, built by a former K-State student.

My only regret is that our words that evening and otherwise could not come close to conveying the appreciation we felt for the years of generous support, the presence of these good friends, and their expressions.

There was also a reception in Topeka. Many in both the legislative and executive branches of state government had been helpful to me and to K-State and I wanted an opportunity to express appreciation. So, we hosted our own reception for that purpose. Many who had become professional friends were on hand to convey their best wishes.

However, none of the comments were as expressive as Burtis'.

* * * * *

Years after a person leaves a public position, someone may ask, "Whatever happened to her or him?" The presidency of K-State is certainly a public position, for both the president and the spouse. What happened to the couple that served the K-State presidency for a decade or so in the late 1970s and early 1980s? The next chapter summarizes, at least to date.

Chapter XIII

After the Presidency

On the Potomac

Early fall of 1986 Shirley was riding the D.C. area Metro three days a week to her work in the White House Volunteer Office. I read the morning paper on my way by Metro to my AID office. Her destination was the ground floor of the Old Executive Office Building, just west of the White House. My destination was first in Arlington and later in the State Department Building, a couple blocks north of the Lincoln Memorial.

We were living in a rented three-bedroom colonial in Vienna, Virginia, a fifteen-minute walk from the end of the Metro Orange Line.

Shirley was developing her calligraphy skills, addressing President and Mrs. Reagan's congratulatory notes and Christmas cards. Some days she would be on the call-in phones, hearing citizen concerns for relay to the appropriate agencies, or would be helping as needed in one of the White House offices. On the days the President received a foreign head of state, she and her fellow volunteers might be on the White House lawn as part of the welcoming group.

At Christmas, I would get drawn in, as volunteer couples helped host invited groups to see the White House Christmas decorations and enjoy a cup of punch. And, at Easter, she would be on the lawn helping with the Easter Egg hunt.

My task in AID was administering and coordinating food and agriculture programs in and for developing countries. As my K-State staff were in various units on campus and across the state, my AID staff were on three continents, in three Washington-based regional bureaus, and some down the hall from my office.

Though my work involved considerable travel to those three continents, I soon found that, as at the University, a major responsibility was "selling the program." In this case my foci were members of Congress, their staff, and politically active interest groups. Environmental groups feared our programs were damaging the developing countries' natural resources. Members of the American Soybean Association (headed, coincidentally, by one who had been a fellow Nebraska vice chancellor) and other U.S. commodity groups feared our programs' success would increase competition for their export markets.

At the close of the Reagan administration, in January of 1989, we headed back to Manhattan, as planned, for the "academic life." We purchased and Shirley renovated a small brick home west of the campus and I helped teach my former specialty, introductory animal science. I also developed and taught a new course in global agriculture. I retained, however, a quarter time AID responsibility to continue "selling the program," including some travel to foreign development projects with Congressional staff, speeches, and D.C. meetings.

Though we enjoyed being back in the University environment, it was not long (late January, 1990) before we were headed back to D.C. New President George H.W. Bush had named a long-time friend, Clayton Yeutter, USDA Secretary, and I accepted a political appointment as administrator of USDA's Office of International Cooperation and Development (OICD).

This time we chose an apartment in Crystal City, overlooking George Washington Parkway and what is now Ronald Reagan Airport. Shirley and her calligraphy skills were immediately back in the White House Volunteer Office, and she would be teaching calligraphy.

OICD's first function was to represent the Secretary in relationships with United Nations and other international organizations. It was also a rather large contracting agency, tapping university and USDA staff to handle collaborative research and development programs financed by AID, the World Bank, several regional development banks, and the State Department. This was before The Wall came down, and much of the State Department funding was to establish U.S. scientist linkages with counterparts in Eastern Europe.

In early 1991, I was asked to also head the Foreign Agricultural Service (FAS), a larger unit of about 700 staff. The Foreign Agricultural Service is known primarily for its agricultural attaches and export promotion staff located around the world. It also helps the U.S. Trade Representative's Office negotiate bilateral and multilateral trade agreements, handles the logistics and financing of U.S. food aid, and provides federal credit guarantees to assist commercial sales of U.S. commodities and products to importing countries.

I found several K-State Finance grads in that FAS credit guarantee office. Their job was to assess the credit worthiness of foreign governments to which U.S. banks would loan money for purchase of U.S. commodities. On their word—and sometimes a few political considerations—FAS would guarantee the loans.

As administrator of both agencies, I began the steps to merge the two. The actual merger would happen only after appropriate Congressional committees could give their nods of approval. Before that could happen, early 1992, USDA's new secretary, Ed Madigan of Illinois, asked me to move across the street to serve as his assistant secretary for science and education.

Though I had relished the OICD and FAS assignments—new and exciting territory—and had many satisfactions and more stories to tell from each, the science and education role put me back in more familiar territory. My portfolio included the Agricultural Research Service, with about 120 laboratories around the country (such as Manhattan's USDA Grain Marketing Laboratory), the two agencies that handled the money to state agricultural experiment stations and Extension services, and the National Agricultural Library near Bethesda, Maryland.

Huddling in my USDA assistant secretary office with, from the left, Assistant Interior Secretary and former Kansas Governor Mike Hayden, USDA Assistant Secretary for Administration Charles Hilty and Extension Service Administrator Myron Johnsrud, June, 1992. We were likely sharing "war stories" about our recent Senate confirmation hearings, a part of the process to become an assistant secretary.

Two academic duties had come along, board member for the USDA Graduate School and a trustee of the American University in Beirut, Lebanon. The USDA Graduate School has its roots in the 1920s to upgrade agency staff. It had earned accreditation and by the 1990s was offering a wide array of graduate courses, serving thousands of professionals in virtually all federal agencies.

Of interest to Kansans is that former Governor Mike Hayden was then assistant secretary of Interior for wildlife and fisheries. This was at a time when wildlife interests were pressing to make USDA's Conservation Reserve Program (CRP) more beneficial to wildlife. Our good relationship let us help USDA agencies address that issue. (Years later, in the spring of 2009, Shirley and I would place ninety acres in such a CRP program, eligible because the land is within three miles—the feeding range for pheasants and wild turkeys—of a county-owned wildlife preserve. The ninety acres was seeded to ten species of native grasses plus herbs and wildflowers.)

Less than a year later, November of 1992, Bill Clinton won over George H.W. Bush. As a political appointee, my D.C. job would end, and my thoughts turned to Number Five on that list of goals that we had recorded in November of 1976. It was to operate my home farm for five years. Now was the time!

Corn, Beans, and Alfalfa

On January 21, 1993, in a pick-up loaded with books and personal effects, Shirley and I headed west from D.C. toward our Iowa farm, a few miles off I-80 in western Iowa.

We custom farmed 120 acres that year, land not already committed by lease to others, and built a new home on the farm. We had lived in a home of our own less than thirty months in the previous twenty-seven years. It was time for Shirley to have one she designed.

We also wrote a seven-page business plan, signed a $200,000 line of credit note for operating funds, and with the help of a young man who would join our operation for 1994, bought a line of mostly used equipment and a small cow herd. For the next three years we would handle about two sections of cropland—corn, beans, and alfalfa—and that cow herd.

Shirley and me near completion of the fourth corn harvest on our Iowa family farm, early November, 1996.

My farmer schoolmates and friends, ready to retire, could not understand why we would start farming. However, for me, forty-five years after leaving the farm for college, it would be new and challenging. It would also yield some surprises and more stories to tell.

I enjoyed the work and the operation was profitable, but after four years my work ethic and satisfactions became victims of government social policy! In this case, earned farm income was subject to social security taxes and that earned income precluded receipt of social security checks by both Shirley and me. However, IRS classifies cash rent as passive income, not subject to the social security taxes and not precluding our receiving social security checks. Calculations made it clear we should rent the land to others and accept the checks.

Community and Rural Development

By that time, Shirley had been named by the Iowa governor to the Iowa Arts Council and was also on the Board of the Wesley Foundation, which owns and operates retirement and extended care facilities in five Iowa communities. And, she had gotten back to her lifelong interest, painting. She had studied under K-State's Oscar Larmer during our years on campus and, with friends

Wy Johnson and Marion Larson, had used the Flint Hills for some water colors.

This time, though, she moved to a far more complex art, fired oils on porcelain. After each successive application of paint, the piece is fired at a temperature above 1400 degrees. The interaction of pigment, oil type, and firing temperature is a challenge far beyond the scene or design perspective. In a short time, she was winning blue ribbons in State Fair and other competitions.

I had also become involved with a local rural development action committee, the Iowa Department of Economic Development, and a steering committee considering an egg production business. For the latter, our group sold equity shares to 275 parties, built a 650,000-bird complex, and contracted with a source of pullets, by coincidence, the Wilburn and Greg Nelson Poultry Farms at Manhattan, Kansas.

Our egg business sells about 15 million dozen eggs a year. As a rural community project, we count success two ways, jobs (a dozen new full-time and a dozen part-time) and return on equity for the 275 owners (an average of 13 per cent annual cash return at the end of ten years and, with appreciated stock value included, 22 per cent return).

In 1998 the Iowa Legislature authorized an Iowa Agricultural Finance Corporation and a $25 million loan to help develop value-added food and agriculture businesses. I was one of seven asked to form the operating corporation and served on that board the limit of seven years, most of the time as vice chair or chair. We attracted an additional $16 million of private funds and invested in several young businesses.

Professor Again

My "home department" of Animal Science at Iowa State, where I had earned two degrees and taught seven years, had given me a collaborative professor title soon after we moved back to Iowa. I appreciated that formal affiliation after a thirty-plus year break, and served as a guest lecturer and on several department committees. My introductory textbook was by then in its sixth edition and in need of another revision. Though major responsibility had been handed on to others, I was now closer to the poultry and livestock industries and could not turn down the invitation to rewrite and update several chapters.

I also chaired of a futuring project for the National Vocational Agriculture Council and co-chaired the same for Iowa State University Extension. For several other land grant universities, I served as a visiting lecturer and reviewed experiment station programs, and even served as an expert witness in a case that involved Mississippi's relative allocations to 1862 and 1890 land grant universities.

There have been several international involvements, including project reviews and lectures in Belarus, the Republic of Georgia, Ukraine, Costa Rica, and twice more in China. Shirley traveled with me for several of these. And, since 2004, I have been a part of 25x'25, a national effort focused on 25 per cent of total U.S. energy consumption to come from the land—renewable fuels, wind, solar and geothermal conversion—by 2025. And, just recently, I have been drawn into a U.N. Foundation effort to consider global agriculture's relationships to perceived climate change.

The philosophy that has guided both Shirley and me is that "we try to work where we can be most useful." And, regardless of where we might be, we encounter K-State people. For example, in early summer of 2009 I interrupted work on this book to join a college roommate for a two-day cruise on the Mississippi. The afternoon before boarding, while walking through the John Deere pavilion at Moline, I heard my name called. The caller was Kent Stone, who had been a student in the orientation class I taught during my associate dean years at K-State. He and his wife were there to pick up a new combine for their farm at Lebanon, Kansas. The next night, on a motel elevator in Dubuque, Iowa, I met Dr. Barry Bradford, a new K-State faculty member, in Dubuque for a regional dairy nutrition conference. And, the next morning at breakfast, Steve Larson, who had helped me grade papers in that orientation class and now managing editor of Hoard's Dairyman, and his wife stopped by my table to visit.

Taking up the Pen—and the Laptop

It was not until late 2003 that I had time to think about recording from memory and notes some anecdotes from our K-State presidency. We could provide details and perspectives not found in University or media archives and I should get to work on the task. By then we were spending four months each winter in a Florida condo. Away from farm maintenance duties I would have more time to do it.

Midway through that process, another thought struck. Perhaps I could do more good for higher education as a whole, and for those now in state university leadership, by putting together some concepts and guidance based largely on my and others' experiences. Might it be an earlier priority to influence forward direction than record where one has been?

The result was a 204-page book, *Can State Universities be Managed? A Primer for Presidents and Management Teams,* published in 2006 as part of the American Council of Higher Education Series on Higher Education.

The limited market for such a book does not justify a promotional budget and the publisher made it clear the author carries responsibility for letting people know about it. Consequently I periodically check web sites and the *Chronicle of Higher Education* for names of people chosen for state university leadership roles or finalists for such positions. I send each a short e-mail note with the book's table of contents attached.

Early on a recent afternoon I sent notes to twelve and before evening I had four responses:

- From a finalist for a presidency in Texas: "Thanks! I do have the book and am reading it—very helpful!"
- From a finalist for a presidency in Louisiana (sent from his Blackberry): "Thanks, will ask _____ in our office to order a copy."
- From a newly-named president in North Dakota: "Thank you for the kind note. I'll pick up the book. I'll need the help!"
- From a newly-named president in Indiana: "Thank you for your kind message. I've already purchased the book and find its content very informative! Thank you again?"

From our years in state university leadership, especially of K-State, satisfactions continue.

CITATIONS

Chapter I

1. Eisenhower, Milton S. 1974. The President is Calling. Doubleday & Co., Inc., Garden City, New York, p. 151.
2. Beadle, Muriel. 1972. Where Has All the Ivy Gone? Doubleday & Co. Inc., Garden City, New York, pp. IX,X.

Chapter II

1. A Summary of Legislative and Related Actions Regarding Nichols Reconstruction, Duane Acker, June 21, 1982, and From Nichols Gym to Nichols Hall, Duane Acker, August 16, 1985.
2. Summary of President Acker's comments regarding Nichols Gym to a rally on the north side of Nichols Gym, September 29, 1975, and a September 30, 1975, DA letter to Kent Foerster.
3. Mold on Library Wall, notes from DA files, undated.
4. DA April 30, 1976, letter to members of the Kansas Board of Regents.
5. DA July 7, 1976, letter to Booster Club Chairmen and Representatives and Members of Alumni Association Athletics Committee.
6. DA Notes at a Glance, Pocket Book 1, Page 65.
7. DA Notes at a Glance, Pocket Book 1, Page 63.
8. DA Notes at a Glance, Pocket Book 1, Page 62, and Pocket Book 2, Page 80.
9. Media release, Office of University News, Kansas State University, mailed July 1, 1977.
10. DA October 17, 1977, letter to Ms. Juliane Hoover, Lawrence, KS.
11. DA Notes at a Glance, Pocket Book 2, Page 80.

12. DA Notes at a Glance, Pocket Book 2, Page 84.
13. DA June 30, 1976, letter to members of the Kansas Board of Regents.

Chapter IV.

1. Our 25th Wedding Anniversary, notes from DA files, dated July 31, 1978.
2. DA February 22, 1977, letter to Robert Snell.
3. DA March 29, 1977, letter to Mark Reiner.
4. Ellis Rainsberger's Start at Kansas State, notes from DA files, dated February 14, 1986.
5. DA October 15, 2009, letter from John Graham.
6. DA August 7, 1978, letter to Citizen Forum Participants, KSU Endowment Association Board of Trustees, KSU Alumni Association Officers and Directors.
7. Personal correspondence from Elizabeth Unger, August 25, 2009.
8. DA November 21, 1979, letter to Members of the 1202 Commission, with attachments.
9. Kansas State University, "Facts" and "Achievements," an 18-page multilith document, dated November 22, 1985.

Chapter V.

1. Agricultural Research - - Where to Send the Bill. Speech delivered to the 1977 Annual Meeting of the American Society of Agricultural Consultants, St. Louis, MO, September 26, 1977.
2. DA April 6, 1976, letter to members of Kansas Board of Regents.
3. A Summary of Legislative and Related Actions Regarding Nichols Reconstruction, Duane Acker, June 21, 1982, and From Nichols Gym to Nichols Hall, Duane Acker, August 16, 1985.
4. K-Staters Debate Fate of Nichols in Halls of Kansas Statehouse, April, 1979, K-Stater.
5. In a brief description of this saga in Can State Universities be Managed? I erroneously identified Stites with this phone call. Notes I found later told me it was Sands.
6. DA Notes at a Glance, Pocket Book 1, Page 65.
7. DA Notes at a Glance, Pocket Book 2, Page 59.
8. Statement on Financial Exigency, by Duane Acker, President, delivered to Kansas State University Faculty Senate, November 14, 1978. The financial exigency plan was formally approved in the fall of 1980.

9. DA Notes at a Glance, Pocket Book 1, Page 68.
10. Chamber of Commerce Retreat, notes from DA files, December 5, 1980.
11. DA November 17, 1980, letter to members, Kansas Board of Regents.
12. Kansas in the Fall, notes for presentations in the Kansas City area, October, 1984.
13. Notes from DA file, dated August 29, 1985, and regarding Governor Landon.
14. Notes from DA files dated August 29, 1985, President Reagan Landon Lecture.
15. Notes from DA files dictated August 29, 1985, from notes taken May, 16, 1983.
16. Notes from DA files dated August 29, 1985, Cutting the Trees.
17. Notes from DA files, dated August 29, 1985, A Spare Axe Handle.
18. Personal communication, November 6, 1984, from Phil Finley.
19. Notes from DA files, August 29, 1985, Facilitator or Blocker
20. Notes from DA files, June 28, 1985, Dinner for Creech.
21. Personal communication, July 14, 2009, from Dr. Ronald Downey, Professor of Psychology and former staff member in the Office of Institutional Research.
22. DA Notes at a Glance, Pocket Book 2, Page 61.
23. Good for K-State, April, 2009, Page 4.

Chapter VI.

1. Goals and Objectives, 1984-85, Kansas State University, Duane Acker, President, October 24, 1984. (Though the budget policies were established in early 1976, I find no record in my files except this document.)
2. March 17, 1978, Minutes, Kansas Board of Regents, and DA March 20, 1978, letter to Jerry Maddox, Head, Department of Art.
3. DA May 27, 1977, letter to members of the Kansas Board of Regents.
4. Items for Talk. "Offense and Defense in Administration." Undated.
5. DA May 8, 1980, letter to members of the Kansas Board of Regents, vice presidents, deans, directors, heads of related departments, branch station superintendents, county extension

directors, chairs of county extension councils, and related college, research and extension advisory councils.

6. DA Presentation to Opening Faculty Meeting, August 22, 1980.
7. Games Universities Play, notes from Duane Acker files, undated.
8. Personal communication, July 14, 2009, from Dr. Ronald Downey, Professor of Psychology and former staff member in the Office of Institutional Research.
9. Notes from DA files, April 4, 1984, A Long Day.
10. Kansas State University Collegian, February 11, 1986.
11. DA March 5, 1985, letter to members of Kansas Board of Regents. More detail in DA June 25 and August 15, 1985, letters to board members.

Chapter VII.

1. DA August 7, 1978, letter to members of the Kansas Board of Regents.
2. DA September 25, 1975, letter to members of the Kansas Board of Regents.
3. DA September 24, 1976, letter to members of the Kansas Board of Regents.
4. DA seven-page January, 1977, letter to Roger Mitchell, Carroll Hess, and Vernon Larson.
5. DA April 20, 1978, letter to Ambassador David D. Newsome.
6. DA January 25, 1977, letter to members of the Kansas Board of Regents.
7. Konza Prairie Research Natural Area, Chronology, 1872-1999. Kansas State University Archives and Manuscripts.
8. National Parks, Summer, 2007, issue. Pages 44-48.
9. A Terminal Report on Contract AID/afr830 at Ahmadu Bello University, Zaria, Nigeria, 1963-64, International Agricultural Programs, Kansas State University, August 31, 1974.
10. Establishing a Veterinary Faculty at Ahmadu Bello University, Zaria, Nigeria. A terminal report, International Agricultural Programs, Kansas State University, undated, but apparently written in late 1977.
11. A 38-page "summary of impressions" gained from a 10-day visit to the People's Republic of China as a member of the Kansas Trade Delegation led by Governor John Carlin, August, 1979.
12. DA Notes from China Visit, May 17, 1985.

13. Chinese Commuters Embrace the Bike, Omaha World Herald, July 26, 2009, Page 11A.
14. DA May 17, 1985, letter to Provost Koeppe, deans, and department heads.
15. DA November 15, 1982, letter to members of the Kansas Board of Regents.
16. Agricultural Improvement Project, Annual Report Number 8, September, 1990, Department of Agricultural Research, Ministry of Agriculture, Botswana, and Mid America International Agricultural Consortium (MIAC), and personal correspondence from David Norman, July 27, 2009.
17. Agricultural Technology Improvement Project, Technical Summary of ATIP's Activities, 1982-90, ATIP RP6, September, 1990, Department of Agricultural Research, Botswana, and Mid-America International Agricultural Consortium.

Chapter VIII.

1. Acker, Duane. The Importance of Private Philanthropy at a Public University, Presentation at KSU Foundation Trustee Banquet, November 2, 1984.
2. K-Stater, August, 1988, page 9.
3. DA Notes at a Glance, Pocket Book 1, Page 92.
4. DA June 24, 1980, letter to members of Kansas Board of Regents, and January25, 2010, personal communication from Jennifer Fabrizius, K-Sate Foundation.

Chapter IX.

1. The Landon Lectures: Perspective from the First Twenty Years, William L. Richter and Charles E. Reagan, editors. Friends of the Libraries of Kansas State University. Undated, but published in 1987.
2. The One and Only Non-Landon Lecture, Notes from DA files, dated August 19, 1985.

Chapter X.

1. DA Notes at a Glance, Pocket Book 1, Page 35, and Book 2, Page 102.
2. KSU Graduate Commencement, notes from DA files, May 19, 1978.
3. Manhattan Mercury, undated DA file copy, content suggests early January, 1979.

4. Address to Graduates, Kansas State University President Duane Acker, Kansas State University Graduate Commencement, May 15, 1981.
5. Speech delivered by President Duane Acker, Kansas State University, Overland Park, October 19, 1981, and Academic Freedom: Protecting the Right to Learn, for delivery by President Duane Acker, Kansas State University, at Wichita Rotary Club, November 23, 1981.
6. Acker, Duane, Can State Universities be Managed? A Primer for Presidents and Management Teams. 2006. American Council on Education/Praeger Series on Higher Education.
7. DA May 28, 1982, letter to "Dear Colleagues," about 85 staff in their first to fifth year of employment and directly affected by the policy change.
8. DA Notes at a Glance, Pocket Book No. 2, Page 87.
9. DA July 11, 1984, letter to members of the Kansas Board of Regents and a July 12, 1984, K-State News press release by Charles R. Hein, Director of Communication.
10. DA Notes at a Glance, Pocket Book 1, Page 63.
11. DA Notes at a Glance, Pocket Book 2, Page 79.
12. DA Notes at a Glance, Pocket Book 2, Page 84.

Chapter XI.

1. August 2, 1982, letter to Deans and Department Heads by Owen J. Koeppe, Provost.
2. DA Commencement Address, May 19, 1979.
3. DA Presentation to American Association for Higher Education (AAHE), The National Conference on Higher Education, Washington Hilton, Washington, D.C., March 6, 1980.
4. Supreme Court of Kansas, STATE of Kansas, Appellee v. Mustafa Abdulla ABU-ISBA, Appellant, No. 55,891, July 13, 1984, and personal communication from Stanley Dennis, January 2, 2010.
5. The Kansas State Collegian, December 13, 1989, Page 2B, and www.K-State.edu/media/achievements/majorscholarshipwins.
6. DA Notes at a Glance, Pocket Book 2, Page 80.
7. Notes from DA files dated September 23, 1984.
8. DA Notes at a Glance, Pocket Book No. 2, Pages 63, 69 and 70.
9. DA Notes at a Glance, Pocket Book No. 2, Page 86.

10. DA April 1, 1977, letter to members of the Kansas Board of Regents.
11. Personal communication from Dr. Miles McKee, July 14, 2009
12. K-State Engineering Impact, Fall, 1979, Page 3.
13. State of the University, FY 1976-1977, Kansas State University, Page 3.
14. Kansas State University, "Facts" and "Achievements," an 18-page multilith document carrying the date, November 22, 1985.
15. Personal communication from Craig Brown, Director of Forensics, and Charlie Griffin, Head of Communication Studies, Kansas State University, July 24, 2009
16. DA notes from the files, dated August 30, 1985.

Chapter XII.

1. Duane Acker, From A University Presidency, The Next Step, May 1, 1986.
2. Commencement remarks by President Duane Acker, May 17, 1986.
3. The New Century Dictionary of the English Language, a two-volume work edited by H.G. Emery and K.G. Brewster, 1934, D. Appleton-Century Company, New York and London.
4. DA August 7, 1978, letter to members of the Kansas Board of Regents.
5. DA June 10, 1977, letter to members of the Kansas Board of Regents.
6. DA February 27, 1976, letter to members of the Kansas Board of Regents.
7. DA May 28, 1976, letter to members of the Kansas Board of Regents.
8. A Million Strong . . . and Going Strong. Commemorating the Acquisition of One Million Volumes by the Kansas State University Libraries, Manhattan, Kansas, April 3, 1986.
9. Librarian: University Archivist, a position description dated June 8, 1982.

INDEX

4-H Style Show, 95
Academic advising, 230-233
Academic freedom, 205-208
Acker, Shirley
  Board service, 200, 239, 259, 276
  Calligraphy, 272-273
  Hosting, 35, 41-44, 104, 117, 140, 179, 199-200, 241, 259
  Oil painting, 276-277
  Pictured, 114, 185, 219, 276
  Representing K-State, 24, 71, 85, 106, 155-157, 161, 166, 204
  Role and satisfactions, xiv, 6, 117, 258-260
  Student interactions, 41, 87, 178, 218, 229, 233-234, 238-239, 244
  White House volunteer, 272-273
Agency for International Development (AID), 120, 155, 161, 168, 249-253, 258, 262, 272-273
Agriculture, College of, 126-129, 232, 243-244
Agricultural Economics, Department of, 145-147, 161
Agricultural Engineering, Department of, 3, 123, 161, 245
Agricultural Experiment Station, 3, 99, 123, 152-154, 264
Agricultural research, 19, 177
Ahearn Field House, 24, 32, 59-61, 69, 92, 106, 177
Ahmadu Bello University, 161
Akers, Judy, 32, 67, 73-75
Alumni Association, 31, 53, 89, 113, 160, 174-176, 205, 220
Ameche, Don, 257
American Institute of Baking, 263
Animal Science, Department of, 179, 204, 223, 244-245
Anniversary dinner, 63
Arbuthnot, Robert, 115
Architecture and Design, College of, 3, 30, 88-89, 264
Archivist, 268
Armstrong, John "Junior," 127, 166-177
Armstrong, Rex, 165
Arnold, Roy, 149
Arthur, Tom, 103
Arts and Sciences, College of, 3, 88, 232
Association for Intercollegiate Athletics for Women (AIAW), 72-74, 77
Athletics
  Athletic Council, 2, 15, 33, 55-56, 67-73, 76-78, 103
  Department of, 31, 44-46, 53, 69, 72, 76
  Dormitory, 46-47, 70
  Finances, 1-2, 6-8, 15-17, 20, 33-34, 46, 58, 265

Goals and posture, 20-22, 57, 66
The Web, 53
Women's programs, 32-33, 46, 67, 72-73, 77
Auditor, 125-126, 210-211
Authorship, 222-223, 278
Barnaby, Art, 171
Barrett, Ernie, 1-2, 6-8, 11, 16, 20, 33, 39-40, 44, 54-56, 68, 76-78, 118
Bartley, Erle, 127
Basham, Jim, 17, 111
Beatty, Dan, 5-10, 29, 56, 78, 126, 143-145, 152, 210
Beck, Glenn, 5, 122-123, 127, 161, 204-205, 263
Bennett, Olivia, 36
Bennett, Robert, 28, 35-38, 97, 166-167
Bibb, Jim, 37
Bickford, Max, 29, 35, 37, 134
Big 8 Conference, 4, 21, 33, 47, 57, 71-77, 266
Big 8 Women's League, 72-73
Bingham, Cindy, 9
Black, Shirley Temple, 184
Blackman, Merrill, 246
Block, Jack, 249
Bluemont Central College, 152
Board of Regents, 6, 25, 54, 84, 89, 121-122, 251, 261, 267
Expectations of, 27
Members, 17-18, 27-30, 46, 70, 99, 103, 106, 111, 175
Role, xiii, 18-19, 54
Bogina, Gus, 115
Bohannon, Robert, 127
Bonnell, Gene, 175
Botswana project, 168-171
Bowl game, 71, 262
Bozworth, Robert, 83
Brack, Mark, 236
Bradford, Barry, 278
Bradley, Bev, 175
Bradley, Kent, 236
Bradley, Tom, 192-194
Bramlage Coliseum, 56, 106-109, 177, 266
Bramlage, Fred, 55, 66, 71, 89, 107-109, 174
Brandeberry, Norman, 46, 111-112, 175
Brethour, John, 152-153
Briggs, Hilton, 241
Brokaw, Tom, 185
Brookover, Earl, 34, 55, 107, 175
Brown, John Lott, 5
Brownback, Sam, 9, 102
Bubb, Henry, 17
Buck, William, Jr. 237
Budget policy, 119
Budig, Gene, 110-111, 212
Buehler, Bruce, 175
Building priorities, 36-38, 104-106
Bulk, Herb, 96
Bulmahn, Heinz, 92
Bunton, Norma, 245
Burtis, Orville, 158, 270-271
Bush, George H.W., 273-275
Business, College of, 3, 123, 140-141, 232, 267
Bussing, Charles, 171
Buster, Donald, 175
Byrne, David, 100, 135
Carlin, David, 237
Carlin, John, 71, 75, 97, 103, 107, 163-164, 194, 211-212
Carlin, Karen, 95-96, 101-102, 156, 163
Carpenter, Frank, 232
Caruthers, Pat, 110
Case, Gregory, 236

Cedar Crest, 95, 101-102
Chalmers, John, 5, 10-12, 56, 78, 121, 132-134, 215, 221, 236
Chamber of Commerce, Manhattan, 87-89, 98, 112-113
Chemistry/Biochemistry Building, 104-106, 265-266
Chemistry, Department of, 93-94, 226
China visits, 156, 163-165, 204, 278
Citizen Forums, 220
Classified employee recognition, 202- 203
Coffman, Jim, 147-149, 163-165, 263
Colbert, Con, 66, 67, 94
Coleman, Ray, 140-141
Coles, Embert, 169
Colvin, Bill, 14
Commencement addresses, 223-339, 255-258
Computer Science, Department of, 114-116
Conard, John, 29
Construction Science, Department of, 115-116, 116, 246
Conservatory, 263
Continuing Education, 88, 126, 138-139
Cooperative Extension Service, 3, 11, 72, 122, 130, 152
Corman, Warren, 29, 37, 107-109
Cox, David, 104
Creech, Tom, 110-111
Cross, Gene, 89, 92, 94, 115, 143-145, 187, 191, 237
Daane, Adrian, 205
Dahl, Robert, 115
Dairy facilities, 81-83, 262
Dale, Melvin, 228
Data dilemma, 113, 137
Dean of Agriculture position, 3
Demographics, 48
Dempsey, Ambrose, 83
Denholm, Frank, 194
Dennis, Stanley, 161, 234-235
Dickens Hall, 115-116
Dickey, Jim, 66-73, 137, 233, 262
Docking, George, Jr. 27-28
Doctor of Education, 99-101
Dodds, DeLoss, 39, 66-67, 71-77
Dodge, Ted, 126
Dole Telecommunications Center, 267
Dole, Robert, 95 148, 249-250
Doner, Dave, 124
Dorsey, Floyd, 75
Doyen, Ross, 83
Duitsman, Bill, 152
Dunbar, John, 105, 123, 127-129, 142, 145-147
Durland Hall, 31, 260-261, 264
Durland, M.A. "Cotton", 14
Dykes, Archie, 103
Ealy, Robert, 263
Eby, Martin, 31
Economics, Department of, 145-147
Education, College of, 3, 36-37, 89, 99-101, 152
Edwards Hall, 58, 70, 268
Egg business, 277
Eisenhower, Milton, 22, 171
Endowment Association (see Foundation)
Energy Center, 264
Engineering, College of, 3, 87, 110, 242-246, 264
Engineering Experiment Station, 3
Engineering Extension, 3
Enrollment

Beating projections, 112-113
By gender, 242-244
Demographics impact, 48
Increases, 4, 86
Inflated data, 137-140
Projected, 87-89
Eusebio, Jose, 156
Everett, Donn, 27, 200-201
Faculty salaries, 211-213
FarmHouse Fraternity, 103, 117
Farmland Industries, 82
Farm operation, 275-276
Farrar, Keith, 106
Farrell Library, 34, 179-180, 200-201
Farrell, Frances David, 200
Feyerharm, Bill, 135
Finance and facilities vice presidency, 268
Fine Arts degree, 121, 266
Finley, Phil, 105
Fire Training Center, 264
Fiser, Dave, 103
Flinchbaugh, Barry, 85-86, 118, 157-158, 175, 187-189, 212, 268
Foerster, Bernd, 13, 31, 135
Foerster, Kent, 30
Ford, Gerald, 117, 185
Foundation,
Executive committee, 1-2, 50, 54, 90, 103, 154, 174-175
Funding athletics, 1-2, 15-16, 34, 39, 46-47, 53-55
Name change, xv, 175
President's Club, 114-117, 179-180, 266
Scholarships, 88, 238
Wish list, 176-177
Franklin, Bernard, 23, 29, 111
Freedom of speech, 266
Freeman, Ross, 175
Frith, Tom, 70, 235
Funk, Marilyn, 34, 42
Gast, Floyd, 61
Geist, Paul and Sharon, 42
Geoffroy, Greg, 149
Gibson, Mike, 237
Goldstein, Jack, 1, 55, 66, 67, 107, 271
Good, Don, 16, 105, 257
Grade inflation, 214-216
Graduate assistants, 221
Graham, John, 73
Griffith, Paul, 123
Grosh, Peggy, 237
Haines, Jordan, 125
Haley, Alex, 181
Ham, George, 171
Hamil, J.R., 81
Harman, Rick, 54
Hartman, Jack, 59-64, 67, 74-75
Hatch Act, 152
Hathaway, Charles, 189-190
Hauser, Mike, 98-99
Hayden, Mike, 165, 274-275
Hays Experiment Station, 152
Hefty, Elaine, 236
Hein, Charles, 239
Hepler land, 153-154
Hess, Carroll, 13, 127-129, 156, 232
Hess, Dean, 173, 176
Hewsom, Mary, 175
Heywood, Ken, 1, 16, 173-176
Hiersteiner, Walter, 18
Hilty, Charles, 274
Hipsher, Patty, 236
Hobbs, Art, 171
Hobrock, Brice, 135
Hoeflin Child Development Center, 263
Hoeflin, Ruth, 13, 123, 263

Hoffman, Doretta, 13
Holton Hall, 115-116
Home Economics, College of (see also Human Ecology), xv, 3, 88, 123, 243-245
Hoover, Bill, 102, 184, 263
Hope, Bob, 181-183
Horticulture, Department of, 218, 241
Hostetler, Al, 1-2, 50, 54, 89-91, 175
Hostetler, Charlie, 97-99
Hoyt, Don, 137-139, 216
Hulbert, Lloyd, 158-159, 263
Human Ecology, College of, xv, 103, 135, 243-245
Hussein, Khali, 237
Hutton, Prudence, 18-19, 24-25, 29, 111
Installation ceremony, 24-27
Interior Architecture, Department of, 218, 245
International Grains Program, 267
International Livestock Program, 267
International development, 119
International Trade Institute, 140, 267
Iowa Agricultural Finance Corporation, 277
Jack, Lowell, 238
Jackson, Elmer, 18
Jermier, Jersey, 45-46, 60-69, 73
Johnson, Gwyn, 234
Johnson, Mark, 171
Johnson, Mike, 93, 97, 103-104, 144, 172, 212, 247, 268
Johnson, William "Bill", 123
Johnson, Wy, 277
Johnsrud, Myron, 274
Jones, C. Clyde, 10, 55, 67
Jones, Harold, 67
Jones, Larry, 111-112
Jorns, Ann, 226, 236
Jorns, Jim, 168-171
Journalism, Department of, 89, 218
Junction City *Daily Union*, 54
Jury, Dwight, 237
Kahrs, Amos, 89
Kansas legislature, 75, 137, 149, 208, 263, 267
  Building projects, 36-38, 104-106, 115-117, 143-144, 260
  Influence on, 11, 28-30, 175, 206
  Nichols resolution, 83-86, 115-117
  Faculty salaries, 211-213
Kansas City semester, 264
Kansas Technical Institute, 110
Kassebaum, Nancy, 92, 95, 251
Kershaw, Willard, 175
Keys, Sam, 13
Khalil, Hussein, 237
King International Center, 261-262
King, Ed, 174, 261-262
KKSU, 269
Klabunde, Ken, 104
Klein bottle, 93-94
Koch, Burl, 155, 171
Koeppe, Owen, 100, 128-129, 134-140, 187-188
Koger, John, Sr., 175
Konza Prairie, 158-160, 178, 263
Koplik, Stan, 100, 108
Kottman, Roy, 4, 130
Kruh, Robert "Bob", 14, 120, 135
Krukenberg, Sam, 235
K-State *Collegian*, 41, 64-65, 246
K-State Union, 81-83, 114, 117, 178-180, 196, 204, 218-219
K-Stater, 31, 160
Lady, Wendell, 106-109

Land acquisition, 268
Landon, Alf, 91-95, 184
Landon Lecture Series, 181, 184-197
Landscape Architecture, Department of, 218
Lapping, Mark, 89
Larson, George, 155
Larson, Marion, 277
Larson Steve, 278
Larson, Vernon "Vern", 120, 262
Laurie, David, 69
Leasure, E.E., 147
Lee, Alan and Robert, 98
Leighton, Cindy, 237
Leipold, Horst, 235
Lewis, Lloyd, 41
Lindquist, Grace, 1, 12, 39, 41, 51
Lindsay, Ernest, 81
Loub, Art, 176-178
Lowe, Roger, 29
Lowman, Frank, 38, 111, 116
Lueder, Bob, 116
Lull, Linton, 175
Lundberg, Jim, 228
Lundberg, Lynne, 228, 270
Lyng, Dick, 249
Lynn, Robert "Bob", 13, 135, 140-141
Macdonald Collision Facility, 214
Mackintosh, David "Davie", 204-205
MacVicar, Robert, 129-132
Mattox, Jerry, 122
Mader, Ernest, 155, 169
Madigan, Ed, 274
Manhattan *Mercury*, 14, 55, 60, 192, 203
Manry, Cliff, 162
Marshall Scholars, 236-238
Marshall, Stan, 6
Master of Arts, 122
McCain Auditorium, 84, 189-191, 196, 201, 223
McCain, James, xv, 1-6, 10-11, 16, 47, 56, 82, 161, 173, 260-261
McFadden, Patrick, 237
McFarland, Joe, 29
McMullen, Sandra, 71, 111
McNeal, Don, 55
McNight, David, 159
McPherson, Peter, 249-251
McVey, M.D. "Pete", 226
Milbourn, Max, 5, 11, 24, 39, 64, 78, 82, 83, 268
Miller, George, 103, 145
Mills, Joe, 39
Mitchell, Roger, 5, 10-11, 82, 120, 123, 127-134, 153, 262-265
Montgomery, John D., 18, 54, 111
Montgomery, John G. 111, 147
Montgomery, John G. Jr. 38
Montgomery, Jolana Wright, 38
Morrill Act, 151
Morse, Richard L.D., 17
Mugler, David, 135, 232
Mullin, Dennis, 102
Murphy's Laws, 142, 235-236, 247
Musil, Greg, 85, 115
Nafsinger, Wayne, 169
National Collegiate Athletic Association (NCAA), xii, 4, 20-22, 72-77, 93, 136, 244, 265
National Merit Program, 48-50, 88, 227, 238, 267
Nature Conservancy, 158-160
Neinas, Charles "Chuck", 76
Nellis, Duane, 171
Nelson, Wilburn and Greg, 277
Newsome, David, 156
Nichols Gym, 30-31, 83-86, 114-116, 176, 265

Nichols Hall, 114-116, 180, 265
Nichols, Harold, 245
Niemann, David, 236
Nigeria project, 119-120, 156, 161-162
Nighswonger, Jim, 101
Nolting, Earl, 209
Noonan, John, 120, 234
Nordin, John, 145-147
Norman, David, 168-175
Norton, Charlie, 83, 220
Novak, Mike, 50
Nyhart, Sylvester "Sy", 167
Occupational Safety and Health Center, 264
Oklahoma State University, 59-63, 105, 117, 129, 131, 199, 205, 215, 218
Ollington, Mark, 201
Olsen, Jim, 261
O'Neill, Thomas P. "Tip", 194-196
Ono, Mr., 93
Ordway, Katharine, 160, 178
Oregon State University, 129
Oswald, Liz and John, 205
Palacio, June and Moki, 42, 178-179, 241
Palmer, Cruise, 54
Parks, Robert, 61
Parr, Rolland, 127
Parsons headquarters, 153, 264
Pedersen, Jim, 124,
Perry, Ralph, 8-9, 126
Peters, Chester "Chet", 5, 9, 49, 70, 78, 82, 84, 92, 98, 187, 219-220, 263
  Recreation complex, 9, 262
  Women's athletics, 32-33, 39, 56-62, 99
Philippine project, 120, 155-156, 262
Phillips, Bill, 152
Physical Education, Department of, 69
Physics, Department of, 189, 226, 264
Pi Kappa Alpha, 219
Pickert, Jim, 100, 111, 145
Pine, Wilfred and Beatrice, 42
Plant Science, 31, 36-38
Political Theatre, 79-118
Pomeranz, Y, 163
Pound, Glenn, 130
President's Club, 16, 114-117, 178-180, 266
President's Home, 10, 34-44, 117, 178-179, 187, 200, 241, 252-254, 258-259, 269
Priddle, Harland, 165
Protests, 39, 84-85
Provost position, 132-134, 254, 265
Psychology, Department of, 36-37, 227
Quinlan Gardens, 263
Quinlan, Leon, 263
Rahjes, Doyle, 166-167
Railsback, Lee, 147
Rainsberger, Ellis, 33, 56, 64-70
Rathbone, Don, 13, 87, 135, 243, 260-261, 264
Rathbone Hall, 180, 260-261
Rawson, Tom, 88
Reagan, Charles, 184
Reagan, Ronald, 91-95, 194-197, 272
Reeves, Jack, 38, 70, 111, 122
Reiner, Mark, 63-64
Reinhardt, Richard, 111, 147
Research park, 264
Restaurant Management, Department of, 218, 242, 244
Rhodes Scholars, 225-226, 236-238

Richards, Bill, 201
Richter, Bill, 184
Riley, Jack, 171
Robel, Raydon, 9
Roberts, Pat, 166, 240
Robinson, Dan, 236
Rogenmoser, Bill, 92
Rogers, Richard, 1, 18, 54, 175
Rogler, Wayne, 41
Ross, Lynne, 245
Roth, Janctte, 237
Rothermel, Brad, 7-8
Rowan, Carl, 192
Royal Purple, 246
Russell, Brad, 237
Salaries, faculty, 211-213
Sales, Cheryl, 237
Sand, Ivan, 85-86
Satisfactions, 5, 197, 249, 258-269, 274
Schlesinger, James, 186-187
Schruben, Leonard, 79
Schultz, George, 196-197
Schurle, Bryan, 171
Scribante, Ed, 175
Seaton, Edward "Ed", 55, 185, 192
Seaton Hall, 31, 242
Seaton, Richard "Dick", 31
Seymour, Todd, 174-176
Shellenberger, Lori, 236
Sherriff, Stan, 44
Short, Kristi, 75
Shull, Paul and Joan, 23, 200
Sigma Alpha Epsilon, 233
Sink, Roger and Connie, 239
Sit-in, 75-77
Sjo, John, 168
Skelton, Red, 81-84
Smith, Charles, 162
Smith, Floyd, 127-129, 159
Smith, Glee, 17
Smith, Ian, 187-190
Smith, Virginia, 148
Smith, Walt, 196
Smith-Lever Act, 152
Smoking policy, 36
Snell, Robert, 1, 15, 33-34, 45, 55-56, 60-62, 71-78, 103
Sobring, Fred, 142
Sorrell, Roger, 236
South Dakota State University (SDSU), 4-6, 14, 20, 32, 73, 125, 130, 147-148, 152, 222, 241
Southeast Kansas Center, 153, 264
Speech, Department of, 114-115, 245
Spence, Heather, 42
Spencer, Richard, 56
Spurrier, Mark, 237
Stamey, Bill, 13, 135, 145-147, 236, 264
Stewart, Jess, 18
Stites, John, 85
Stolzer, Bill, 16, 175
Stone, Glen, 62
Stone, Kent, 278
Stowe, Barbara, 135
Sutton, Bill, 267
Switzer, Veryl, 74
Talkington, Robert, 165
Tau Kappa Epsilon, 103
Tenure, 141, 205-209, 213-214, 246
Test scores, 48-50, 214-216, 230
Text revision, 222-223
Thomas, Ken, 5, 11, 78
Thompson, Donna, 15
Thomson, John, 149
Throckmorton Hall, 36-38
Throckmorton, R.I., 173, 266
Tien, Henry, 166
Title IX, 72-75

Titus, Ralph, 78
Tomanek, Jerry, 110
Topeka *Capital-Journal*, 56, 99, 108
Towers, Dick, 71-72, 77, 89, 262
Treadway, Kathy, 71, 77
Trotter, Don, 13, 135
Truman scholars, 236-238
Turner, Tracy, 237
Twiss, Nancy, 236
Uehling, Barbara, 77
Unger, Elizabeth "Beth", 73-77, 103
Union Board, 181, 219
Union National Bank, 16
University of Kansas, 28, 49, 101, 173, 212
University of Mid-America, 52
University of Nebraska, 3-4, 28, 32, 35, 131, 147, 263
Upson, Dan, 56
USDA, 4, 79, 123, 130, 148, 165, 249-251, 273-274
Vanier, Jack, 175
Veterinary Medicine
  College of, 3, 120, 161-162, 237, 243-244, 255
  Kansas-Nebraska College, 147-149, 263
  Separate budget for, 147, 267
Vice president for Agriculture, 3, 10-13
Vice presidents, number of, 142-145
Vogel, John, 82
Walker, Warren, 180
Wall, Hyndman, 44-45
Waters Hall, 133, 146
Weber Hall, 104-106, 144, 204, 265
Weber, A.D. "Dad", 14-15, 55, 270
Weigel, Larry, 89, 173-176
Weltsch, Jack, 174
Werts, Merrill, 115
White House Volunteer Office, 272
White, Chappell, 180
White, Fred, 39
Wiebe, Virgil, 236
Wiles, Don, 162-163
Willard Hall, 104
Willham, Oliver, 117, 255-256
Williams, Helen, 202
Wilson, Barbara, 98
Wilson, Larry, 143
Wilson, Norman, 102
Wilson, Peairs, 156
Wilson, Robert, 1, 54, 91, 98, 175
Winter, Tex, 44-45
Winter, Wint, 83-84
Wintermode, Dick, 174-176
Wish list, 176
Woods, Walter, 128-129, 142
Woodward, Jan, 81, 93, 178
Work time, 51
Wunsch, Paul, 18
Yamani, Ahmaed Zake, 190-192
Yeutter, Clayton, 273
Young, Paul, 5, 9-10, 56, 78, 143
Zumberge, Jim, 65